The multiverse was destroyed!

The heroes of Earth-616 and Earth-1610 were powerless to save it!

Now, all that remains is BATTLEWORLD:

A massive, patchwork planet comp... of the fragments of worlds that no longer exist, maint... iron will of its god and master, V...

WRITERS:
...E DECONNICK
...HOMPSON

DAVID LOPEZ (#1-3) &
LAURA BRAGA WITH PAOLO PANTALENA (#4)

COLOR ARTIST:
LEE LOUGHRIDGE

LETTERER:
VC'S JOE CARAMAGNA

CAPTAIN MARVEL and the CAROL CORPS

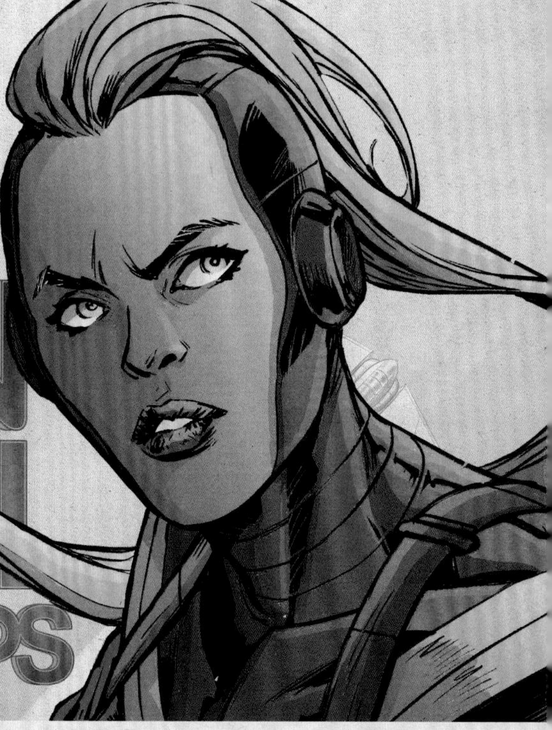

COVER ART: DAVID LOPEZ
ASSISTANT EDITOR: CHARLES BEACHAM
EDITOR: SANA AMANAT

COLLECTION EDITOR: JENNIFER GRÜNWALD
ASSISTANT EDITOR: SARAH BRUNSTAD
ASSOCIATE MANAGING EDITOR: ALEX STARBUCK
EDITOR, SPECIAL PROJECTS: MARK D. BEAZLEY
SENIOR EDITOR, SPECIAL PROJECTS: JEFF YOUNGQUIST
SVP PRINT, SALES & MARKETING: DAVID GABRIEL
BOOK DESIGNER: RODOLFO MURAGUCHI

★

EDITOR IN CHIEF: AXEL ALONSO
CHIEF CREATIVE OFFICER: JOE QUESADA
PUBLISHER: DAN BUCKLEY
EXECUTIVE PRODUCER: ALAN FINE

★

CAPTAIN MARVEL & THE CAROL CORPS. Contains material originally published in magazine form as CAPTAIN MARVEL & THE CAROL CORPS #1-4 and CAPTAIN MARVEL #17. First printing 2015. ISBN# 978-0-7851-9865-9. Published by MARVEL WORLDWIDE, INC., a subsidiary of MARVEL ENTERTAINMENT, LLC. OFFICE OF PUBLICATION: 135 West 50th Street, New York, NY 10020. **Printed in Canada.** ALAN FINE, President, Marvel Entertainment; DAN BUCKLEY, President, TV, Publishing and Brand Management; JOE QUESADA, Chief Creative Officer; TOM BREVOORT, SVP of Publishing; DAVID BOGART, SVP of Operations & Procurement, Publishing; C.B. CEBULSKI, VP of International Development & Brand Management; DAVID GABRIEL, SVP Print, Sales & Marketing; JIM O'KEEFE, VP of Operations & Logistics; DAN CARR, Executive Director of Publishing Technology; SUSAN CRESPI, Editorial Operations Manager; ALEX MORALES, Publishing Operations Manager; STAN LEE, Chairman Emeritus. For information regarding advertising in Marvel Comics or on Marvel.com, please contact Jonathan Rheingold, VP of Custom Solutions & Ad Sales, at jrheingold@marvel.com. For Marvel subscription inquiries, please call 800-217-9158. **Manufactured between 9/25/2015 and 11/2/2015 by SOLISCO PRINTERS, SCOTT, QC, CANADA.**

10 9 8 7 6 5 4 3 2 1

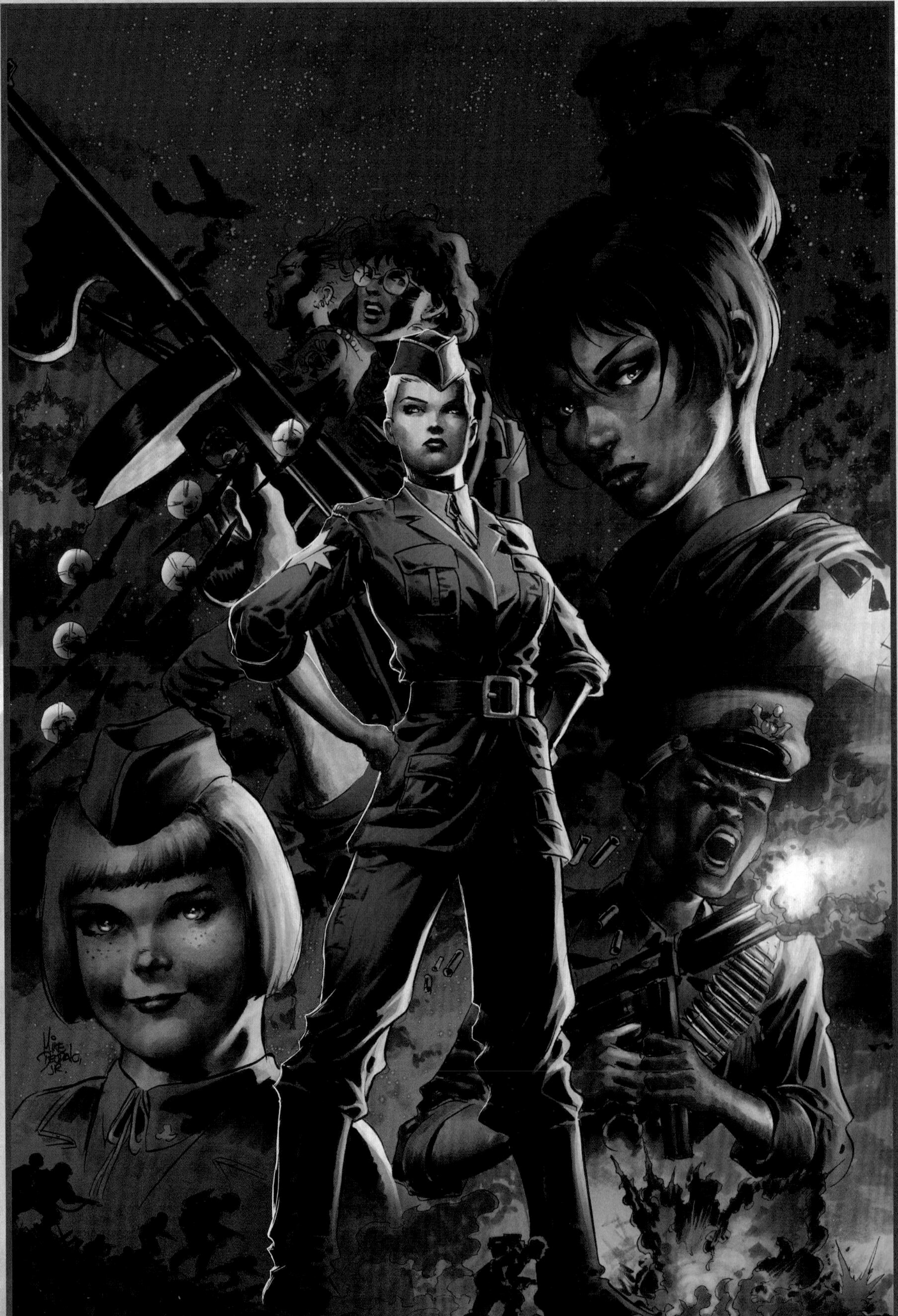

#1 VARIANT BY MIKE DEODATO & FRANK MARTIN

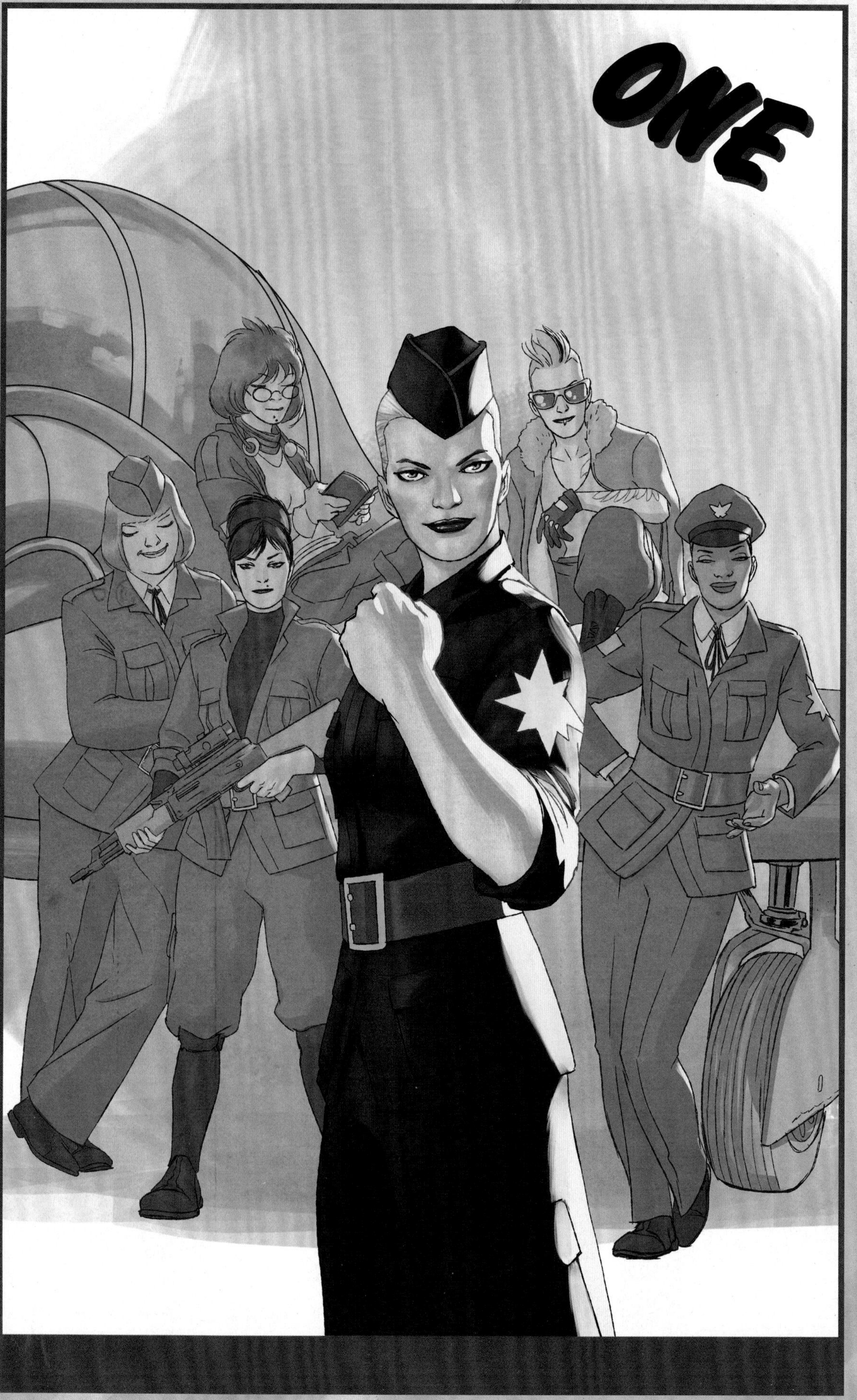
ONE

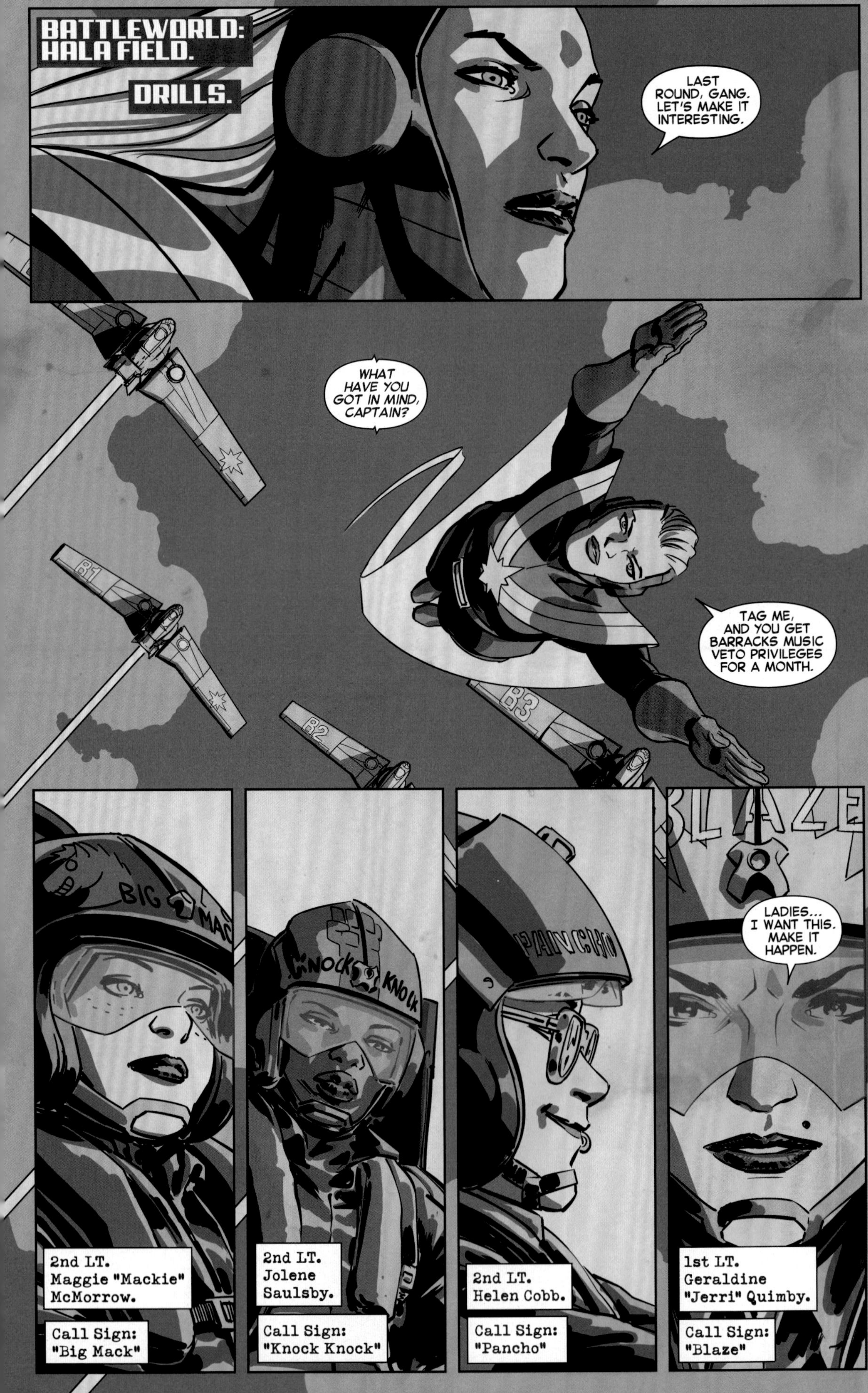
BATTLEWORLD: HALA FIELD.
DRILLS.
LAST ROUND, GANG. LET'S MAKE IT INTERESTING.
WHAT HAVE YOU GOT IN MIND, CAPTAIN?
TAG ME, AND YOU GET BARRACKS MUSIC VETO PRIVILEGES FOR A MONTH.
B1
B2
B3
BIG MAC
2nd LT. Maggie "Mackie" McMorrow.
Call Sign: "Big Mack"
KNOCK KNOCK
2nd LT. Jolene Saulsby.
Call Sign: "Knock Knock"
PANCHO
2nd LT. Helen Cobb.
Call Sign: "Pancho"
BLAZE
LADIES... I WANT THIS. MAKE IT HAPPEN.
1st LT. Geraldine "Jerri" Quimby.
Call Sign: "Blaze"

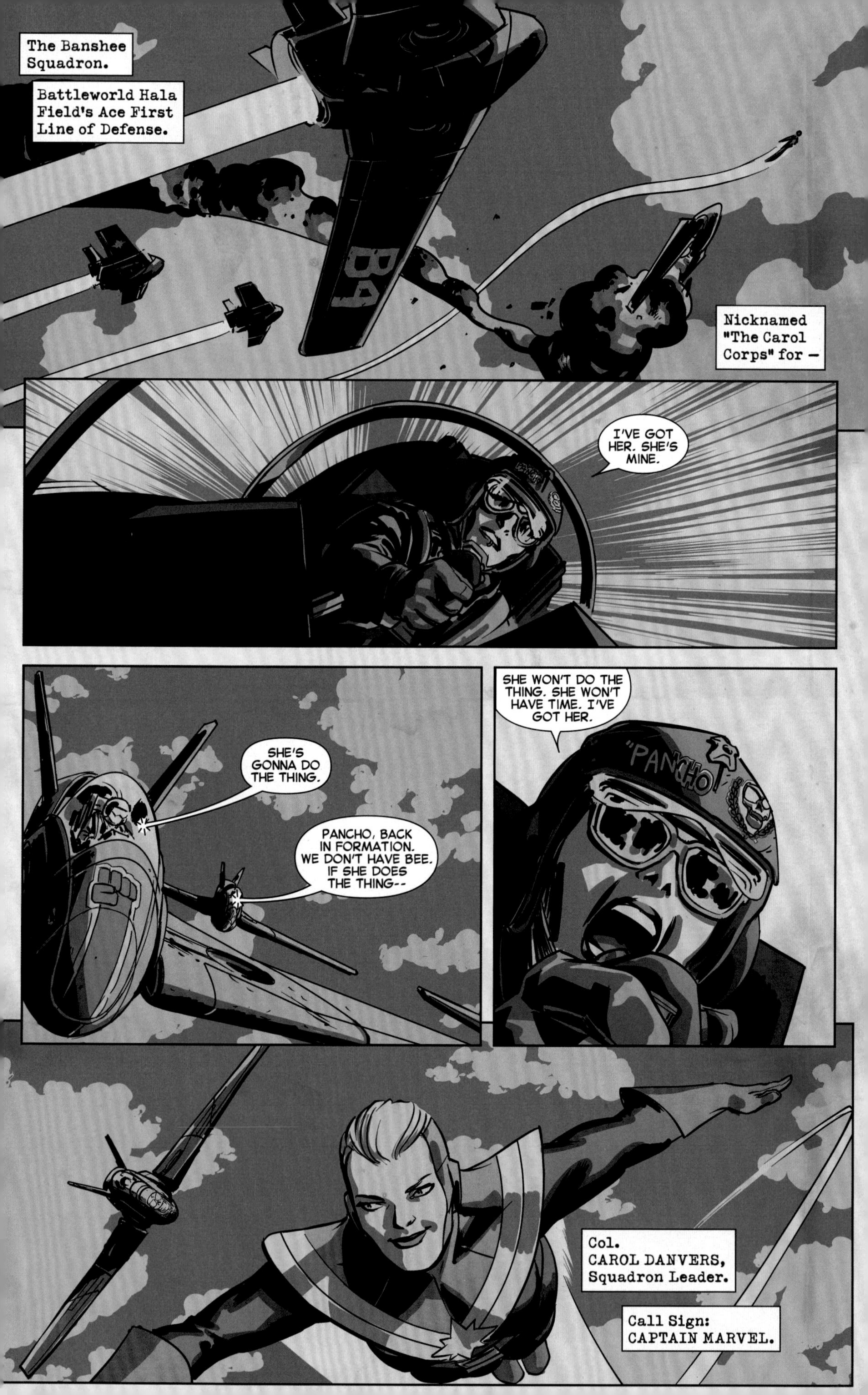
The Banshee Squadron.
Battleworld Hala Field's Ace First Line of Defense.
Nicknamed "The Carol Corps" for —
I'VE GOT HER. SHE'S MINE.
SHE'S GONNA DO THE THING.
PANCHO, BACK IN FORMATION. WE DON'T HAVE BEE. IF SHE DOES THE THING--
SHE WON'T DO THE THING. SHE WON'T HAVE TIME. I'VE GOT HER.
"PANCHO"
Col. CAROL DANVERS, Squadron Leader.
Call Sign: CAPTAIN MARVEL.

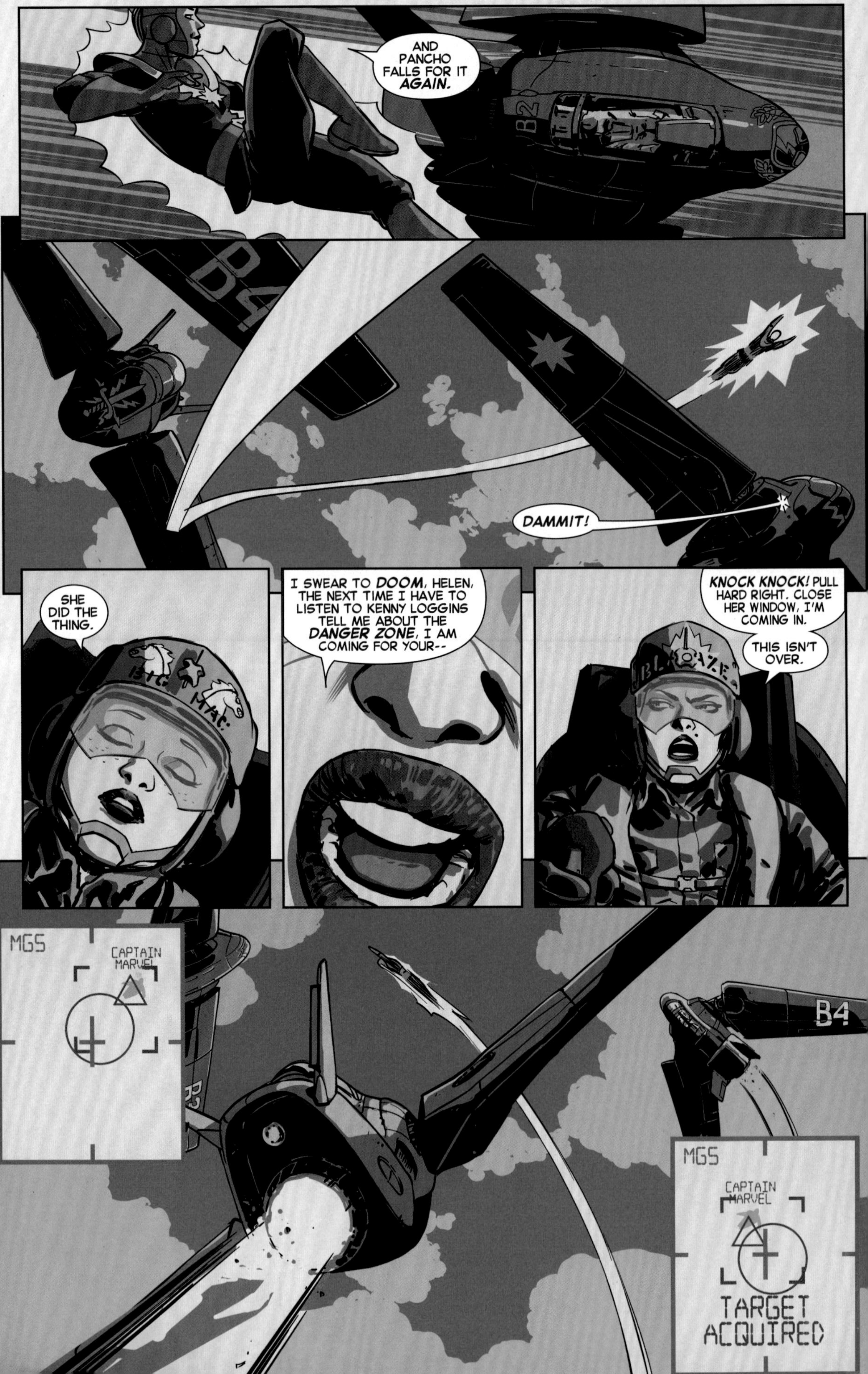
AND PANCHO FALLS FOR IT AGAIN.
B2
B4
DAMMIT!
SHE DID THE THING.
I SWEAR TO DOOM, HELEN, THE NEXT TIME I HAVE TO LISTEN TO KENNY LOGGINS TELL ME ABOUT THE DANGER ZONE, I AM COMING FOR YOUR--
KNOCK KNOCK! PULL HARD RIGHT. CLOSE HER WINDOW, I'M COMING IN.
THIS ISN'T OVER.
MGS
CAPTAIN MARVEL
B4
MGS
CAPTAIN MARVEL
TARGET ACQUIRED

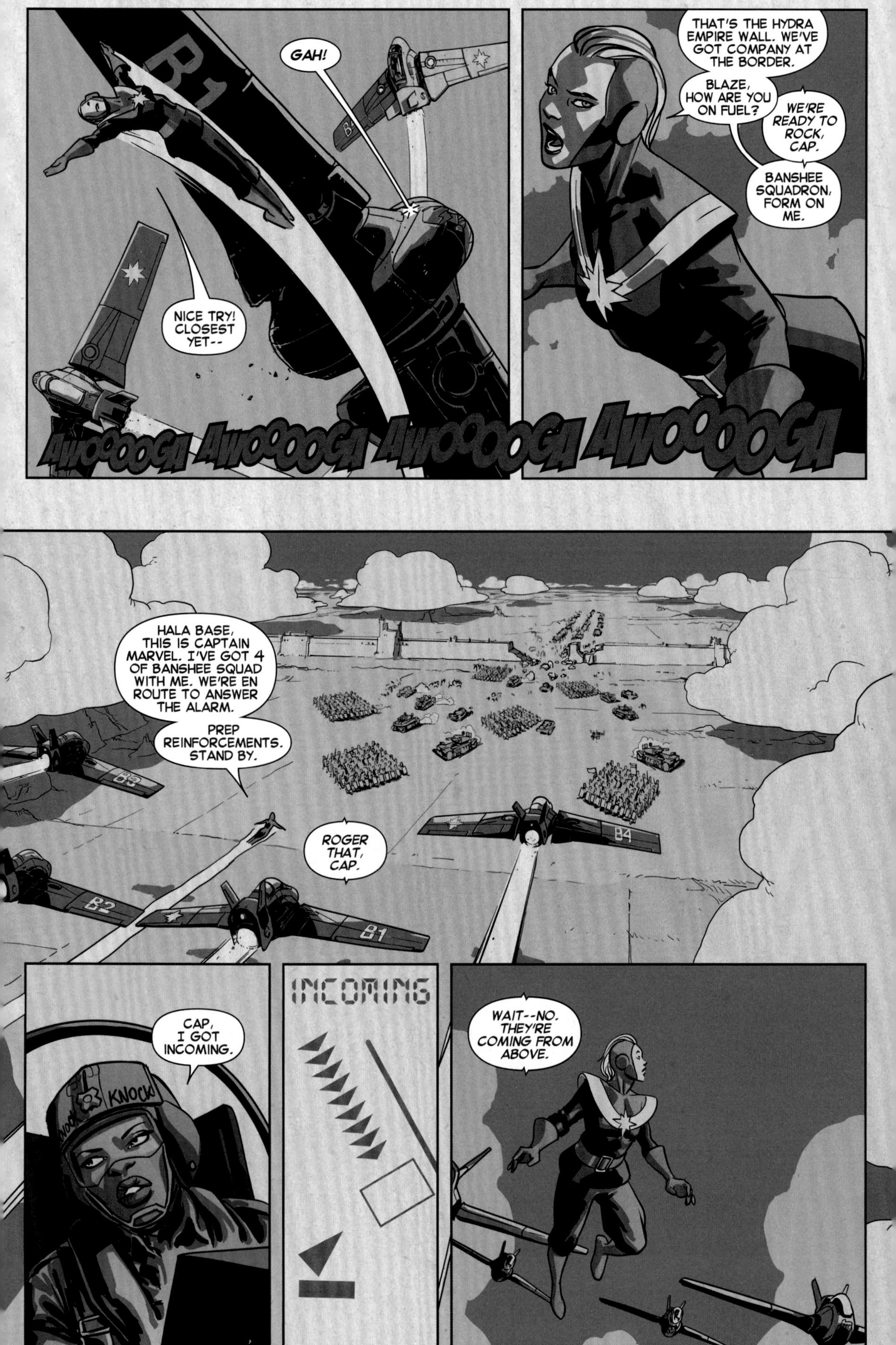
GAH!
NICE TRY! CLOSEST YET--
THAT'S THE HYDRA EMPIRE WALL. WE'VE GOT COMPANY AT THE BORDER.
BLAZE, HOW ARE YOU ON FUEL?
WE'RE READY TO ROCK, CAP.
BANSHEE SQUADRON, FORM ON ME.
AWOOOOGA AWOOOOGA AWOOOOGA AWOOOOGA
HALA BASE, THIS IS CAPTAIN MARVEL. I'VE GOT 4 OF BANSHEE SQUAD WITH ME. WE'RE EN ROUTE TO ANSWER THE ALARM.
PREP REINFORCEMENTS. STAND BY.
ROGER THAT, CAP.
CAP, I GOT INCOMING.
INCOMING
WAIT--NO. THEY'RE COMING FROM ABOVE.

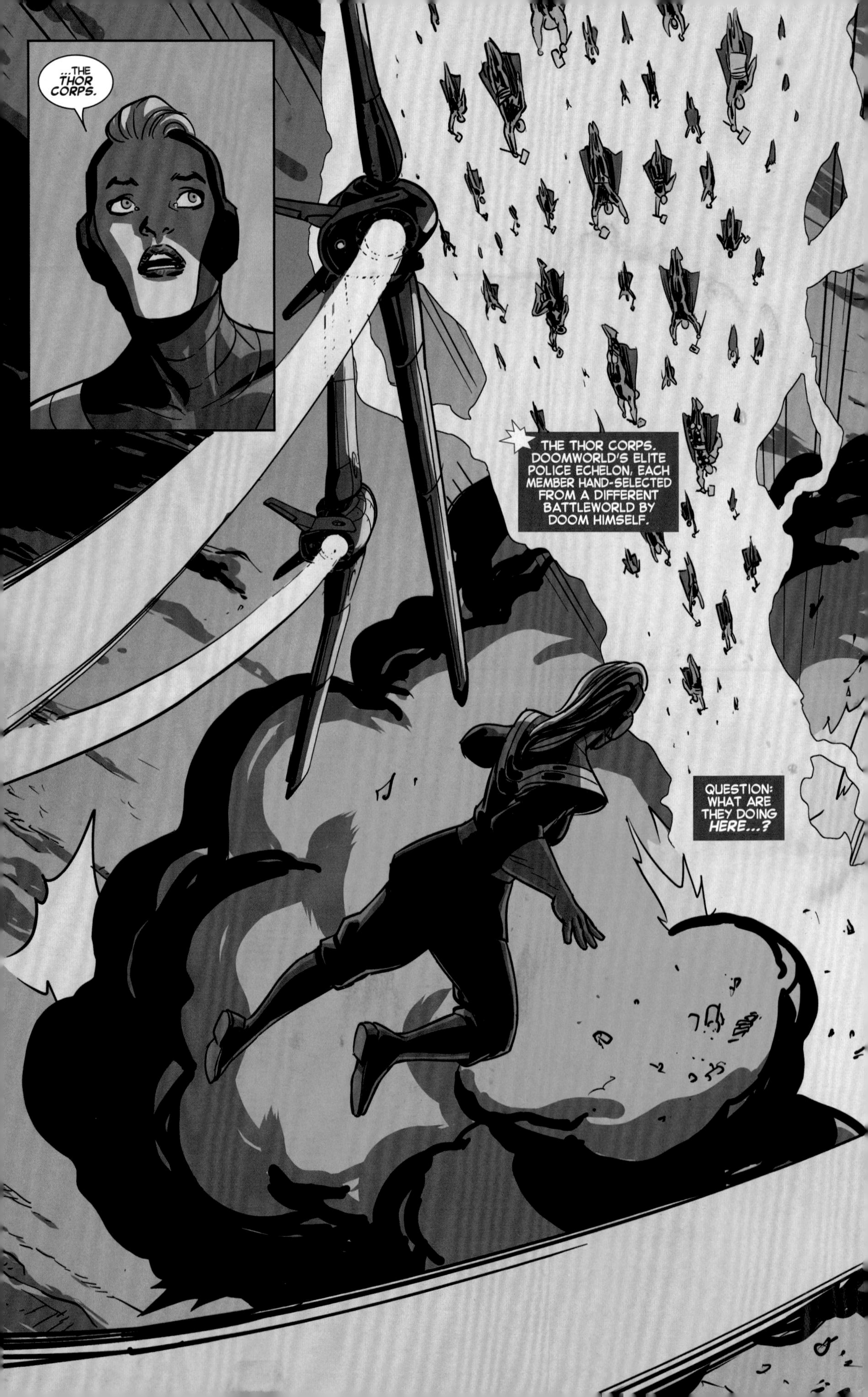
...THE THOR CORPS.
THE THOR CORPS. DOOMWORLD'S ELITE POLICE ECHELON, EACH MEMBER HAND-SELECTED FROM A DIFFERENT BATTLEWORLD BY DOOM HIMSELF.
QUESTION: WHAT ARE THEY DOING HERE...?

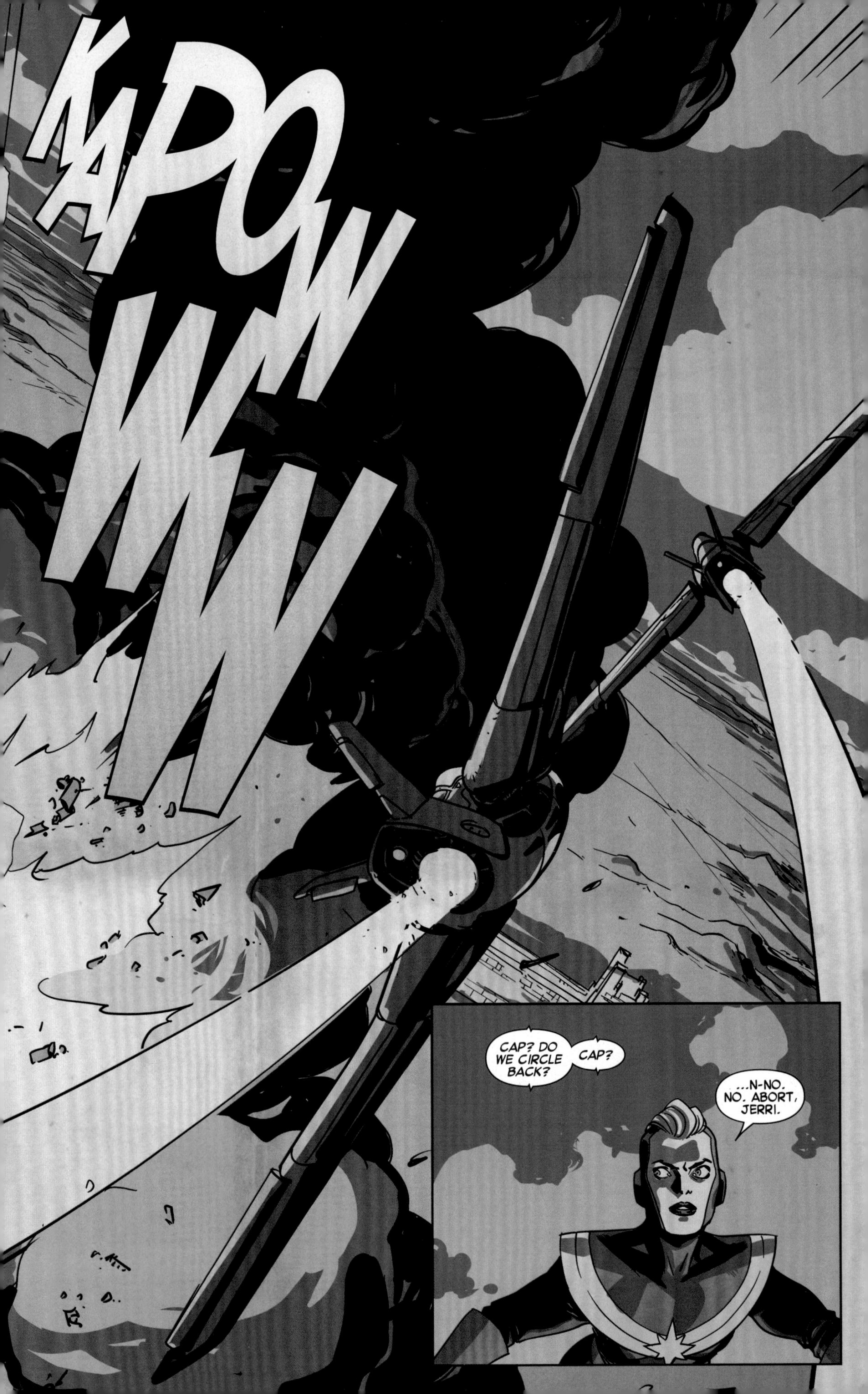
KAPOWWW
CAP? DO WE CIRCLE BACK?
CAP?
...N-NO. NO. ABORT, JERRI.

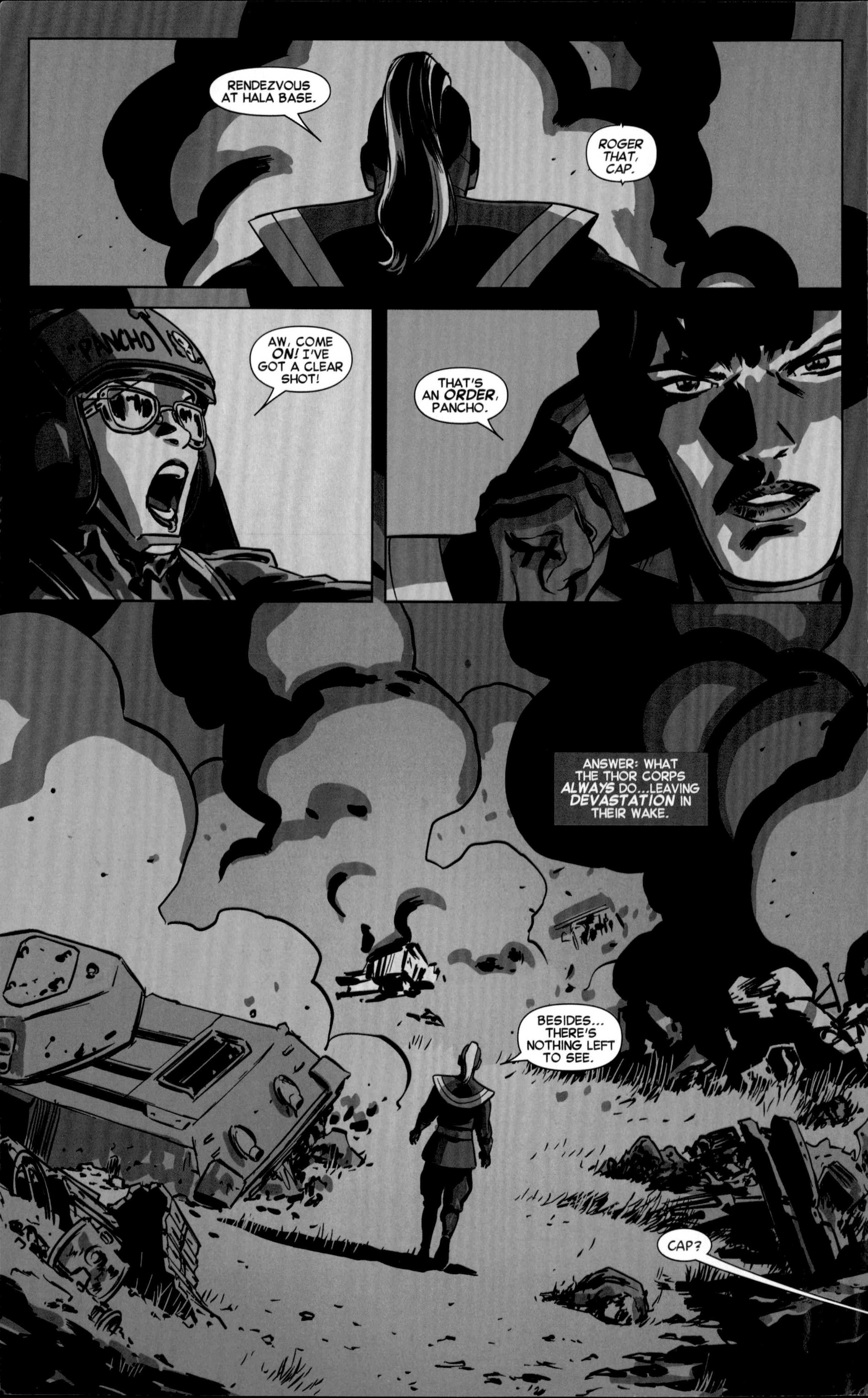
RENDEZVOUS AT HALA BASE.
ROGER THAT, CAP.
AW, COME ON! I'VE GOT A CLEAR SHOT!
THAT'S AN ORDER, PANCHO.
ANSWER: WHAT THE THOR CORPS ALWAYS DO...LEAVING DEVASTATION IN THEIR WAKE.
BESIDES... THERE'S NOTHING LEFT TO SEE.
CAP?

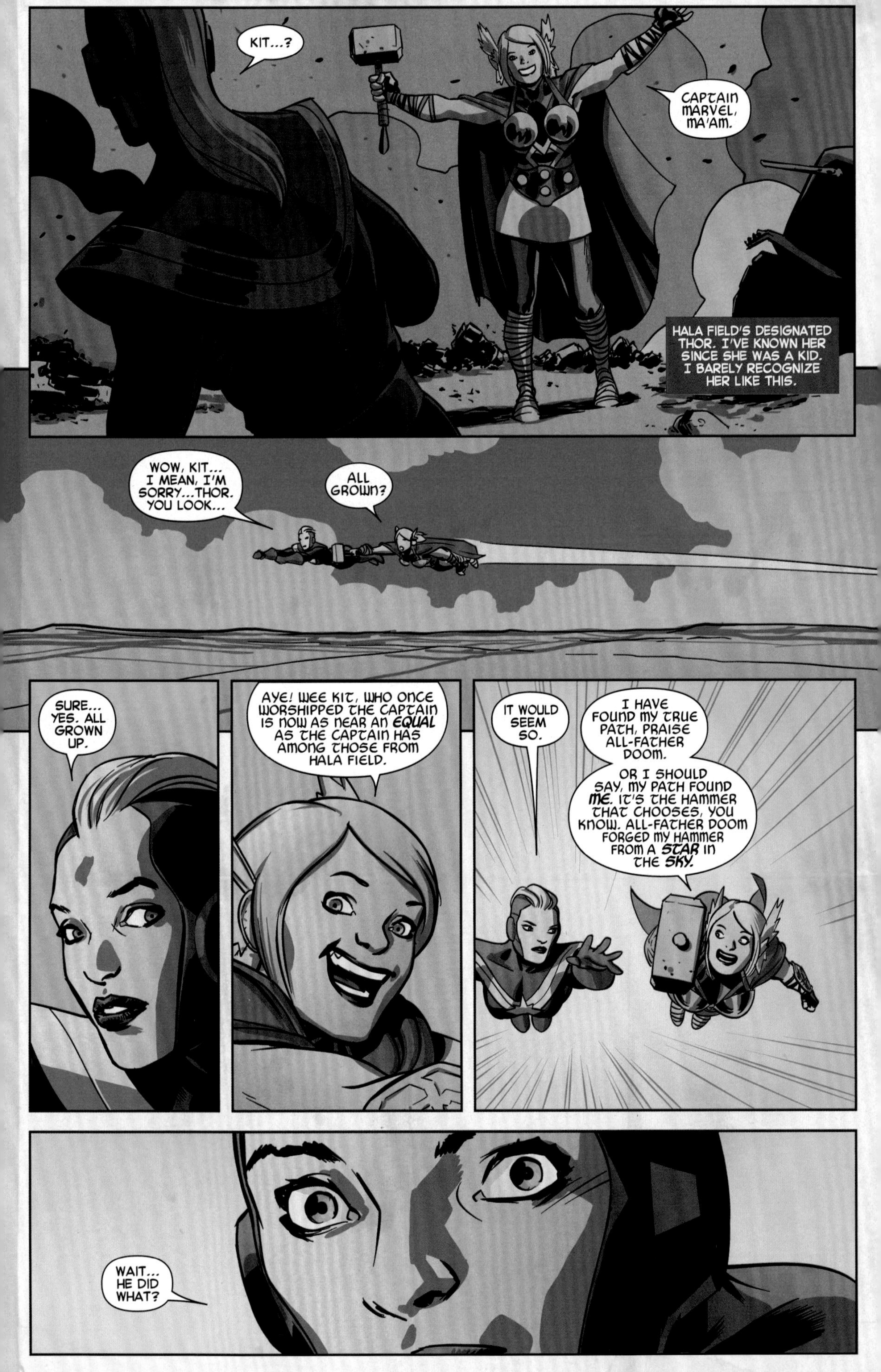
KIT...?
CAPTAIN MARVEL, MA'AM.
HALA FIELD'S DESIGNATED THOR. I'VE KNOWN HER SINCE SHE WAS A KID. I BARELY RECOGNIZE HER LIKE THIS.
WOW, KIT... I MEAN, I'M SORRY...THOR. YOU LOOK...
ALL GROWN?
SURE... YES. ALL GROWN UP.
AYE! WEE KIT, WHO ONCE WORSHIPPED THE CAPTAIN IS NOW AS NEAR AN *EQUAL* AS THE CAPTAIN HAS AMONG THOSE FROM HALA FIELD.
IT WOULD SEEM SO.
I HAVE FOUND MY TRUE PATH, PRAISE ALL-FATHER DOOM.
OR I SHOULD SAY, MY PATH FOUND *ME*. IT'S THE HAMMER THAT CHOOSES, YOU KNOW. ALL-FATHER DOOM FORGED MY HAMMER FROM A *STAR* IN THE *SKY*.
WAIT... HE DID WHAT?

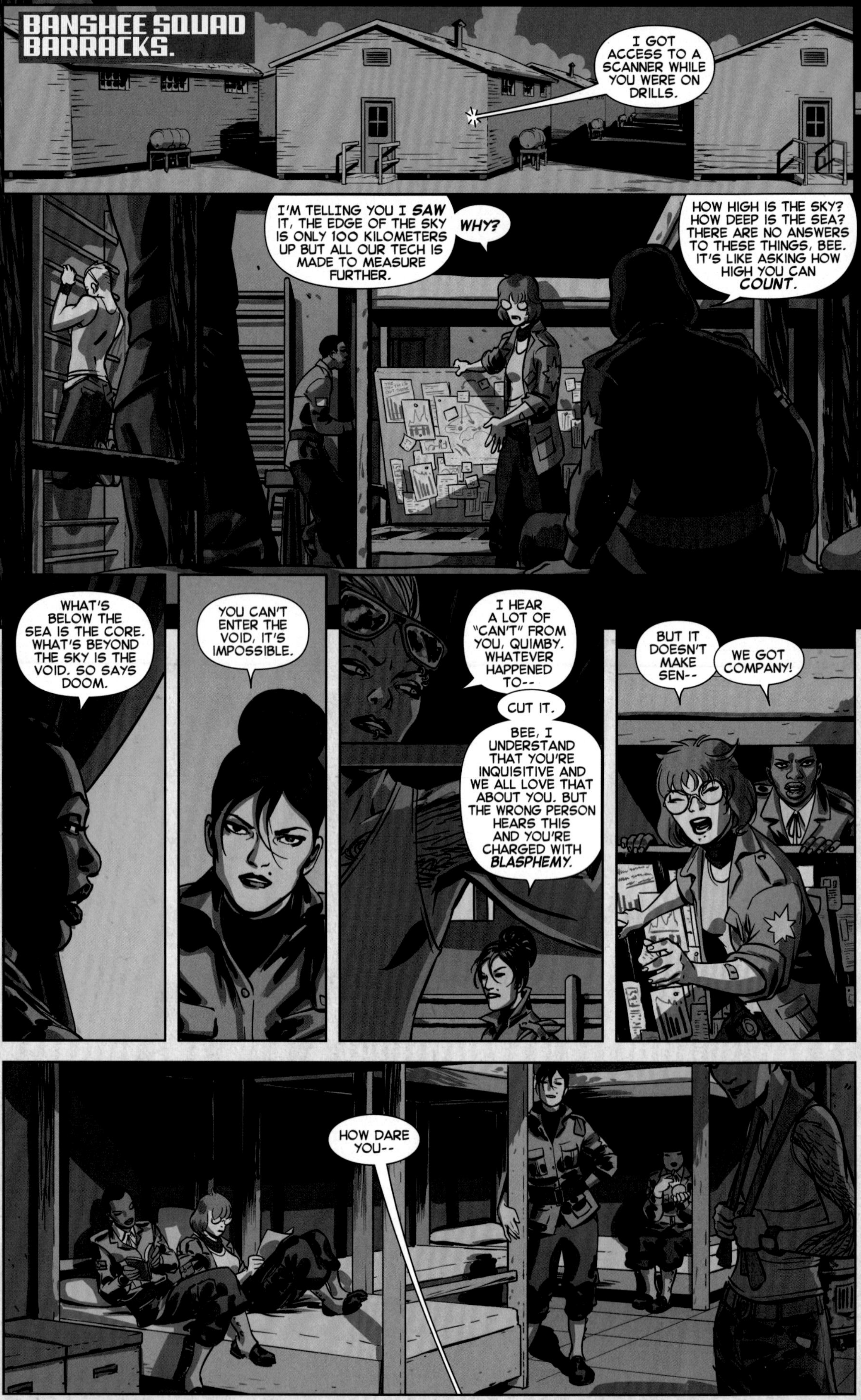
BANSHEE SQUAD BARRACKS.
I GOT ACCESS TO A SCANNER WHILE YOU WERE ON DRILLS.
I'M TELLING YOU I SAW IT, THE EDGE OF THE SKY IS ONLY 100 KILOMETERS UP BUT ALL OUR TECH IS MADE TO MEASURE FURTHER.
WHY?
HOW HIGH IS THE SKY? HOW DEEP IS THE SEA? THERE ARE NO ANSWERS TO THESE THINGS, BEE. IT'S LIKE ASKING HOW HIGH YOU CAN COUNT.
WHAT'S BELOW THE SEA IS THE CORE. WHAT'S BEYOND THE SKY IS THE VOID. SO SAYS DOOM.
YOU CAN'T ENTER THE VOID, IT'S IMPOSSIBLE.
I HEAR A LOT OF "CAN'T" FROM YOU, QUIMBY. WHATEVER HAPPENED TO--
CUT IT.
BEE, I UNDERSTAND THAT YOU'RE INQUISITIVE AND WE ALL LOVE THAT ABOUT YOU. BUT THE WRONG PERSON HEARS THIS AND YOU'RE CHARGED WITH BLASPHEMY.
BUT IT DOESN'T MAKE SEN--
WE GOT COMPANY!
HOW DARE YOU--

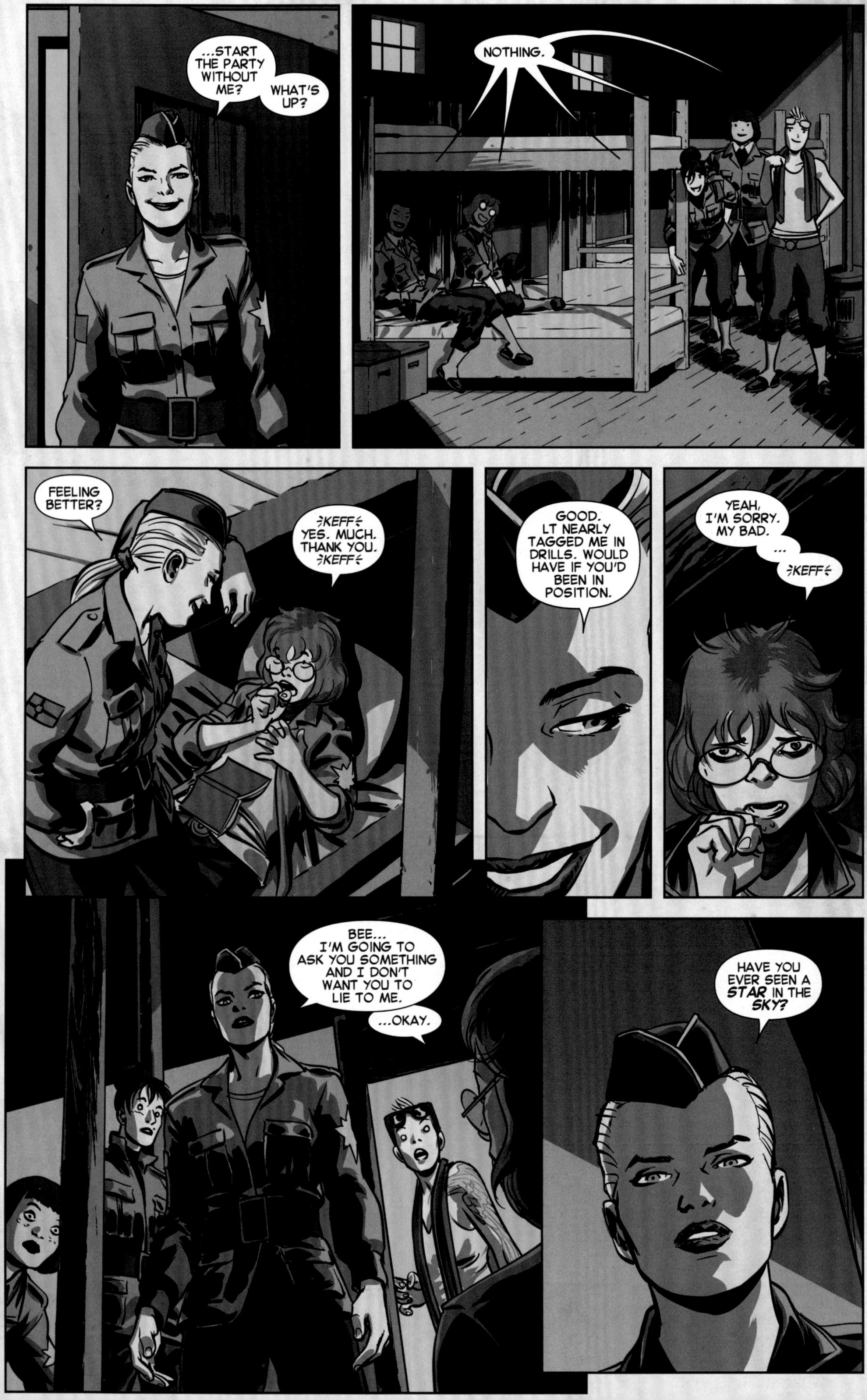
...START THE PARTY WITHOUT ME?
WHAT'S UP?
NOTHING.
FEELING BETTER?
KEFF YES. MUCH. THANK YOU. *KEFF*
GOOD. LT NEARLY TAGGED ME IN DRILLS. WOULD HAVE IF YOU'D BEEN IN POSITION.
YEAH, I'M SORRY. MY BAD.
...
KEFF
BEE... I'M GOING TO ASK YOU SOMETHING AND I DON'T WANT YOU TO LIE TO ME.
...OKAY.
HAVE YOU EVER SEEN A STAR IN THE SKY?

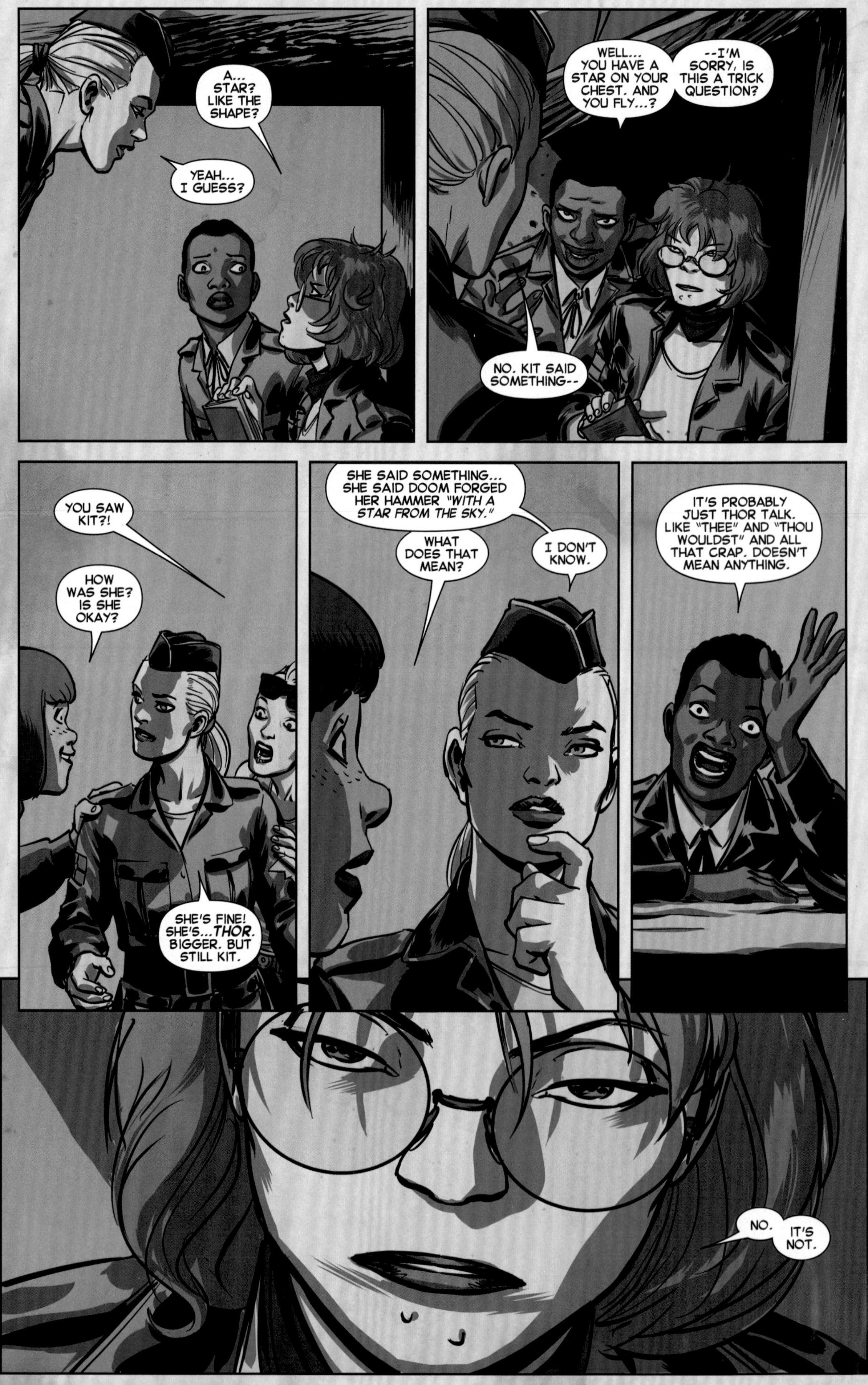
A... STAR? LIKE THE SHAPE?
YEAH... I GUESS?
WELL... YOU HAVE A STAR ON YOUR CHEST. AND YOU FLY...?
--I'M SORRY, IS THIS A TRICK QUESTION?
NO. KIT SAID SOMETHING--
YOU SAW KIT?!
HOW WAS SHE? IS SHE OKAY?
SHE'S FINE! SHE'S...THOR. BIGGER. BUT STILL KIT.
SHE SAID SOMETHING... SHE SAID DOOM FORGED HER HAMMER "WITH A STAR FROM THE SKY."
WHAT DOES THAT MEAN?
I DON'T KNOW.
IT'S PROBABLY JUST THOR TALK. LIKE "THEE" AND "THOU WOULDST" AND ALL THAT CRAP. DOESN'T MEAN ANYTHING.
NO.
IT'S NOT.

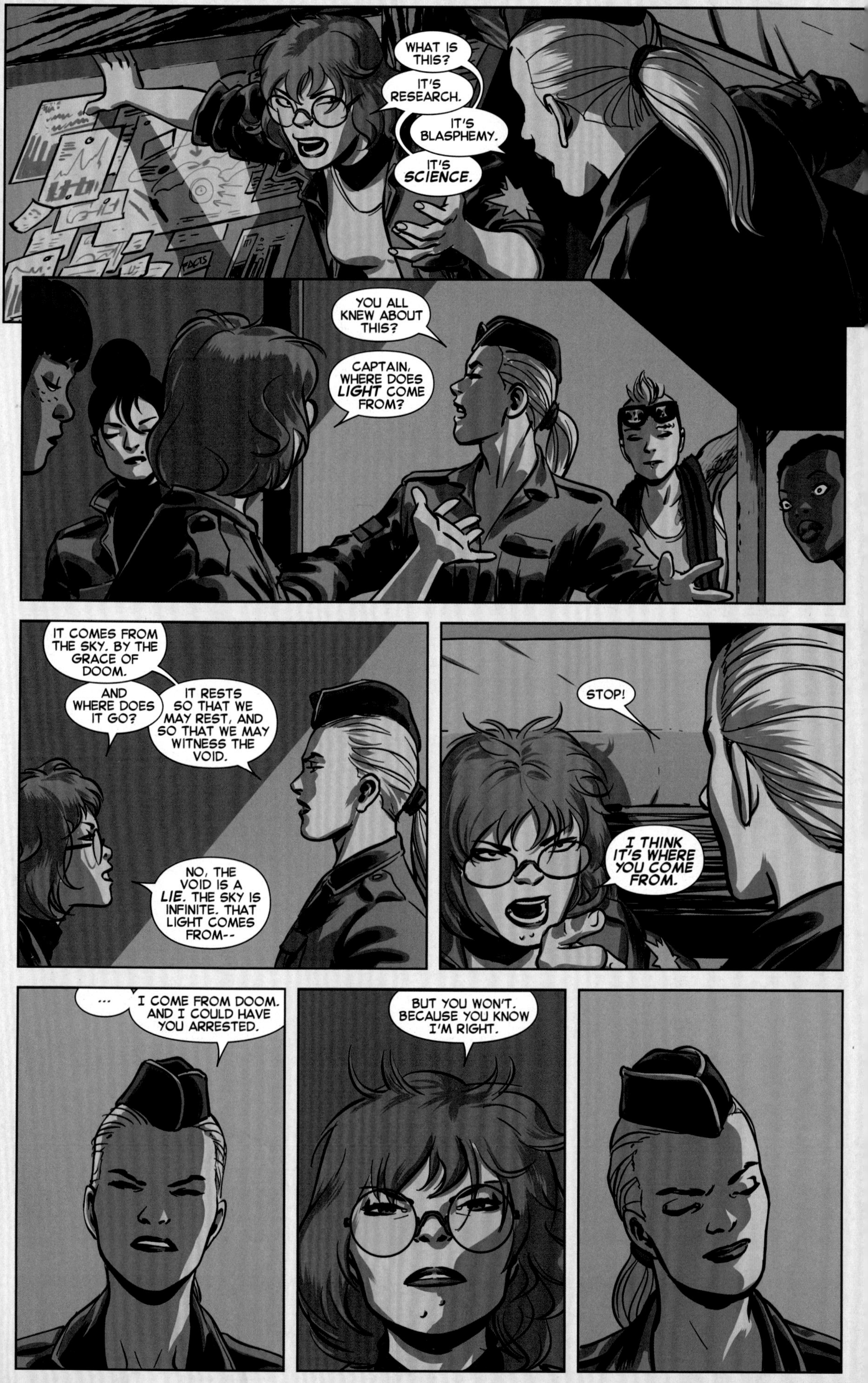
WHAT IS THIS?
IT'S RESEARCH.
IT'S BLASPHEMY.
IT'S SCIENCE.
FACTS
YOU ALL KNEW ABOUT THIS?
CAPTAIN, WHERE DOES LIGHT COME FROM?
IT COMES FROM THE SKY. BY THE GRACE OF DOOM.
AND WHERE DOES IT GO?
IT RESTS SO THAT WE MAY REST, AND SO THAT WE MAY WITNESS THE VOID.
NO, THE VOID IS A LIE. THE SKY IS INFINITE. THAT LIGHT COMES FROM--
STOP!
I THINK IT'S WHERE YOU COME FROM.
...
I COME FROM DOOM. AND I COULD HAVE YOU ARRESTED.
BUT YOU WON'T. BECAUSE YOU KNOW I'M RIGHT.

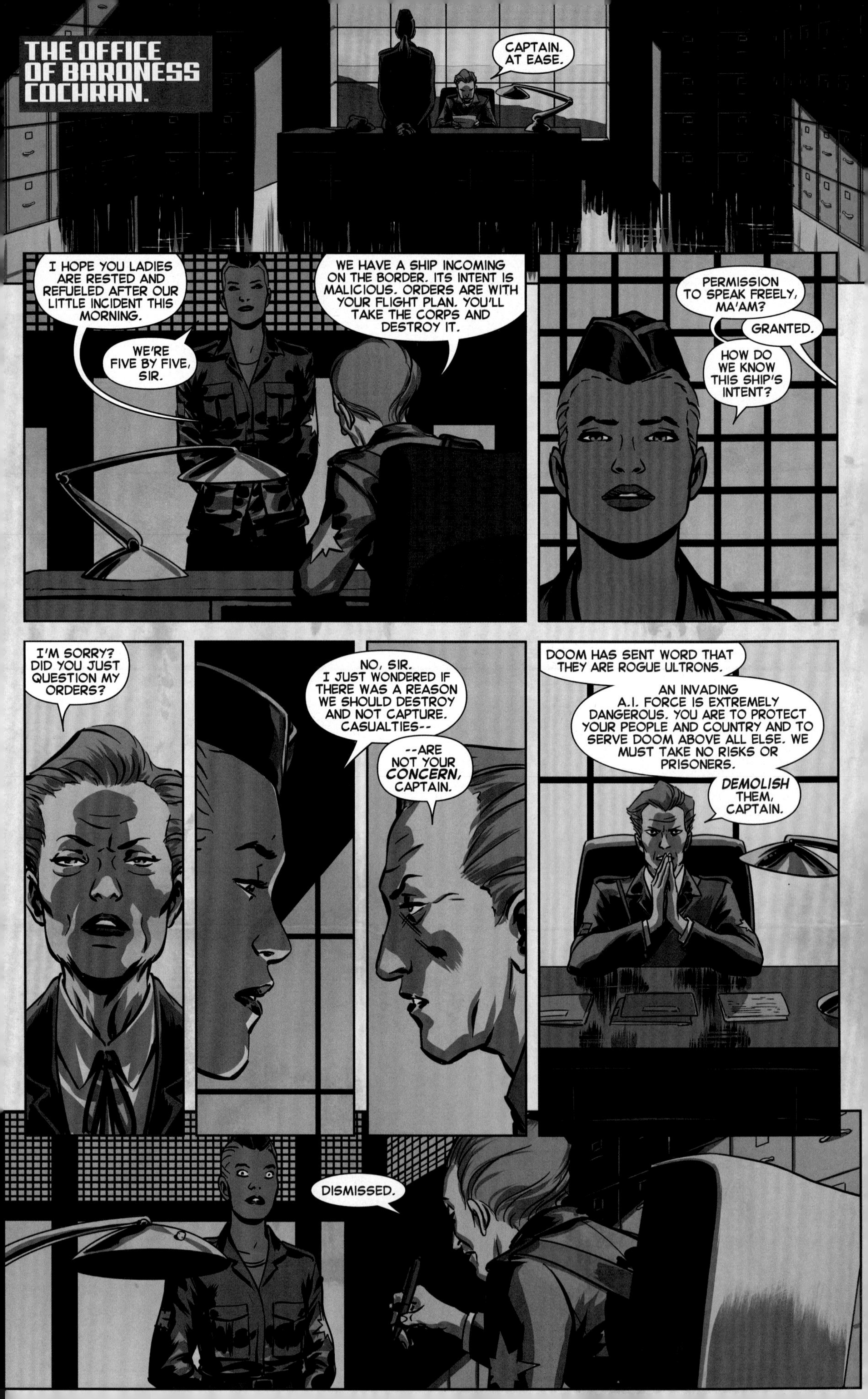
THE OFFICE OF BARONESS COCHRAN.
CAPTAIN. AT EASE.
I HOPE YOU LADIES ARE RESTED AND REFUELED AFTER OUR LITTLE INCIDENT THIS MORNING.
WE'RE FIVE BY FIVE, SIR.
WE HAVE A SHIP INCOMING ON THE BORDER. ITS INTENT IS MALICIOUS. ORDERS ARE WITH YOUR FLIGHT PLAN. YOU'LL TAKE THE CORPS AND DESTROY IT.
PERMISSION TO SPEAK FREELY, MA'AM?
GRANTED.
HOW DO WE KNOW THIS SHIP'S INTENT?
I'M SORRY? DID YOU JUST QUESTION MY ORDERS?
NO, SIR. I JUST WONDERED IF THERE WAS A REASON WE SHOULD DESTROY AND NOT CAPTURE. CASUALTIES--
--ARE NOT YOUR CONCERN, CAPTAIN.
DOOM HAS SENT WORD THAT THEY ARE ROGUE ULTRONS.
AN INVADING A.I. FORCE IS EXTREMELY DANGEROUS. YOU ARE TO PROTECT YOUR PEOPLE AND COUNTRY AND TO SERVE DOOM ABOVE ALL ELSE. WE MUST TAKE NO RISKS OR PRISONERS.
DEMOLISH THEM, CAPTAIN.
DISMISSED.

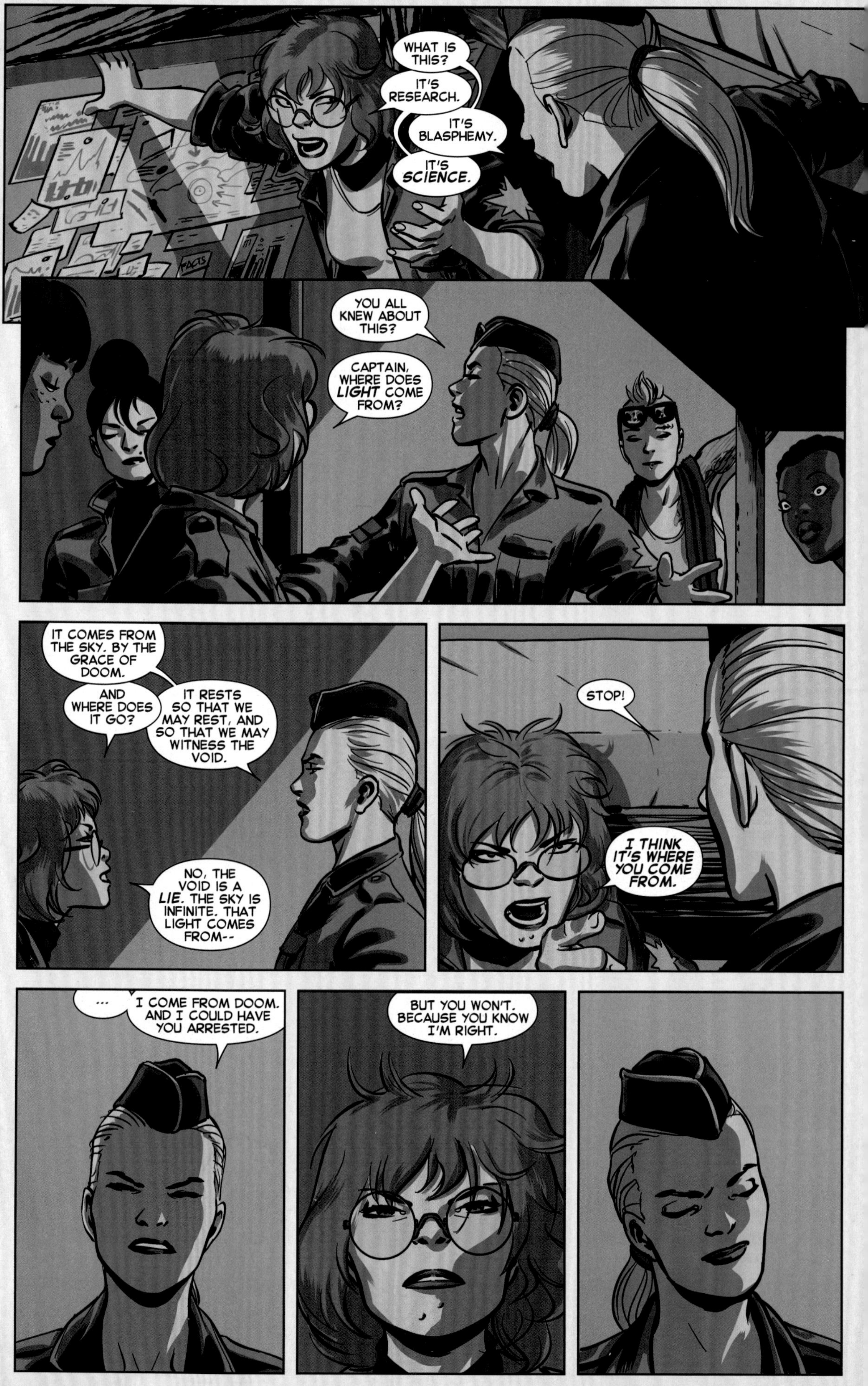
WHAT IS THIS?
IT'S RESEARCH.
IT'S BLASPHEMY.
IT'S SCIENCE.
FACTS
YOU ALL KNEW ABOUT THIS?
CAPTAIN, WHERE DOES LIGHT COME FROM?
IT COMES FROM THE SKY. BY THE GRACE OF DOOM.
AND WHERE DOES IT GO?
IT RESTS SO THAT WE MAY REST, AND SO THAT WE MAY WITNESS THE VOID.
NO, THE VOID IS A LIE. THE SKY IS INFINITE. THAT LIGHT COMES FROM--
STOP!
I THINK IT'S WHERE YOU COME FROM.
...
I COME FROM DOOM. AND I COULD HAVE YOU ARRESTED.
BUT YOU WON'T. BECAUSE YOU KNOW I'M RIGHT.

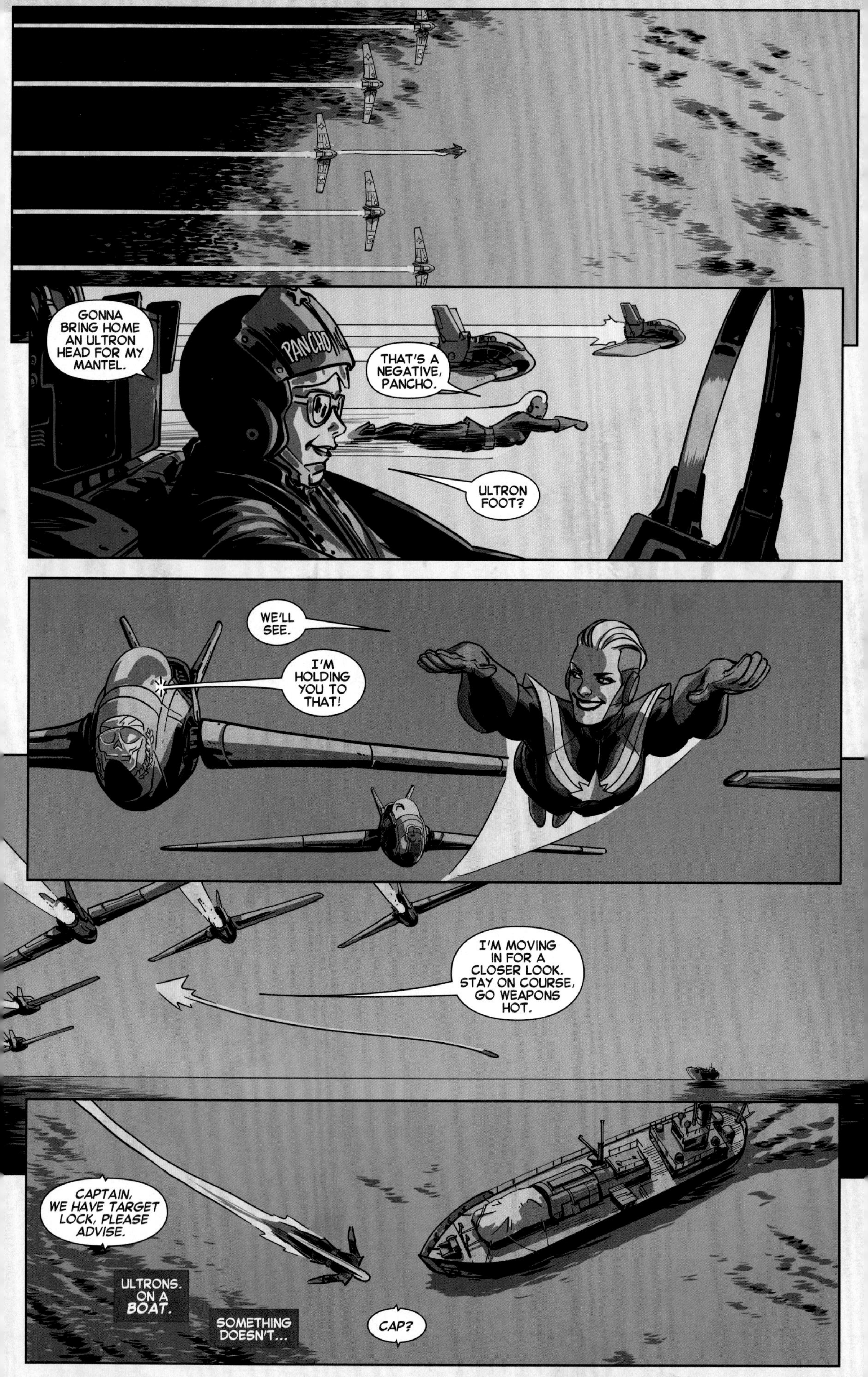

GONNA BRING HOME AN ULTRON HEAD FOR MY MANTEL.
PANCHO
THAT'S A NEGATIVE, PANCHO.
ULTRON FOOT?
WE'LL SEE.
I'M HOLDING YOU TO THAT!
I'M MOVING IN FOR A CLOSER LOOK. STAY ON COURSE, GO WEAPONS HOT.
CAPTAIN, WE HAVE TARGET LOCK, PLEASE ADVISE.
ULTRONS. ON A BOAT.
SOMETHING DOESN'T...
CAP?

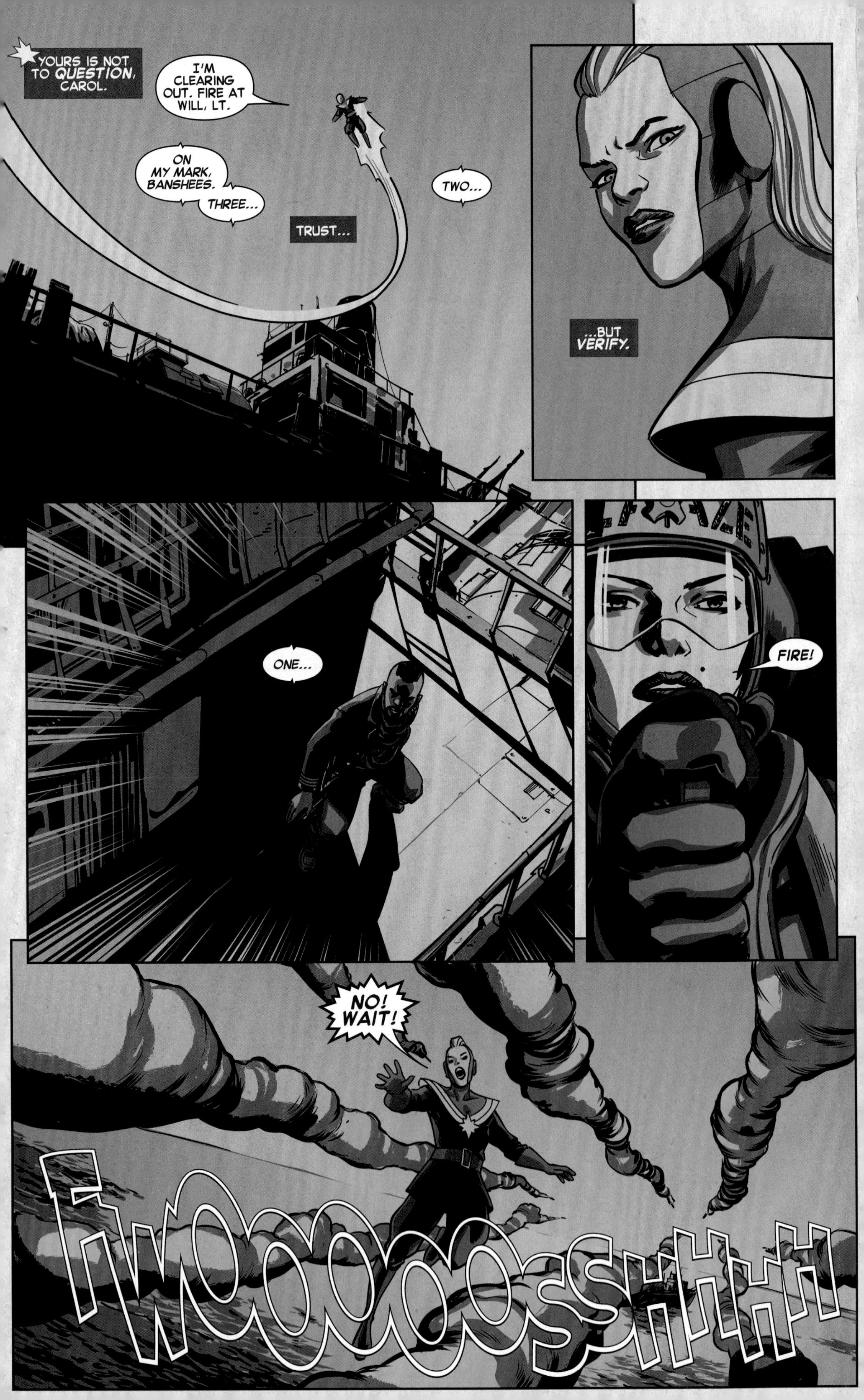
YOURS IS NOT TO QUESTION, CAROL.
I'M CLEARING OUT. FIRE AT WILL, LT.
ON MY MARK, BANSHEES.
THREE...
TRUST...
TWO...
...BUT VERIFY.
ONE...
FIRE!
NO! WAIT!
FWOOOOOOSHHHH

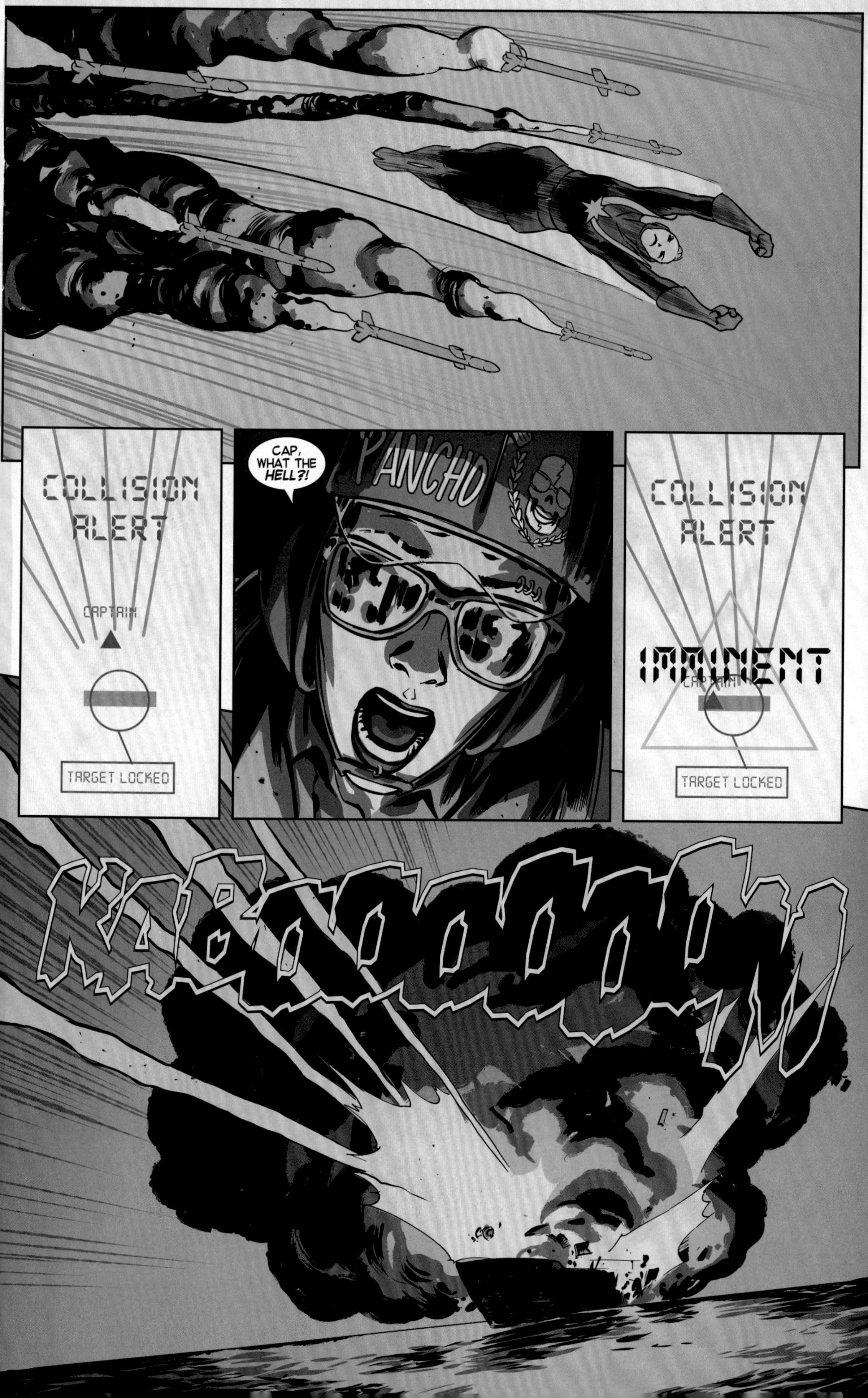
COLLISION ALERT
CAPTAIN.
TARGET LOCKED
PANCHO
CAP, WHAT THE HELL?!
COLLISION ALERT
IMMINENT
CAPTAIN
TARGET LOCKED

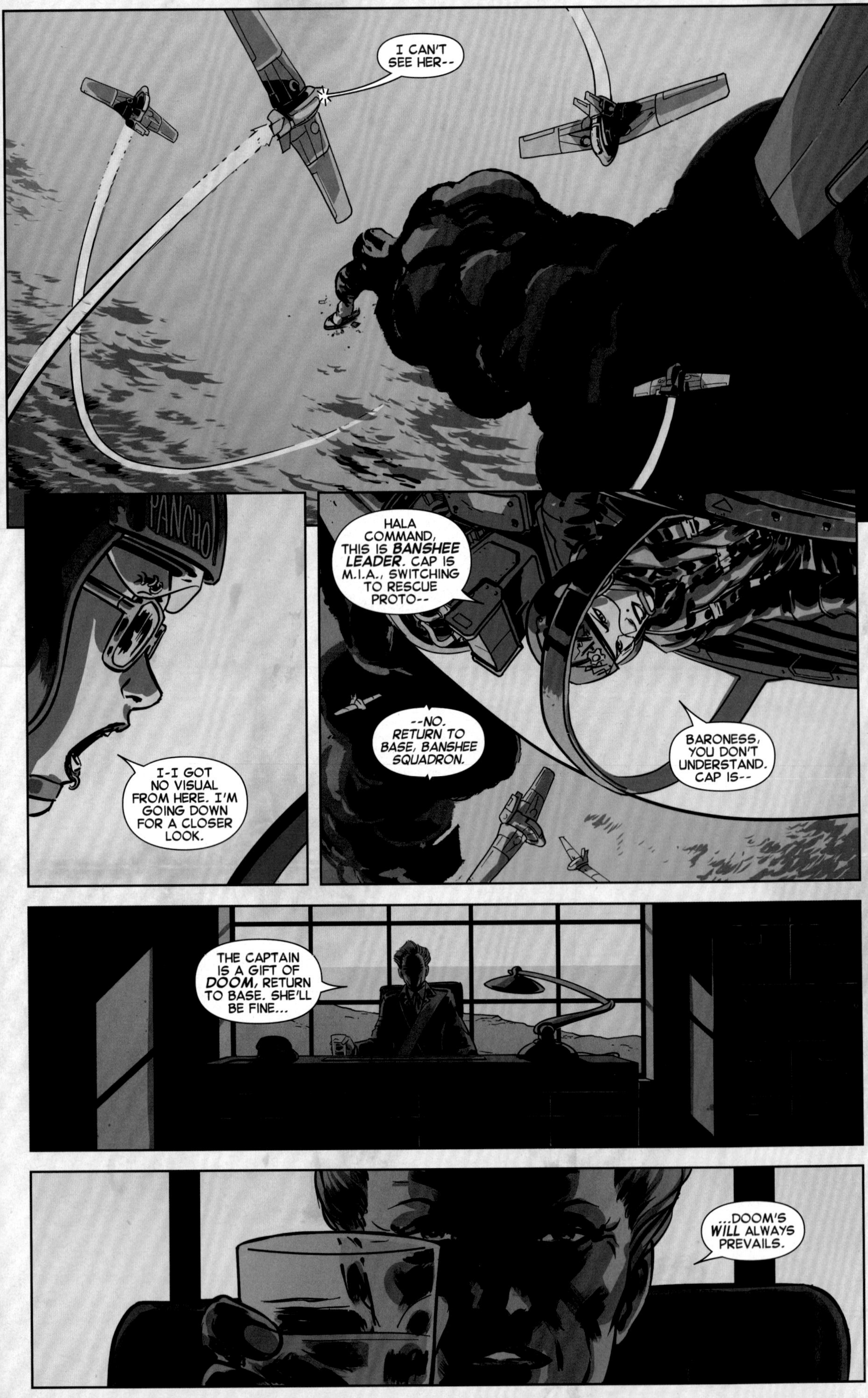
I CAN'T SEE HER--
PANCHO
I-I GOT NO VISUAL FROM HERE. I'M GOING DOWN FOR A CLOSER LOOK.
HALA COMMAND, THIS IS BANSHEE LEADER. CAP IS M.I.A., SWITCHING TO RESCUE PROTO--
--NO. RETURN TO BASE, BANSHEE SQUADRON.
BARONESS, YOU DON'T UNDERSTAND. CAP IS--
THE CAPTAIN IS A GIFT OF DOOM, RETURN TO BASE. SHE'LL BE FINE...
...DOOM'S WILL ALWAYS PREVAILS.

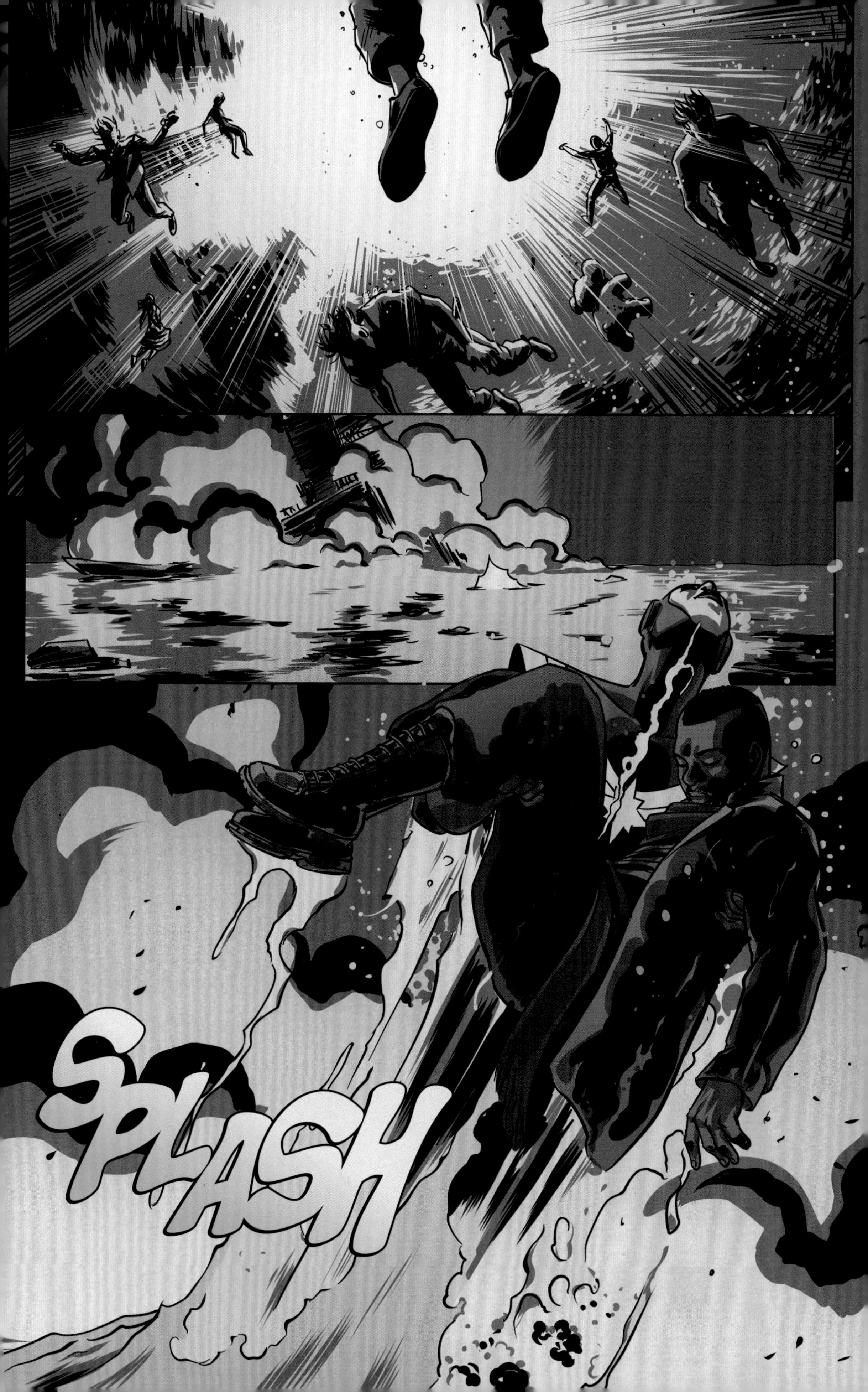
SPLASH

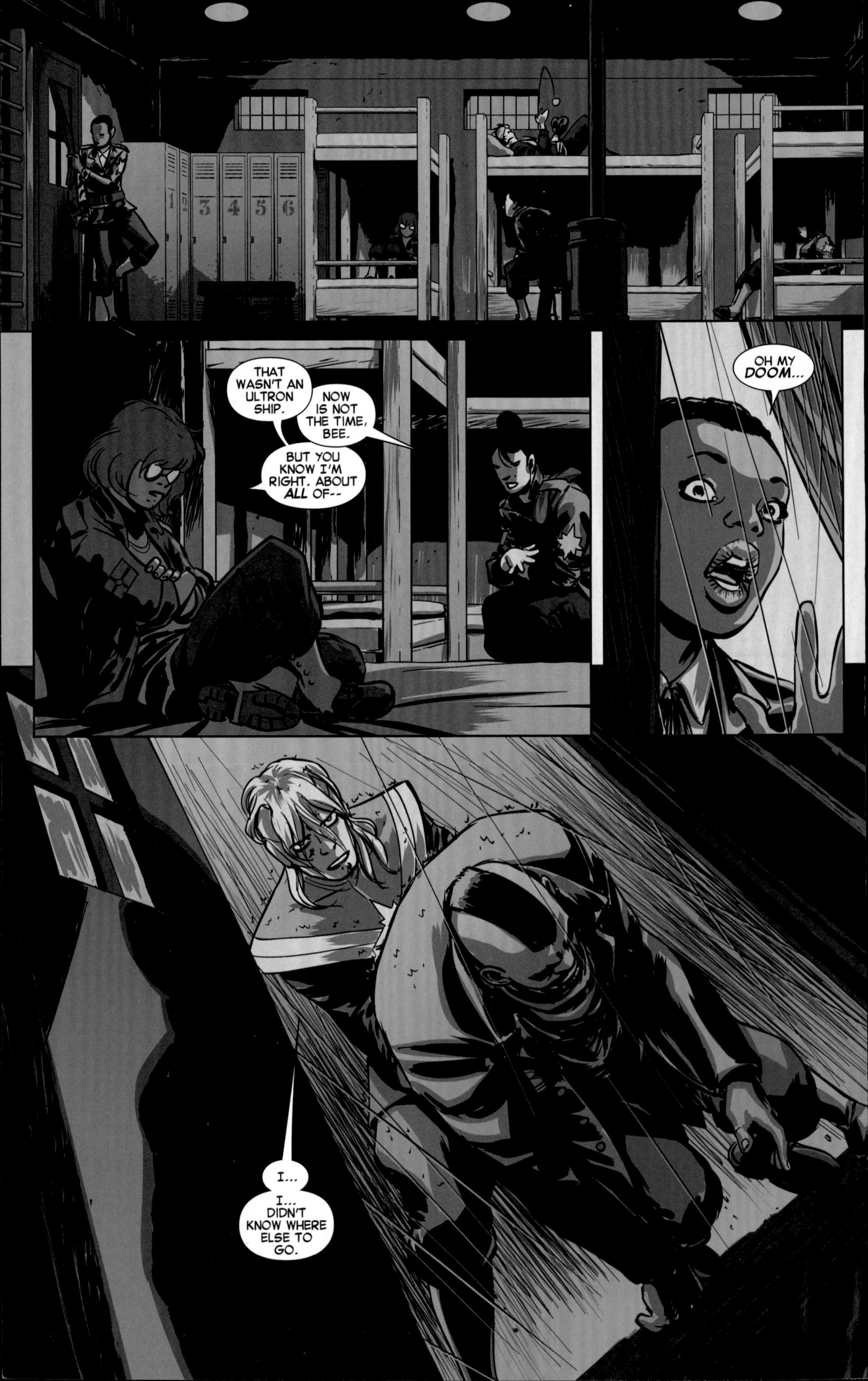
THAT WASN'T AN ULTRON SHIP.
NOW IS NOT THE TIME, BEE.
BUT YOU KNOW I'M RIGHT. ABOUT ALL OF--
OH MY DOOM...
I...
I... DIDN'T KNOW WHERE ELSE TO GO.

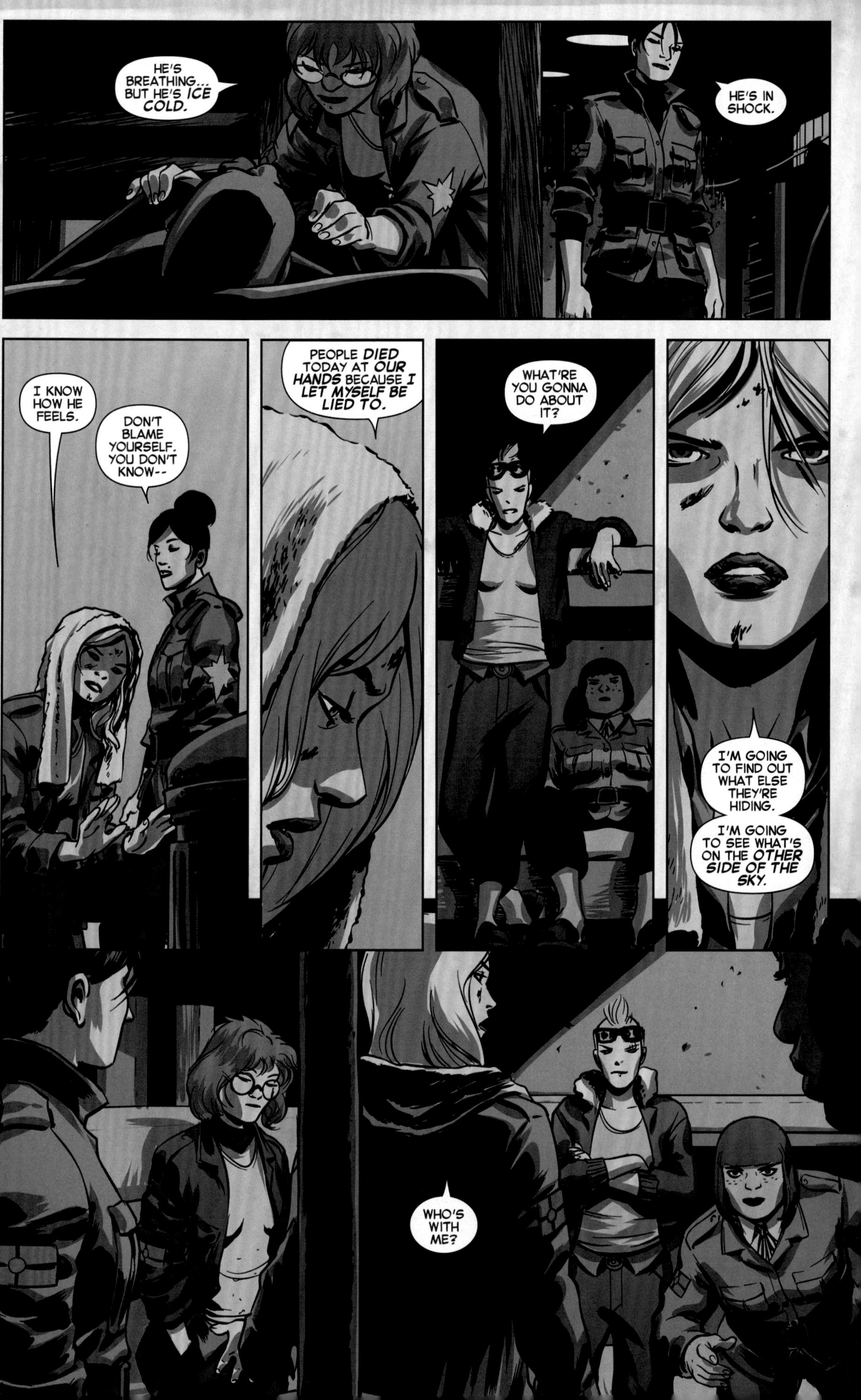
HE'S BREATHING... BUT HE'S ICE COLD.
HE'S IN SHOCK.
I KNOW HOW HE FEELS.
DON'T BLAME YOURSELF. YOU DON'T KNOW--
PEOPLE DIED TODAY AT OUR HANDS BECAUSE I LET MYSELF BE LIED TO.
WHAT'RE YOU GONNA DO ABOUT IT?
I'M GOING TO FIND OUT WHAT ELSE THEY'RE HIDING.
I'M GOING TO SEE WHAT'S ON THE OTHER SIDE OF THE SKY.
WHO'S WITH ME?

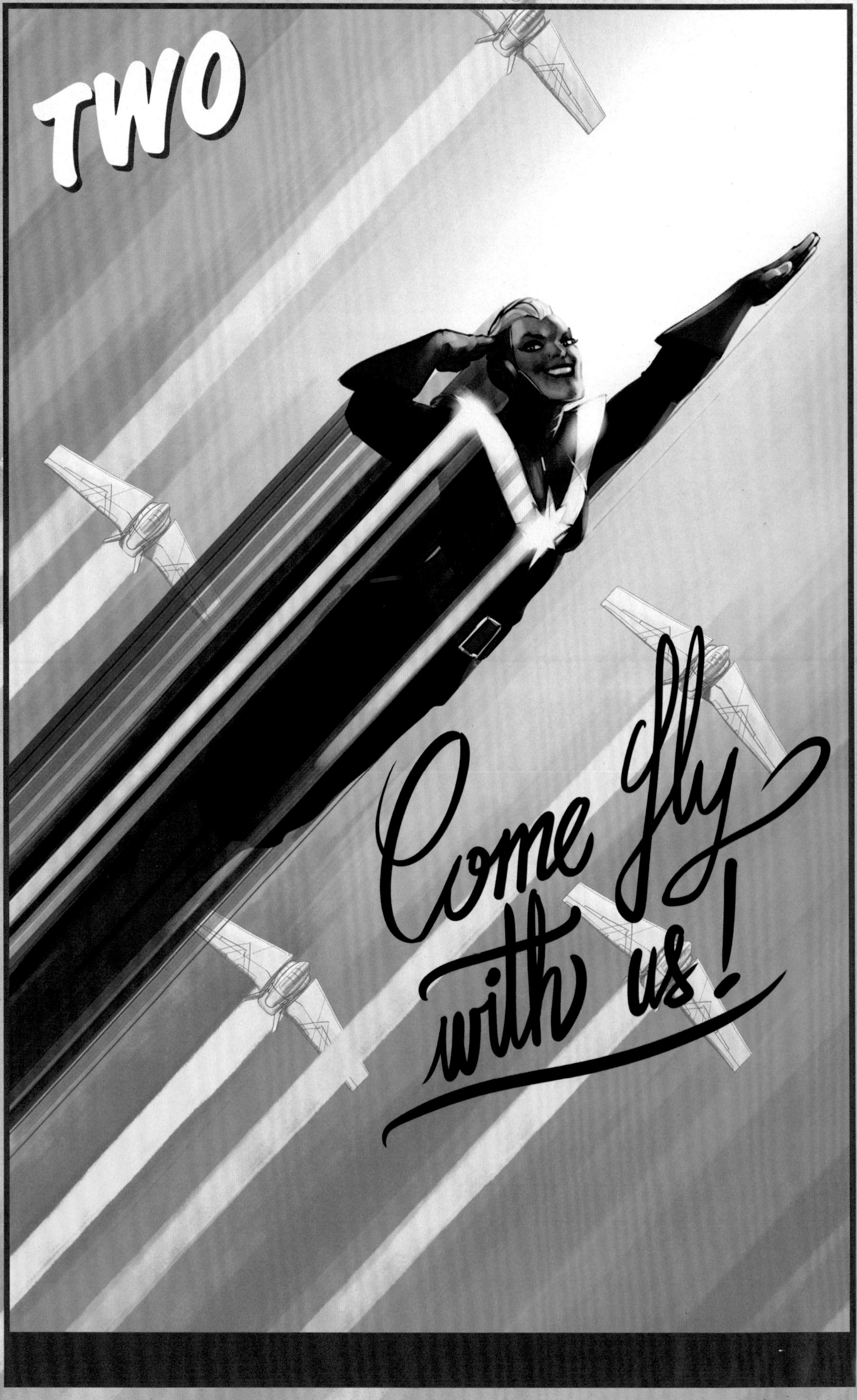
TWO
Come fly with us!

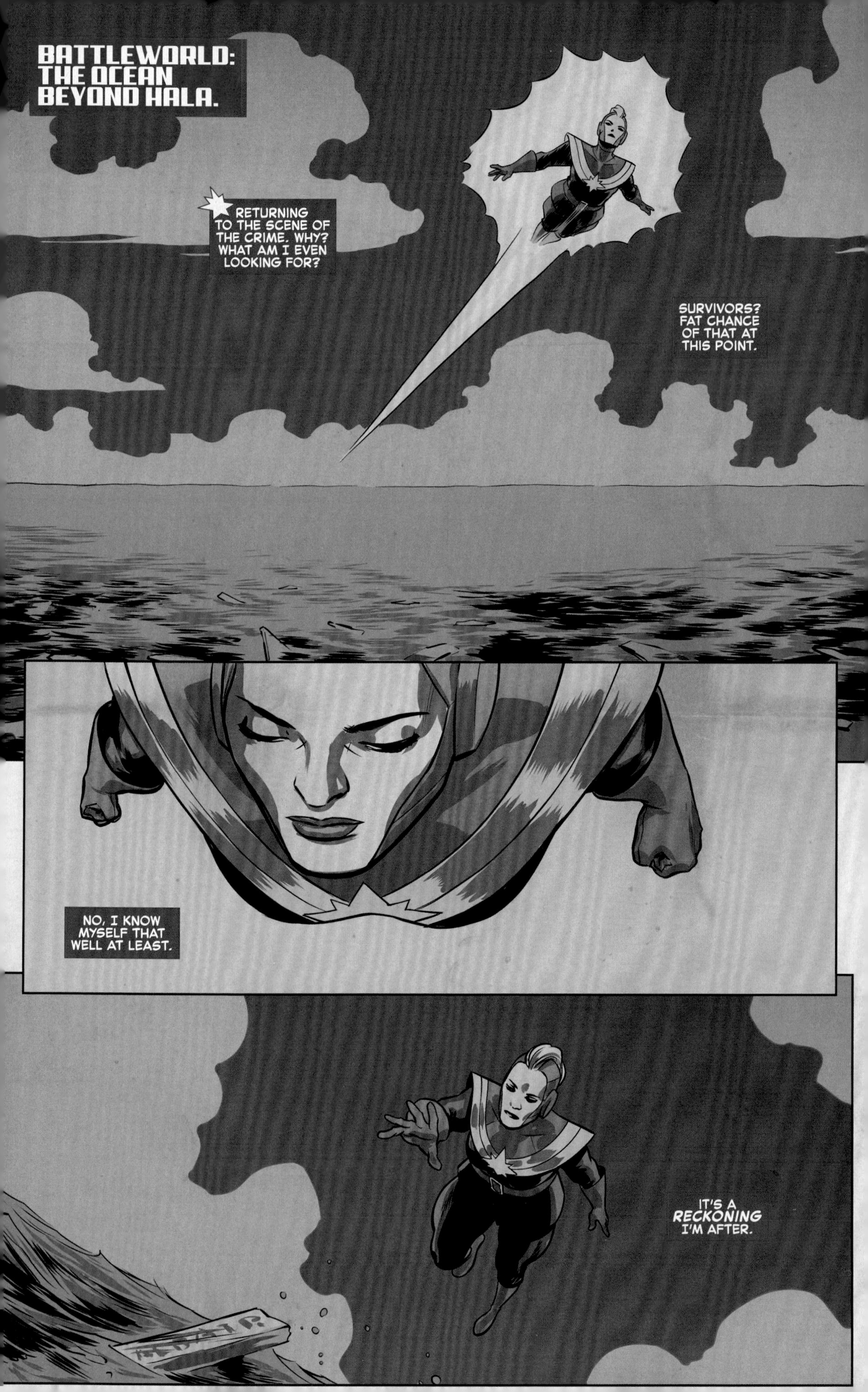
BATTLEWORLD: THE OCEAN BEYOND HALA.
RETURNING TO THE SCENE OF THE CRIME. WHY? WHAT AM I EVEN LOOKING FOR?
SURVIVORS? FAT CHANCE OF THAT AT THIS POINT.
NO, I KNOW MYSELF THAT WELL AT LEAST.
IT'S A *RECKONING* I'M AFTER.

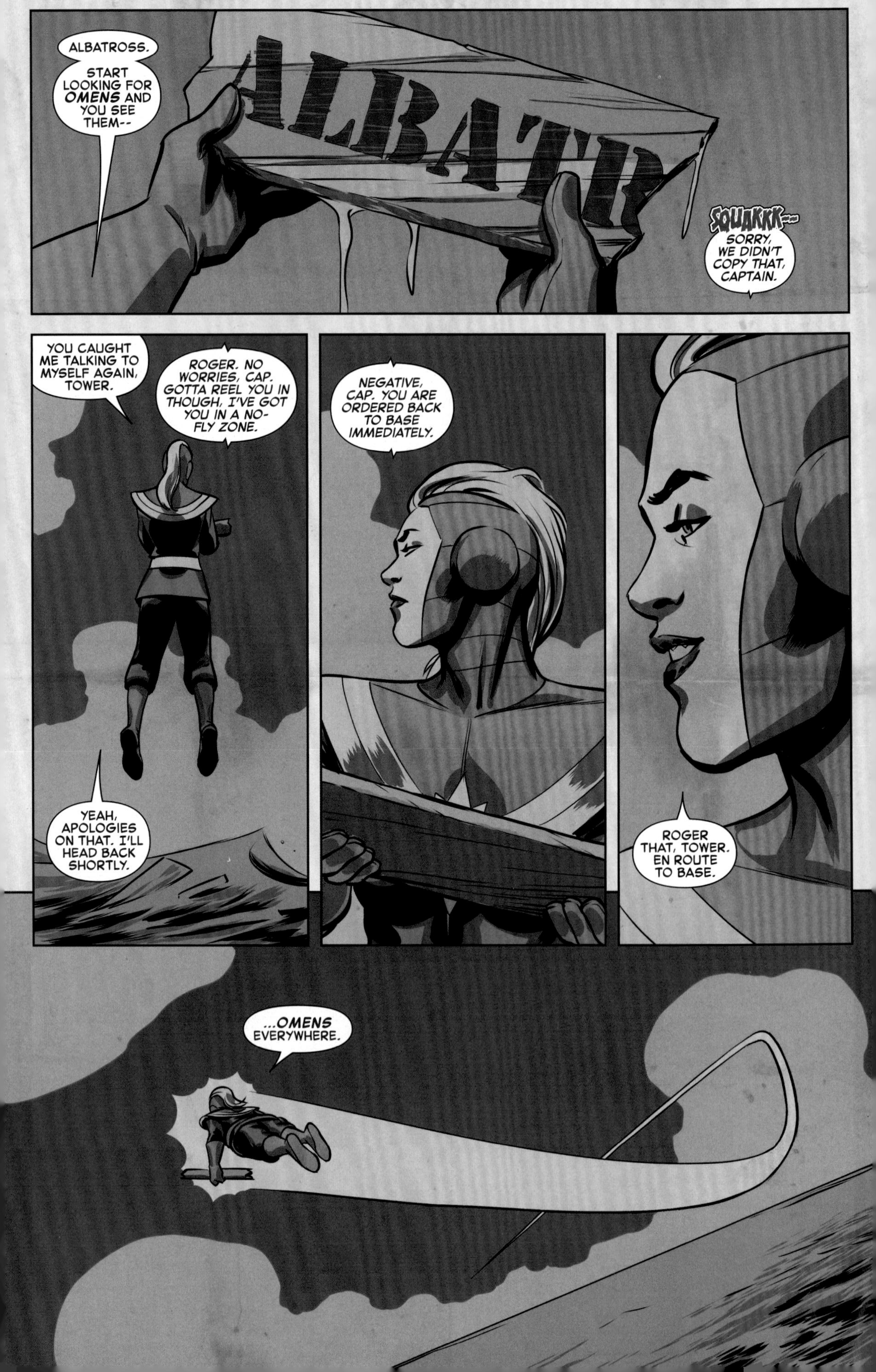
ALBATROSS.
START LOOKING FOR OMENS AND YOU SEE THEM--
ALBATR
SQUAKKK--
SORRY, WE DIDN'T COPY THAT, CAPTAIN.
YOU CAUGHT ME TALKING TO MYSELF AGAIN, TOWER.
ROGER. NO WORRIES, CAP. GOTTA REEL YOU IN THOUGH, I'VE GOT YOU IN A NO-FLY ZONE.
YEAH, APOLOGIES ON THAT. I'LL HEAD BACK SHORTLY.
NEGATIVE, CAP. YOU ARE ORDERED BACK TO BASE IMMEDIATELY.
ROGER THAT, TOWER. EN ROUTE TO BASE.
...OMENS EVERYWHERE.

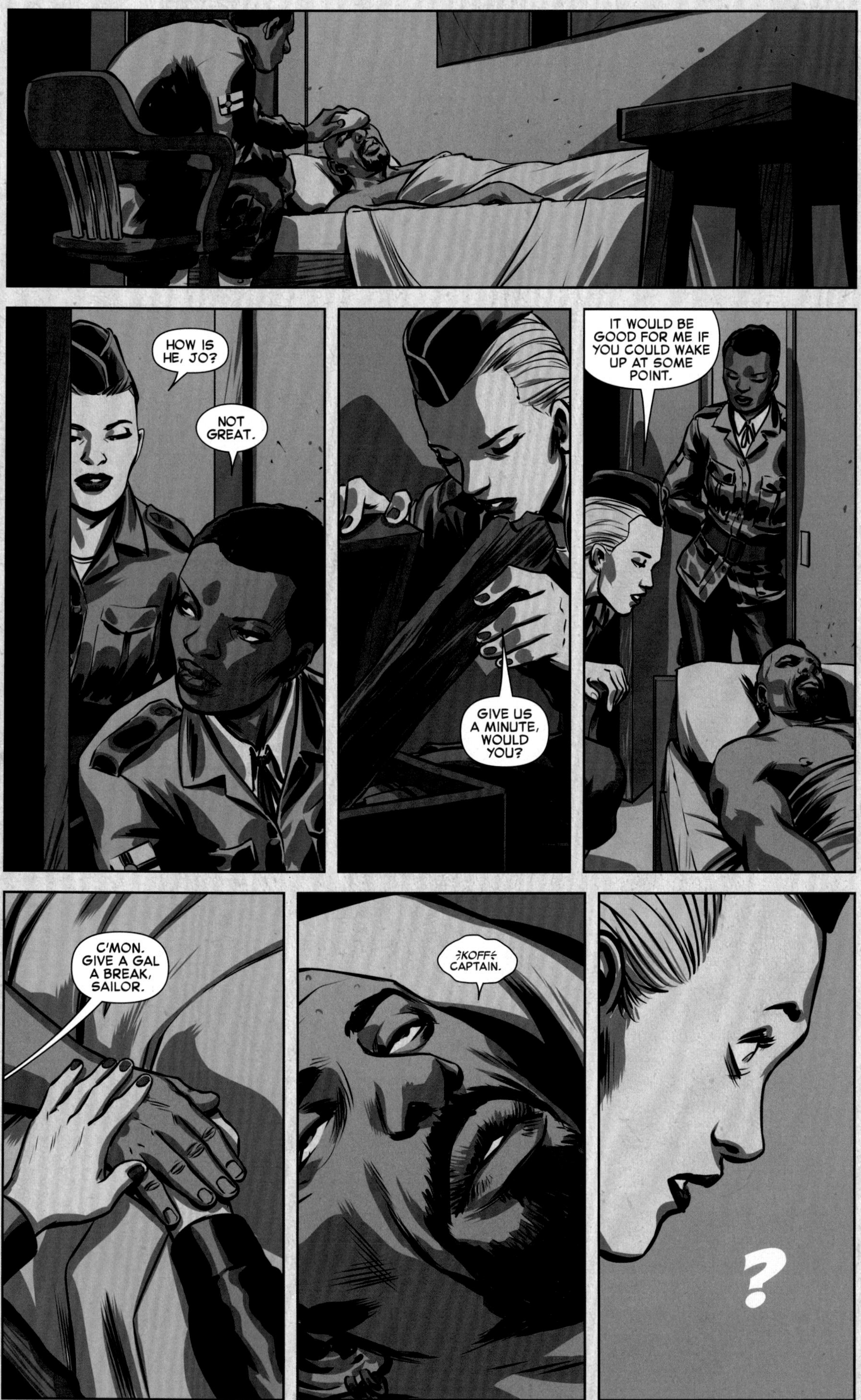
HOW IS HE, JO?
NOT GREAT.
GIVE US A MINUTE, WOULD YOU?
IT WOULD BE GOOD FOR ME IF YOU COULD WAKE UP AT SOME POINT.
C'MON. GIVE A GAL A BREAK, SAILOR.
KOFF CAPTAIN.
?

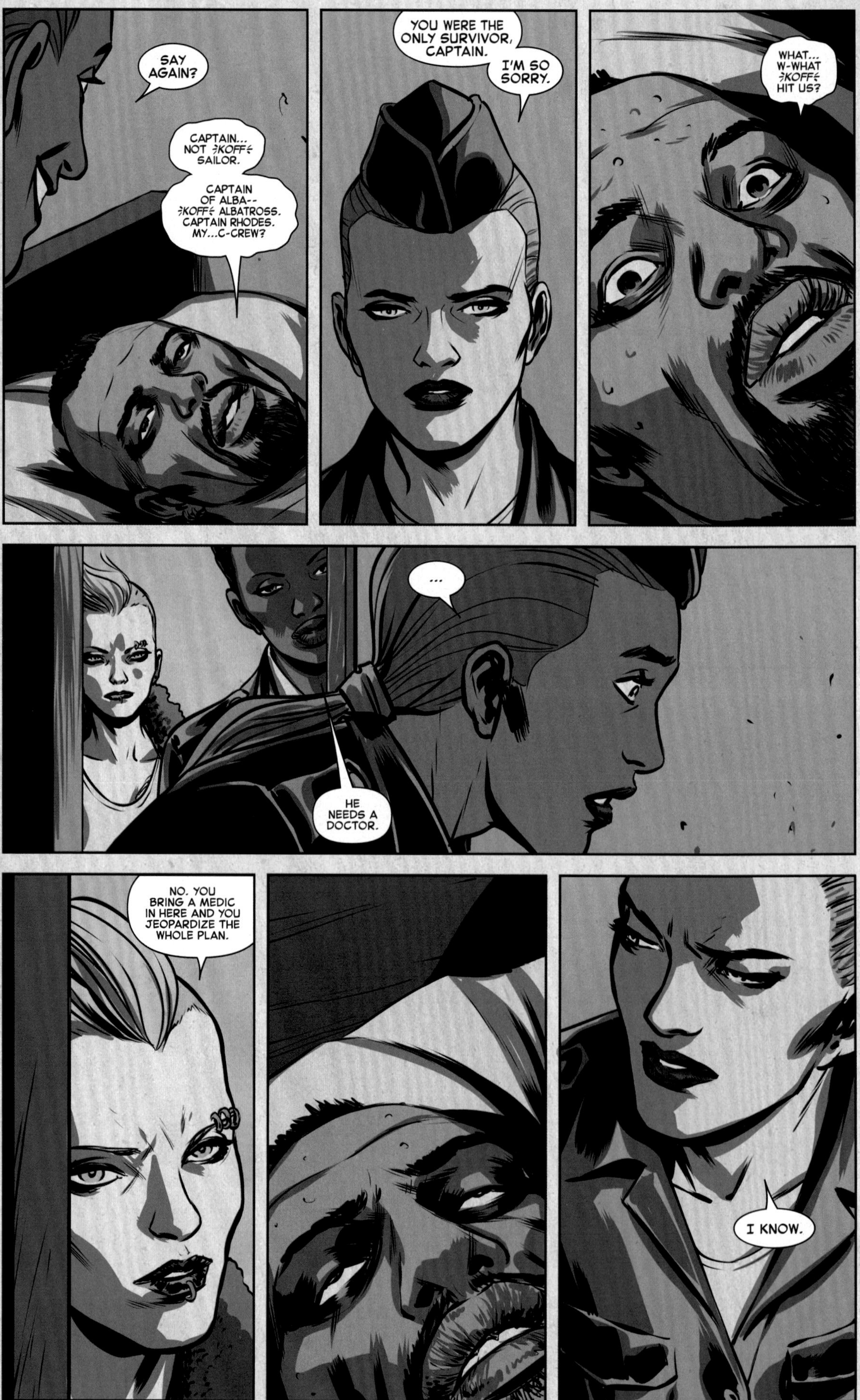
SAY AGAIN?
CAPTAIN... NOT ⸗KOFF⸗ SAILOR.
CAPTAIN OF ALBA-- ⸗KOFF⸗ ALBATROSS. CAPTAIN RHODES. MY...C-CREW?
YOU WERE THE ONLY SURVIVOR, CAPTAIN.
I'M SO SORRY.
WHAT... W-WHAT ⸗KOFF⸗ HIT US?
...
HE NEEDS A DOCTOR.
NO. YOU BRING A MEDIC IN HERE AND YOU JEOPARDIZE THE WHOLE PLAN.
I KNOW.

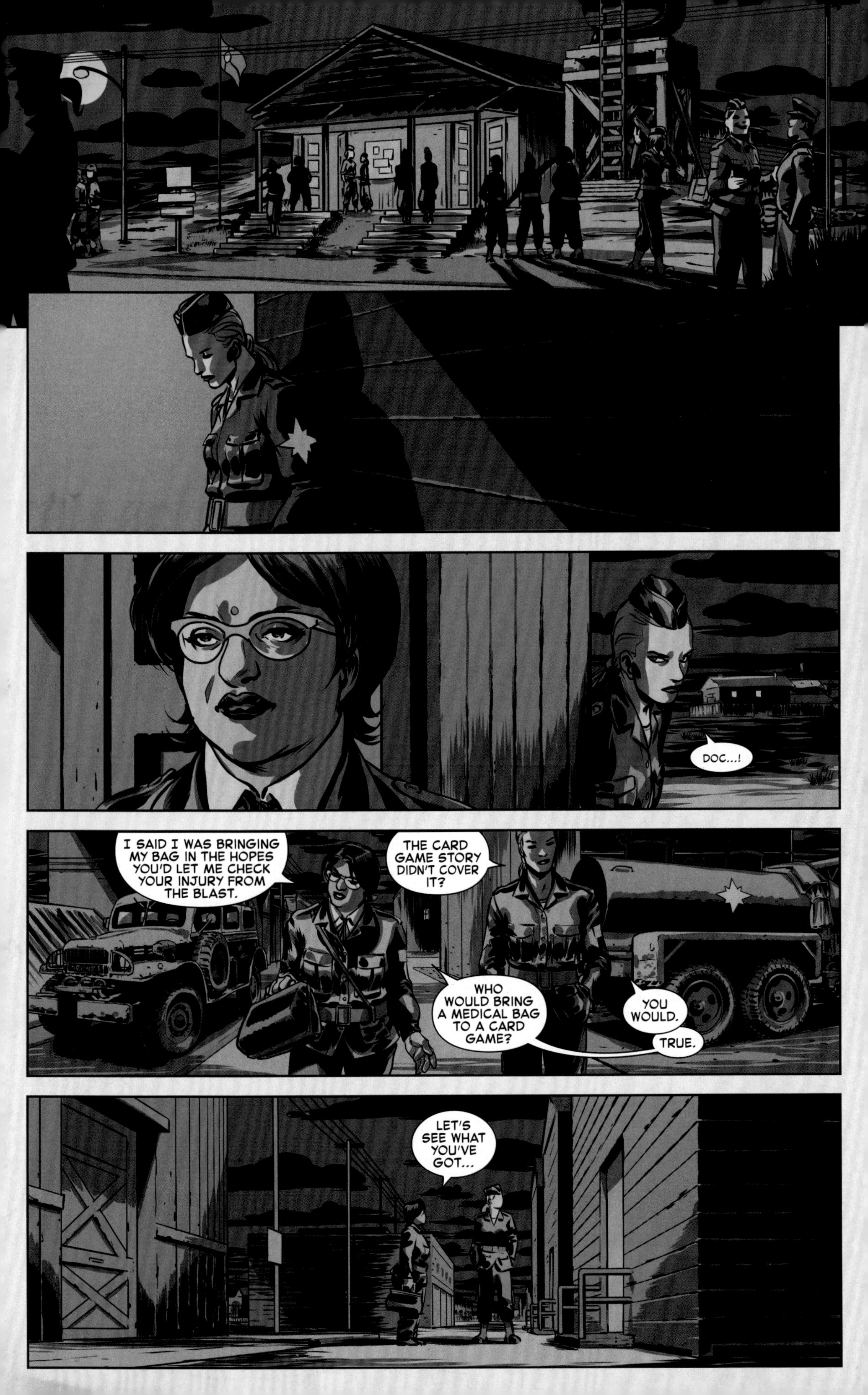
DOC...!
I SAID I WAS BRINGING MY BAG IN THE HOPES YOU'D LET ME CHECK YOUR INJURY FROM THE BLAST.
THE CARD GAME STORY DIDN'T COVER IT?
WHO WOULD BRING A MEDICAL BAG TO A CARD GAME?
YOU WOULD.
TRUE.
LET'S SEE WHAT YOU'VE GOT...

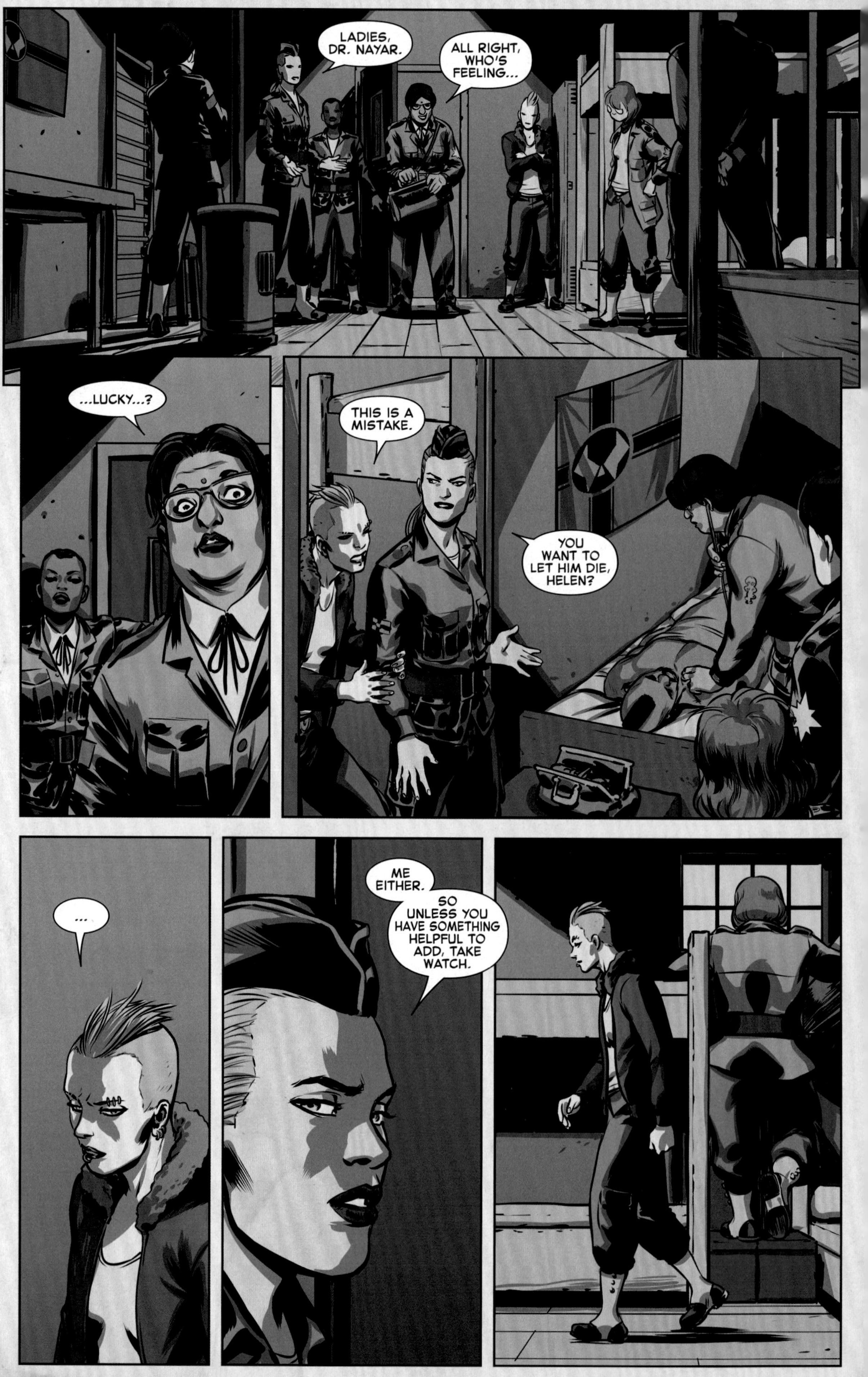
LADIES, DR. NAYAR.
ALL RIGHT, WHO'S FEELING...
...LUCKY...?
THIS IS A MISTAKE.
YOU WANT TO LET HIM DIE, HELEN?
...
ME EITHER.
SO UNLESS YOU HAVE SOMETHING HELPFUL TO ADD, TAKE WATCH.

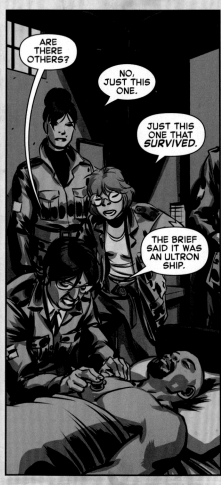

ARE THERE OTHERS?

NO, JUST THIS ONE.

JUST THIS ONE THAT *SURVIVED*.

THE BRIEF SAID IT WAS AN ULTRON SHIP.

HE LOOK LIKE AN ULTRON TO YOU?

NO. NO, HE DOESN'T.

HE'S FIGHTING AN INFECTION. I'M LEAVING YOU ANTIBIOTICS FOR HIM, BUT THAT DOESN'T SOLVE THE GREATER PROBLEM...

...OF WHAT YOU'RE GOING TO DO WITH HIM WHEN HE'S ON HIS FEET AGAIN. THIS IS NOT A *PUPPY*. THIS IS A PERSON-- A *MAN*.

CAROL, PATCHING UP SOMEBODY THAT GOT INTO AN OFF-BASE BRAWL AND KEEPING IT QUIET IS ONE THING, BUT THIS--

HERE WE GO.

I'M THE BARONESS'S PERSONAL *PHYSICIAN*. NOT TO MENTION AN *OFFICER*. I HAVE A RESPONSIBILITY TO *DOOM*--

DOOM IS LIES!

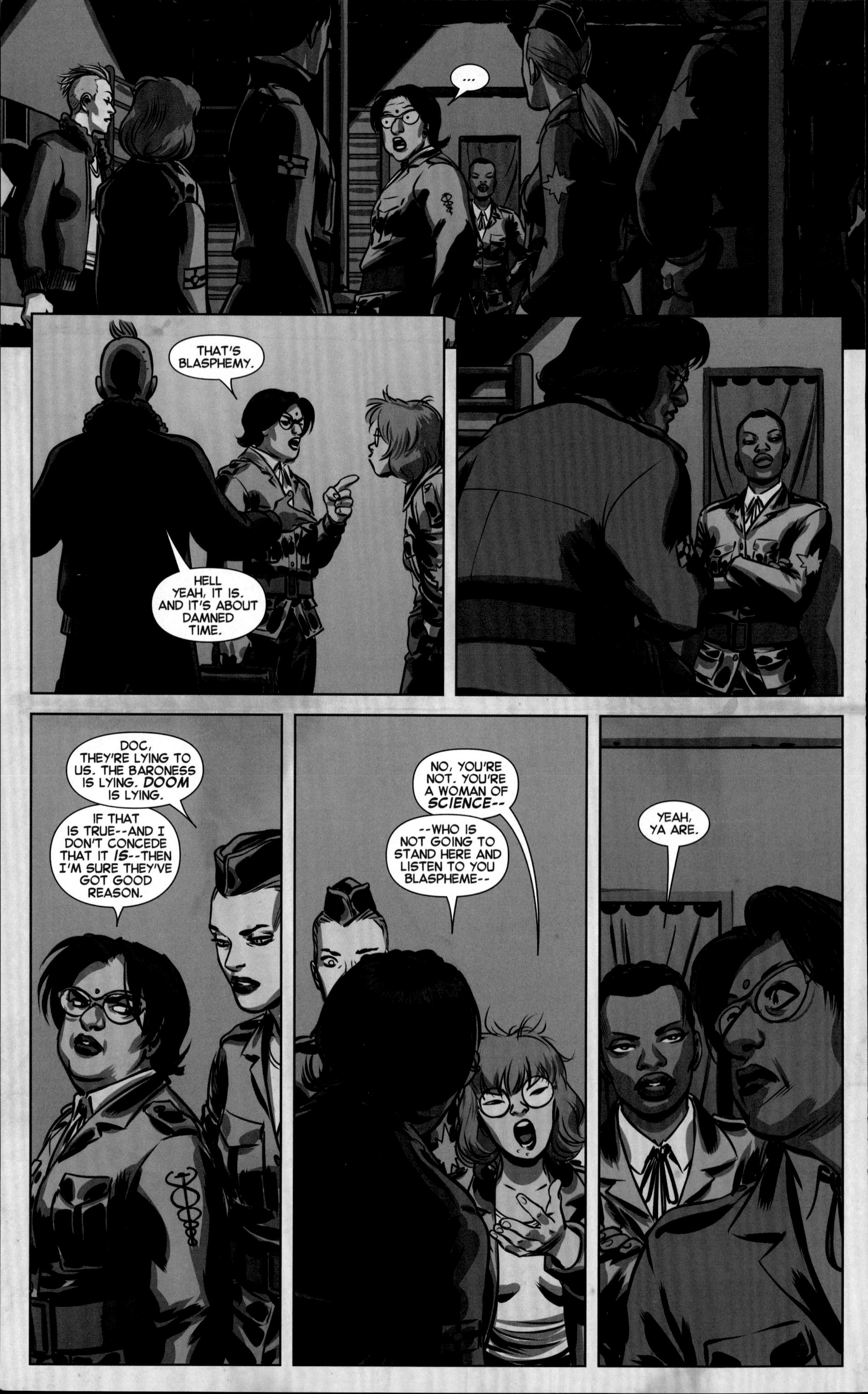
...
THAT'S BLASPHEMY.
HELL YEAH, IT IS. AND IT'S ABOUT DAMNED TIME.
DOC, THEY'RE LYING TO US. THE BARONESS IS LYING. DOOM IS LYING.
IF THAT IS TRUE--AND I DON'T CONCEDE THAT IT IS--THEN I'M SURE THEY'VE GOT GOOD REASON.
NO, YOU'RE NOT. YOU'RE A WOMAN OF SCIENCE--
--WHO IS NOT GOING TO STAND HERE AND LISTEN TO YOU BLASPHEME--
YEAH, YA ARE.

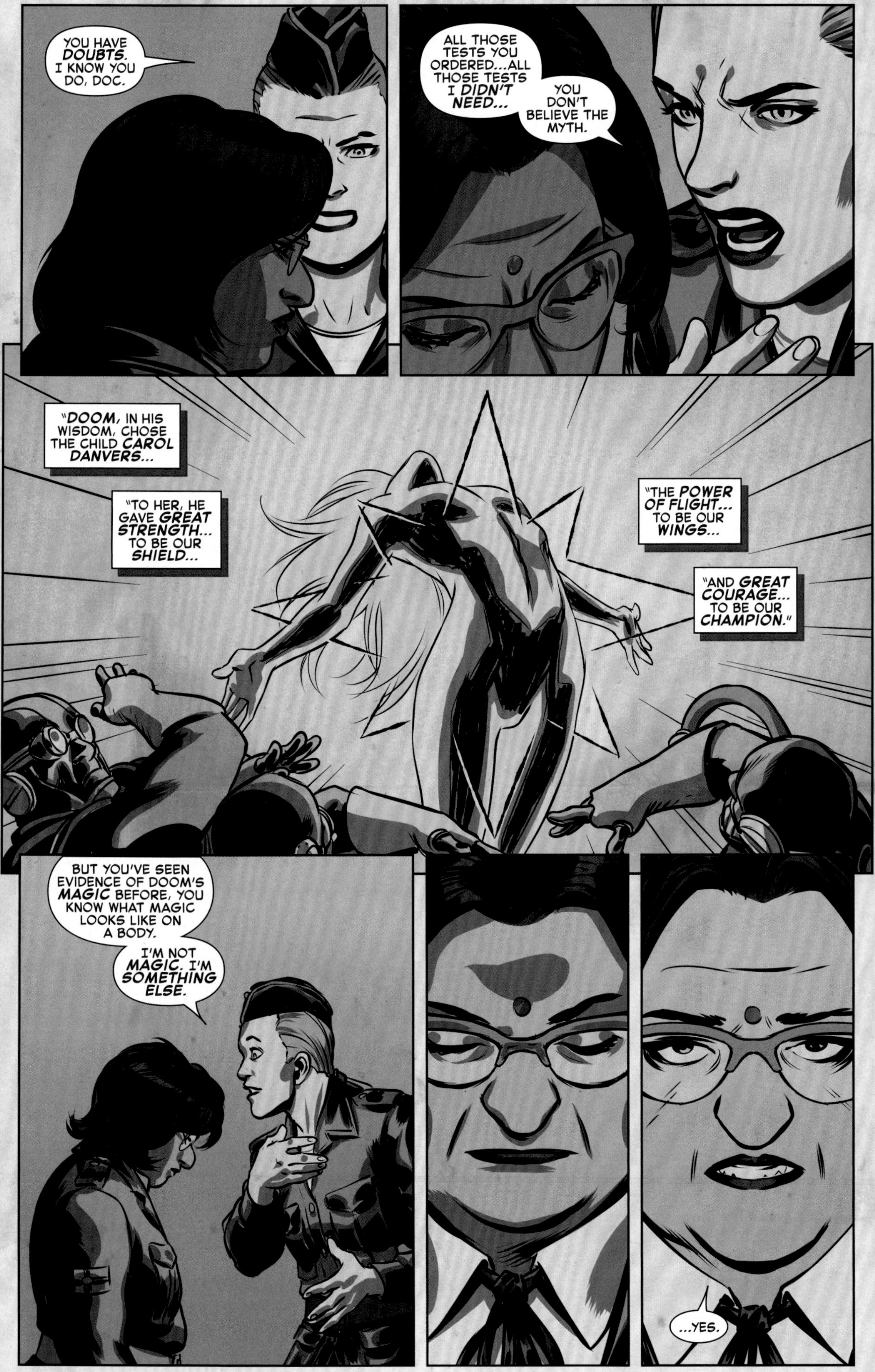
YOU HAVE DOUBTS. I KNOW YOU DO, DOC.
ALL THOSE TESTS YOU ORDERED...ALL THOSE TESTS I DIDN'T NEED...
YOU DON'T BELIEVE THE MYTH.
"DOOM, IN HIS WISDOM, CHOSE THE CHILD CAROL DANVERS...
"TO HER, HE GAVE GREAT STRENGTH... TO BE OUR SHIELD...
"THE POWER OF FLIGHT... TO BE OUR WINGS...
"AND GREAT COURAGE... TO BE OUR CHAMPION."
BUT YOU'VE SEEN EVIDENCE OF DOOM'S MAGIC BEFORE, YOU KNOW WHAT MAGIC LOOKS LIKE ON A BODY.
I'M NOT MAGIC. I'M SOMETHING ELSE.
...YES.

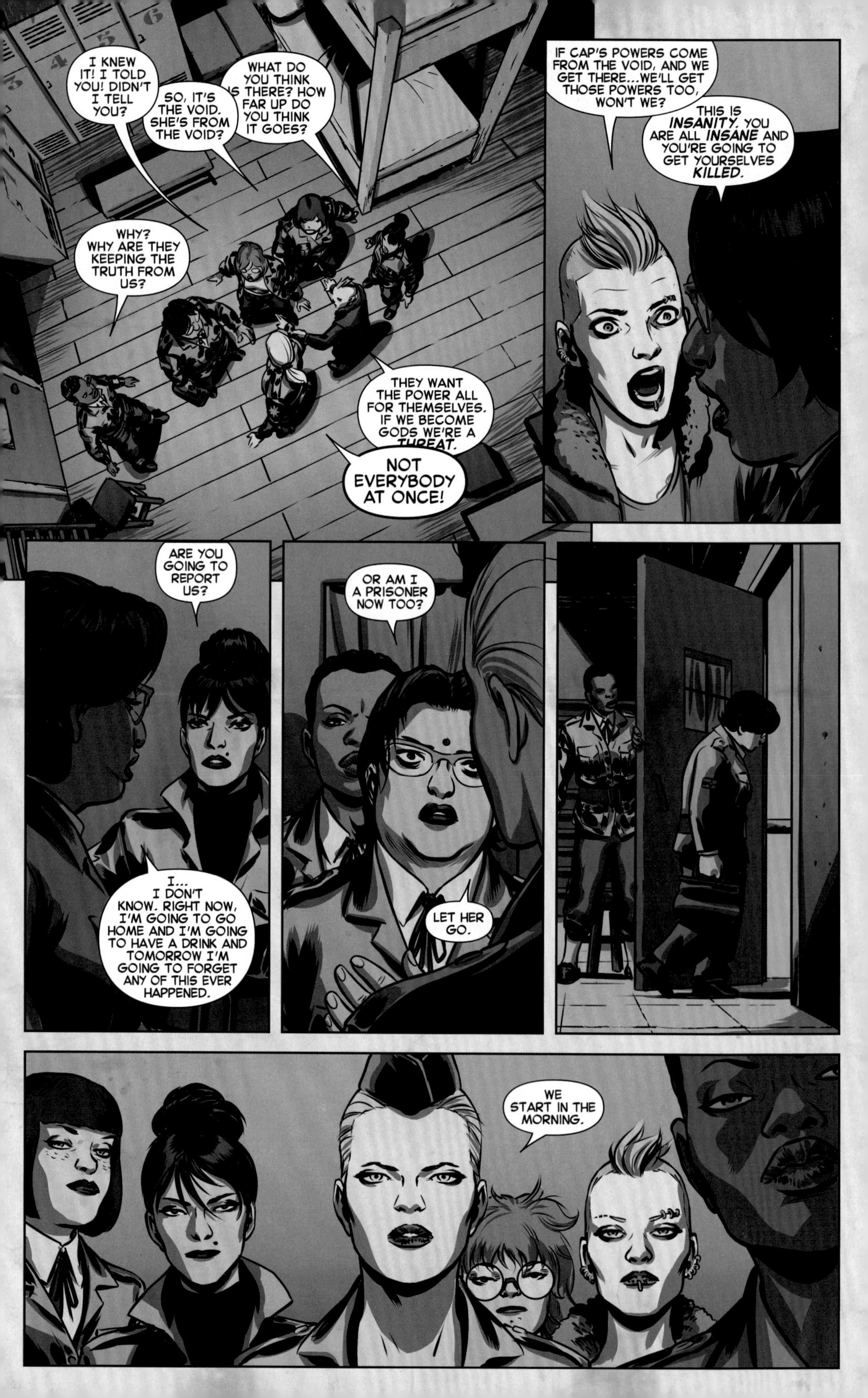

I KNEW IT! I TOLD YOU! DIDN'T I TELL YOU?
SO, IT'S THE VOID. SHE'S FROM THE VOID?
WHAT DO YOU THINK IS THERE? HOW FAR UP DO YOU THINK IT GOES?
WHY? WHY ARE THEY KEEPING THE TRUTH FROM US?
THEY WANT THE POWER ALL FOR THEMSELVES. IF WE BECOME GODS WE'RE A THREAT.
NOT EVERYBODY AT ONCE!
IF CAP'S POWERS COME FROM THE VOID, AND WE GET THERE...WE'LL GET THOSE POWERS TOO, WON'T WE?
THIS IS INSANITY. YOU ARE ALL INSANE AND YOU'RE GOING TO GET YOURSELVES KILLED.
ARE YOU GOING TO REPORT US?
I... I DON'T KNOW. RIGHT NOW, I'M GOING TO GO HOME AND I'M GOING TO HAVE A DRINK AND TOMORROW I'M GOING TO FORGET ANY OF THIS EVER HAPPENED.
OR AM I A PRISONER NOW TOO?
LET HER GO.
WE START IN THE MORNING.

"ALL RIGHT THEN. HERE'S HOW IT'S GOING TO GO..."

"MACKIE IS GOING TO LEAD THE WORK RETROFITTING OUR PLANES, TURNING THEM INTO ROCKETS CAPABLE OF CLEARING THE VOID."

"YOU'LL DO YOUR OWN AND JOLENE'S FIRST, MACK. SINCE THAT WILL GROUND JOLENE, SHE'LL BE YOUR FIRST ASSISTANT."

"YOU PULL THE PARTS FROM THE GRAVEYARD. IF YOU CAN'T FIND WHAT YOU NEED THERE... WELL, GET CREATIVE."

"WHEN JOLENE'S PLANE IS DONE, WE'LL ROTATE OUT. BEE IS NEXT, THEN JERRI, THEN HELEN. MINE IS LAST."

"WHILE MACKIE AND HER ROTATING ASSISTANTS ARE BUSY WITH THE RETROFITS, THE REST OF YOU NEED TO BE STRICTLY S.O.P.

"YOU'RE RUNNING DRILLS. IT'S JUST AN AVERAGE DAY. I WANT THINGS BY. THE. BOOK."

"BUT STILL US. WE'RE NEVER QUITE BY THE BOOK... ARE WE, PANCHO?"

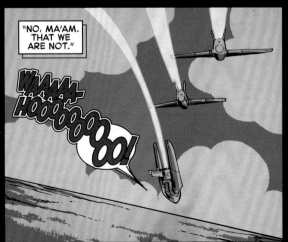

"NO, MA'AM. THAT WE ARE NOT."

WAAAA-HOOOOOOOO!

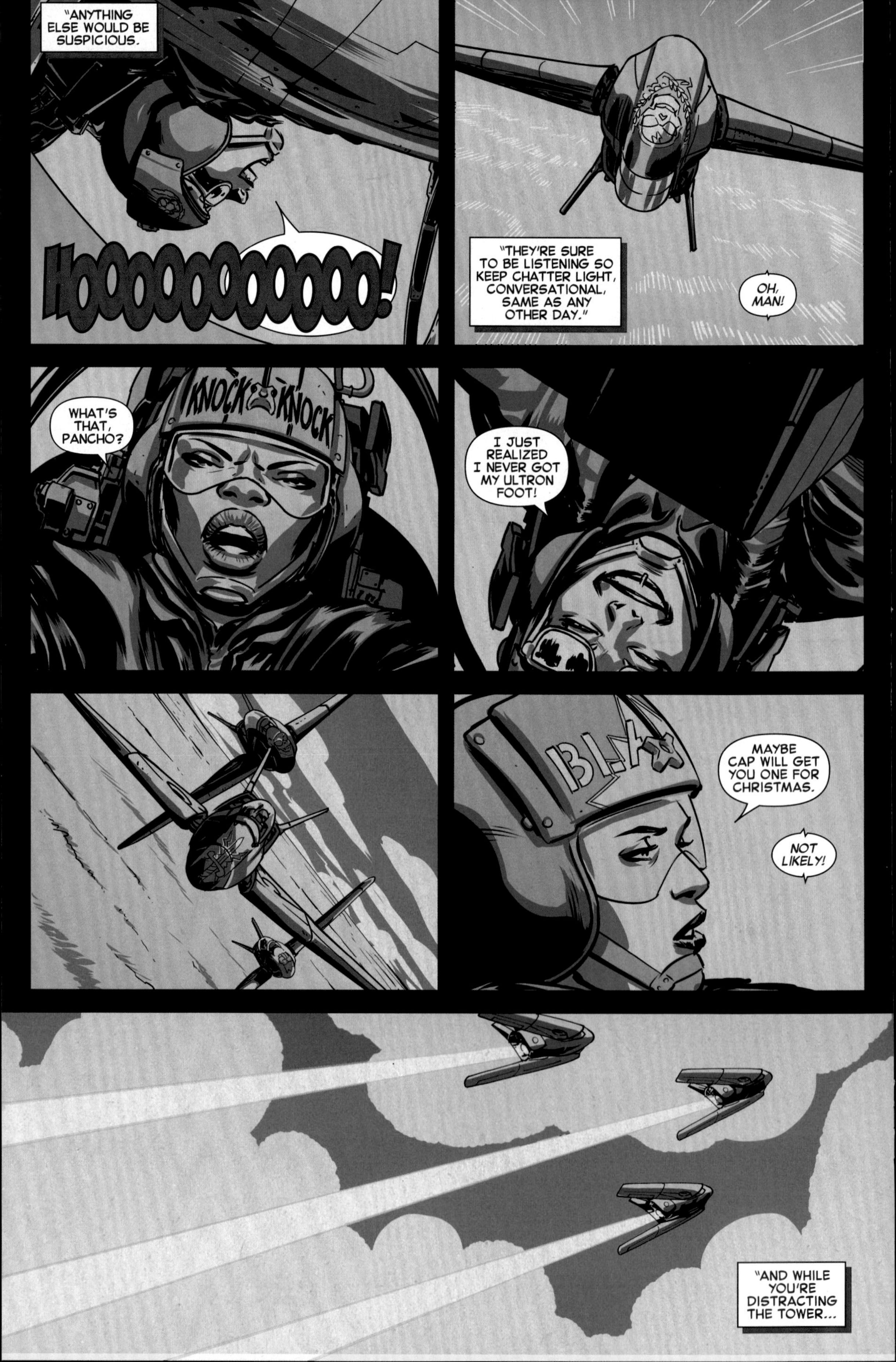
"ANYTHING ELSE WOULD BE SUSPICIOUS.
HOOOOOOOOOOOO!
"THEY'RE SURE TO BE LISTENING SO KEEP CHATTER LIGHT, CONVERSATIONAL, SAME AS ANY OTHER DAY."
OH, MAN!
KNOCK KNOCK
WHAT'S THAT, PANCHO?
I JUST REALIZED I NEVER GOT MY ULTRON FOOT!
MAYBE CAP WILL GET YOU ONE FOR CHRISTMAS.
NOT LIKELY!
"AND WHILE YOU'RE DISTRACTING THE TOWER...

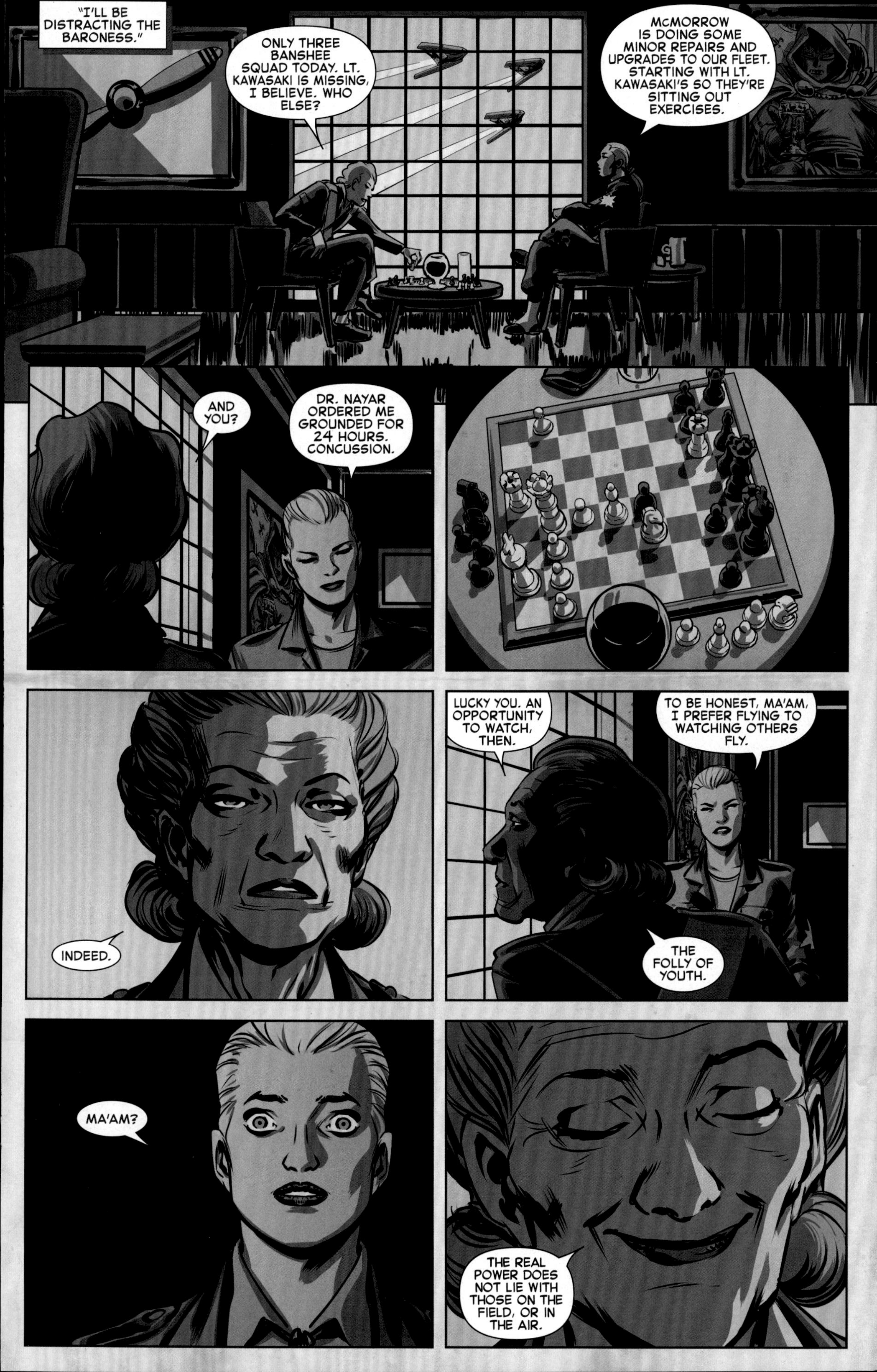
"I'LL BE DISTRACTING THE BARONESS."
ONLY THREE BANSHEE SQUAD TODAY. LT. KAWASAKI IS MISSING, I BELIEVE. WHO ELSE?
McMORROW IS DOING SOME MINOR REPAIRS AND UPGRADES TO OUR FLEET. STARTING WITH LT. KAWASAKI'S SO THEY'RE SITTING OUT EXERCISES.
AND YOU?
DR. NAYAR ORDERED ME GROUNDED FOR 24 HOURS. CONCUSSION.
INDEED.
LUCKY YOU. AN OPPORTUNITY TO WATCH, THEN.
TO BE HONEST, MA'AM, I PREFER FLYING TO WATCHING OTHERS FLY.
THE FOLLY OF YOUTH.
MA'AM?
THE REAL POWER DOES NOT LIE WITH THOSE ON THE FIELD, OR IN THE AIR.

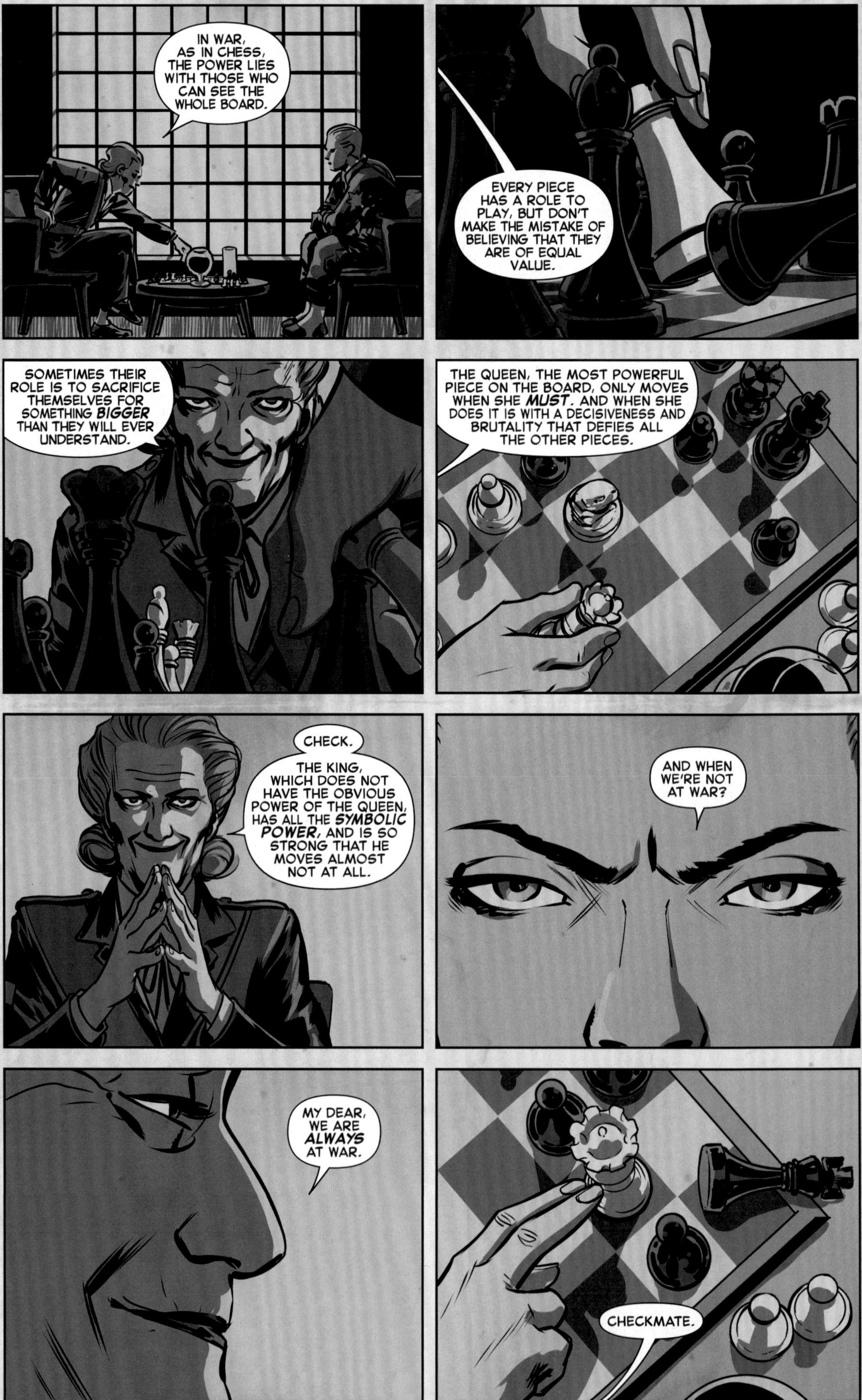
IN WAR, AS IN CHESS, THE POWER LIES WITH THOSE WHO CAN SEE THE WHOLE BOARD.
EVERY PIECE HAS A ROLE TO PLAY, BUT DON'T MAKE THE MISTAKE OF BELIEVING THAT THEY ARE OF EQUAL VALUE.
SOMETIMES THEIR ROLE IS TO SACRIFICE THEMSELVES FOR SOMETHING BIGGER THAN THEY WILL EVER UNDERSTAND.
THE QUEEN, THE MOST POWERFUL PIECE ON THE BOARD, ONLY MOVES WHEN SHE MUST. AND WHEN SHE DOES IT IS WITH A DECISIVENESS AND BRUTALITY THAT DEFIES ALL THE OTHER PIECES.
CHECK.
THE KING, WHICH DOES NOT HAVE THE OBVIOUS POWER OF THE QUEEN, HAS ALL THE SYMBOLIC POWER, AND IS SO STRONG THAT HE MOVES ALMOST NOT AT ALL.
AND WHEN WE'RE NOT AT WAR?
MY DEAR, WE ARE ALWAYS AT WAR.
CHECKMATE.

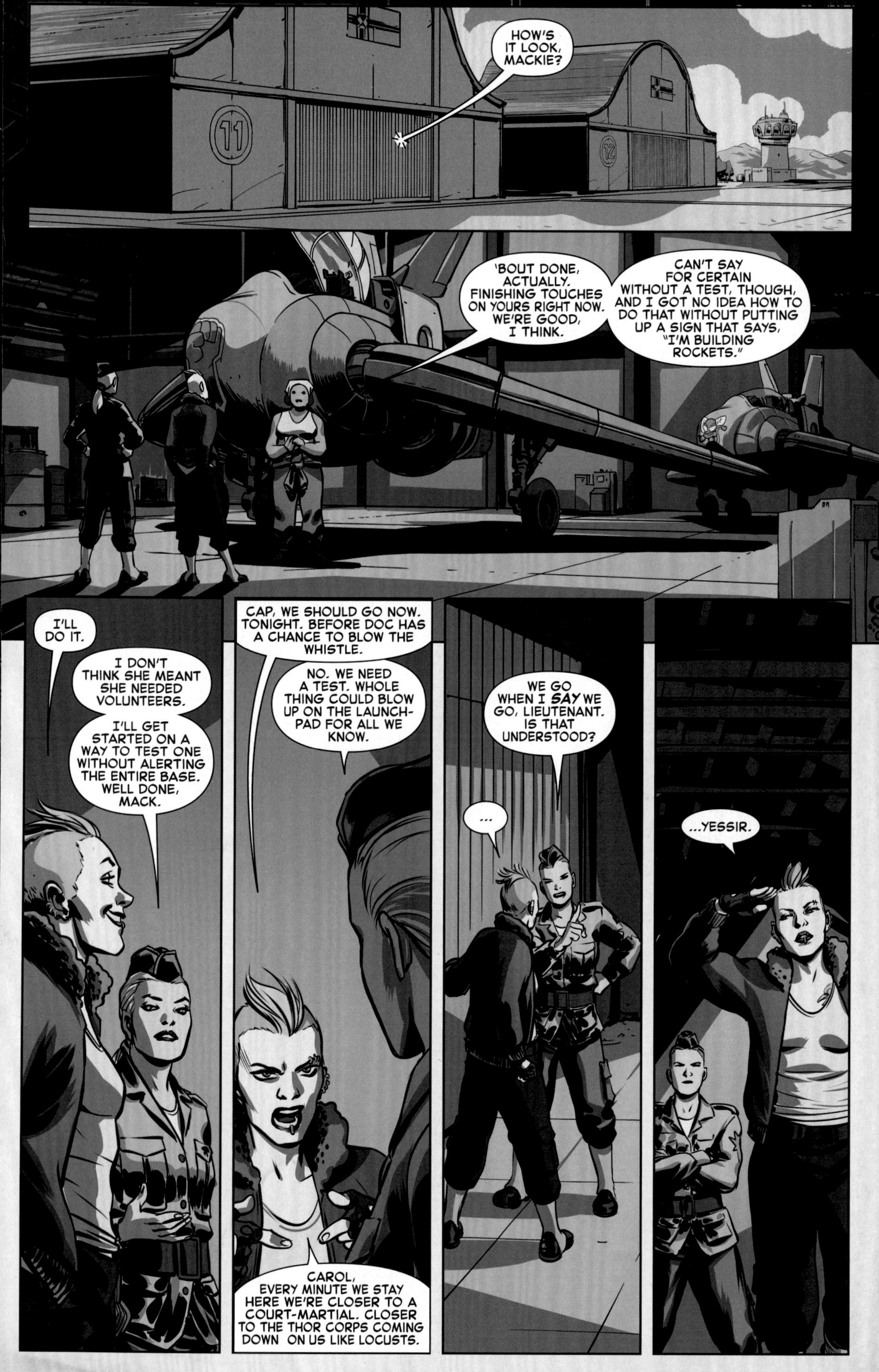
HOW'S IT LOOK, MACKIE?
'BOUT DONE, ACTUALLY. FINISHING TOUCHES ON YOURS RIGHT NOW. WE'RE GOOD, I THINK.
CAN'T SAY FOR CERTAIN WITHOUT A TEST, THOUGH, AND I GOT NO IDEA HOW TO DO THAT WITHOUT PUTTING UP A SIGN THAT SAYS, "I'M BUILDING ROCKETS."
I'LL DO IT.
I DON'T THINK SHE MEANT SHE NEEDED VOLUNTEERS.
I'LL GET STARTED ON A WAY TO TEST ONE WITHOUT ALERTING THE ENTIRE BASE. WELL DONE, MACK.
CAP, WE SHOULD GO NOW. TONIGHT. BEFORE DOC HAS A CHANCE TO BLOW THE WHISTLE.
NO. WE NEED A TEST. WHOLE THING COULD BLOW UP ON THE LAUNCH-PAD FOR ALL WE KNOW.
CAROL, EVERY MINUTE WE STAY HERE WE'RE CLOSER TO A COURT-MARTIAL. CLOSER TO THE THOR CORPS COMING DOWN ON US LIKE LOCUSTS.
WE GO WHEN I SAY WE GO, LIEUTENANT. IS THAT UNDERSTOOD?
...
...YESSIR.

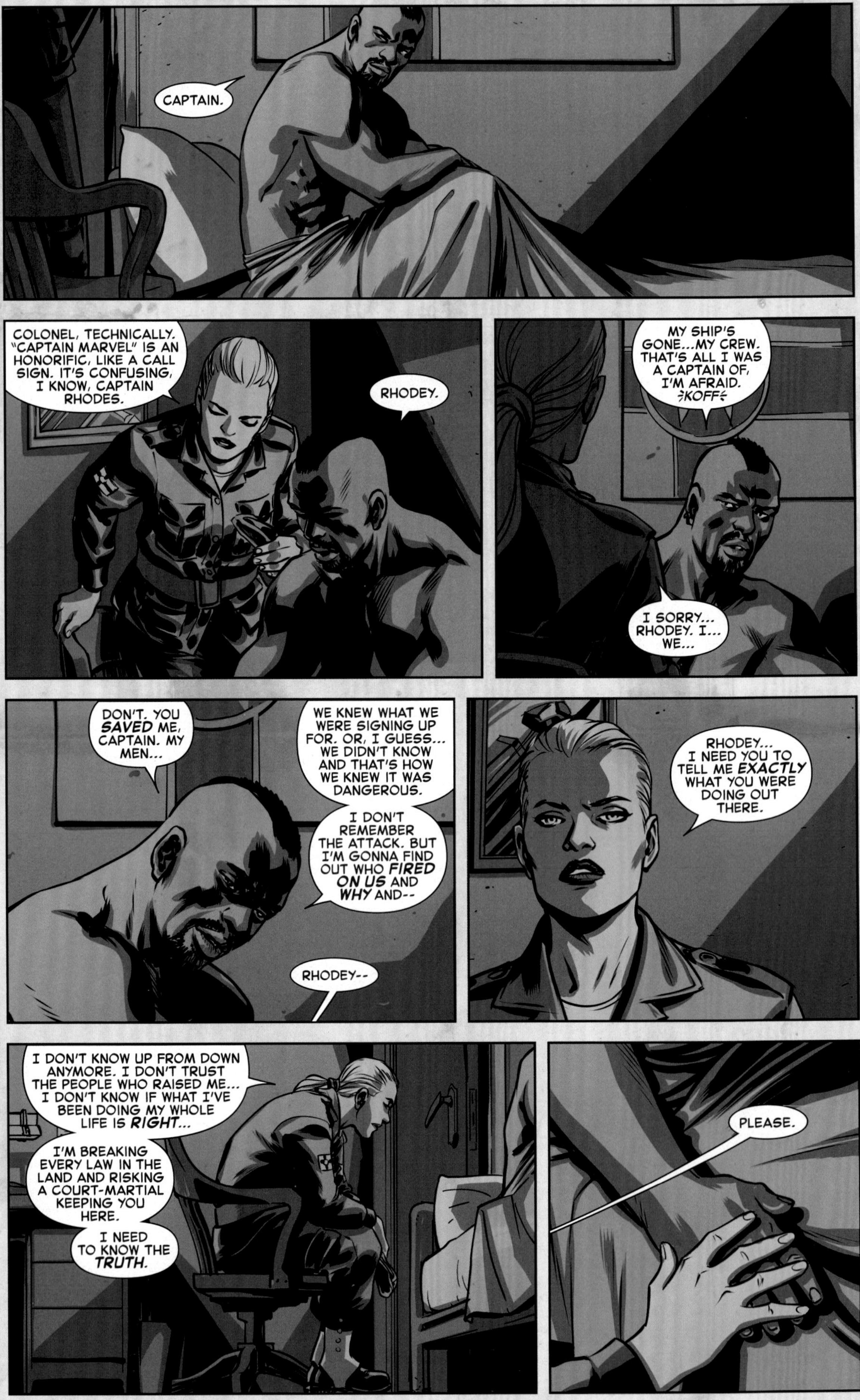
CAPTAIN.
COLONEL, TECHNICALLY. "CAPTAIN MARVEL" IS AN HONORIFIC, LIKE A CALL SIGN. IT'S CONFUSING, I KNOW, CAPTAIN RHODES.
RHODEY.
MY SHIP'S GONE... MY CREW. THAT'S ALL I WAS A CAPTAIN OF, I'M AFRAID. *KOFF*
I SORRY... RHODEY. I... WE...
DON'T. YOU SAVED ME, CAPTAIN. MY MEN...
WE KNEW WHAT WE WERE SIGNING UP FOR. OR, I GUESS... WE DIDN'T KNOW AND THAT'S HOW WE KNEW IT WAS DANGEROUS.
I DON'T REMEMBER THE ATTACK. BUT I'M GONNA FIND OUT WHO FIRED ON US AND WHY AND--
RHODEY--
RHODEY... I NEED YOU TO TELL ME EXACTLY WHAT YOU WERE DOING OUT THERE.
I DON'T KNOW UP FROM DOWN ANYMORE. I DON'T TRUST THE PEOPLE WHO RAISED ME... I DON'T KNOW IF WHAT I'VE BEEN DOING MY WHOLE LIFE IS RIGHT...
I'M BREAKING EVERY LAW IN THE LAND AND RISKING A COURT-MARTIAL KEEPING YOU HERE.
I NEED TO KNOW THE TRUTH.
PLEASE.

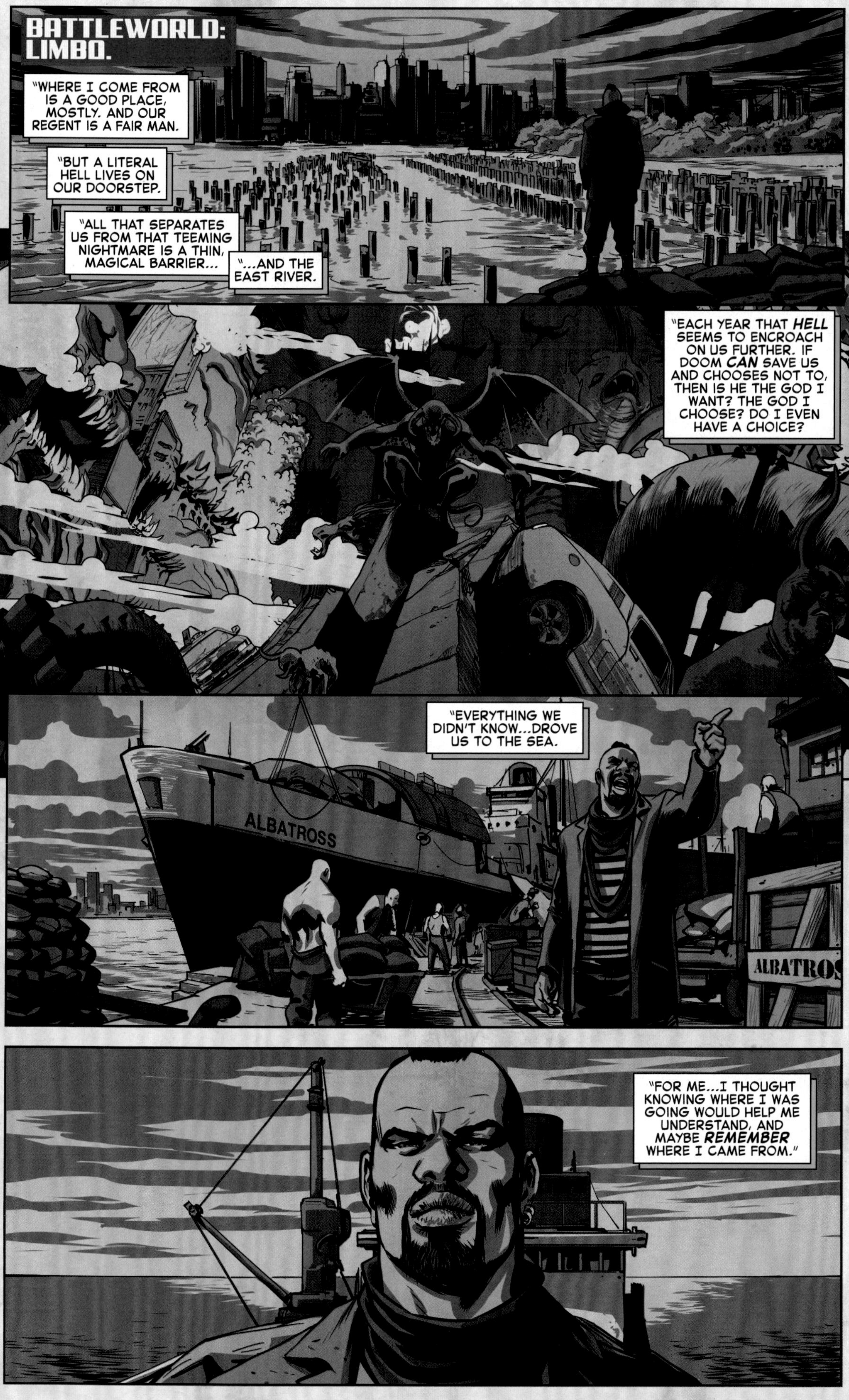
BATTLEWORLD: LIMBO.
"WHERE I COME FROM IS A GOOD PLACE, MOSTLY. AND OUR REGENT IS A FAIR MAN.
"BUT A LITERAL HELL LIVES ON OUR DOORSTEP.
"ALL THAT SEPARATES US FROM THAT TEEMING NIGHTMARE IS A THIN, MAGICAL BARRIER...
"...AND THE EAST RIVER.
"EACH YEAR THAT HELL SEEMS TO ENCROACH ON US FURTHER. IF DOOM CAN SAVE US AND CHOOSES NOT TO, THEN IS HE THE GOD I WANT? THE GOD I CHOOSE? DO I EVEN HAVE A CHOICE?
"EVERYTHING WE DIDN'T KNOW...DROVE US TO THE SEA.
ALBATROSS
ALBATROS
"FOR ME...I THOUGHT KNOWING WHERE I WAS GOING WOULD HELP ME UNDERSTAND, AND MAYBE REMEMBER WHERE I CAME FROM."

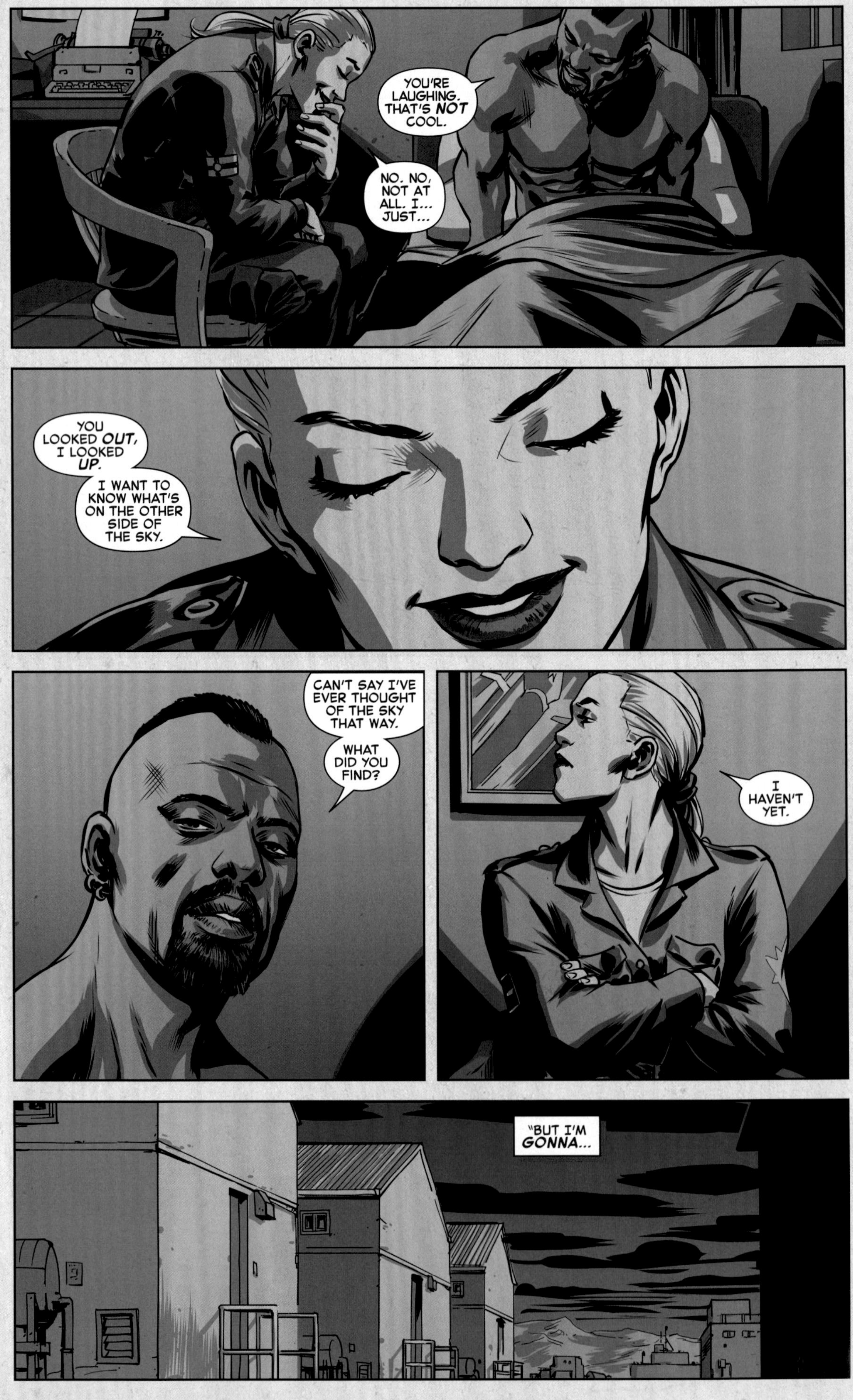
YOU'RE LAUGHING. THAT'S NOT COOL.
NO. NO, NOT AT ALL. I... JUST...
YOU LOOKED OUT, I LOOKED UP.
I WANT TO KNOW WHAT'S ON THE OTHER SIDE OF THE SKY.
CAN'T SAY I'VE EVER THOUGHT OF THE SKY THAT WAY.
WHAT DID YOU FIND?
I HAVEN'T YET.
"BUT I'M GONNA...

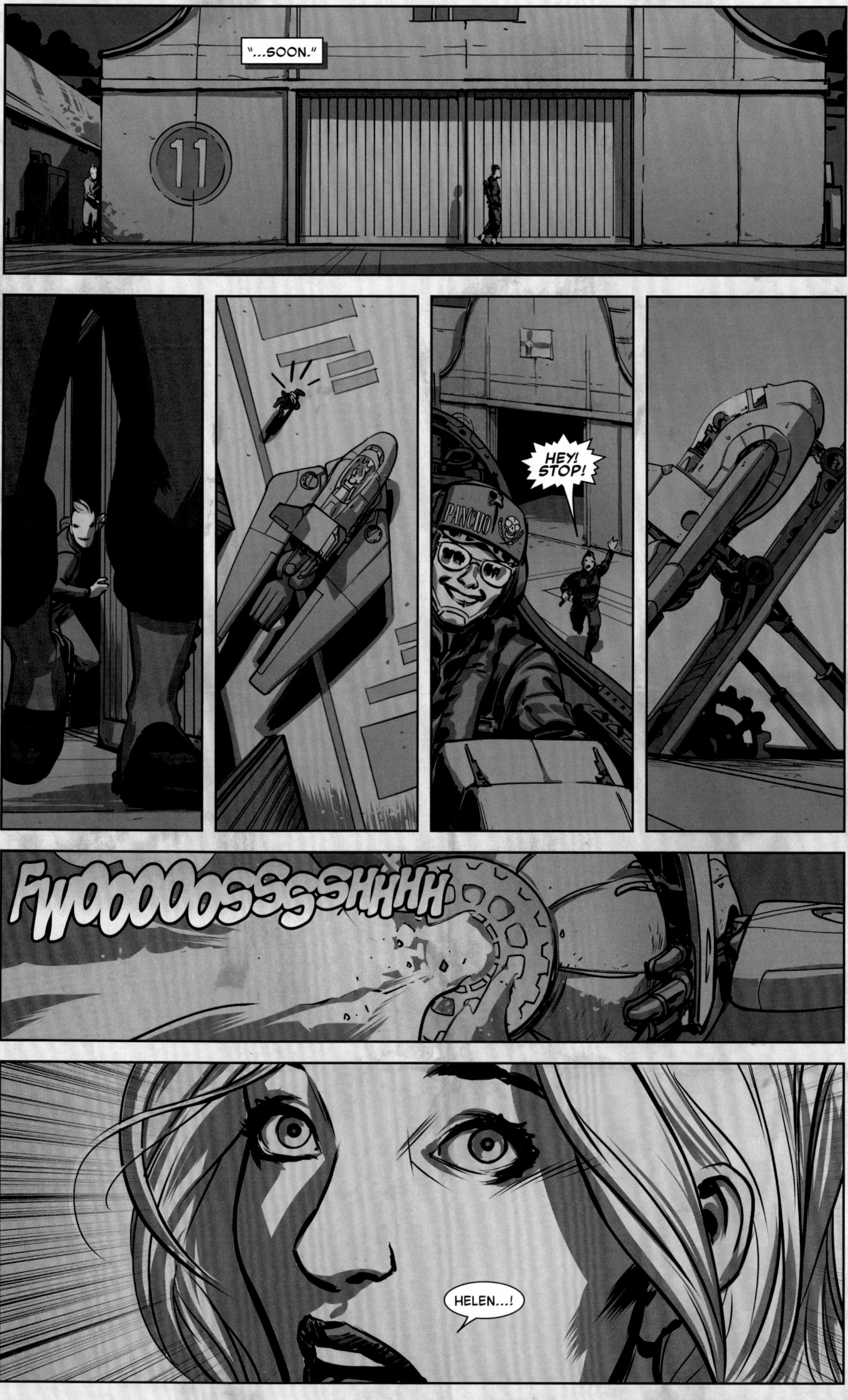
"...SOON."
11
HEY! STOP!
PANCHO
FWOOOOOSSSSHHHH
HELEN...!

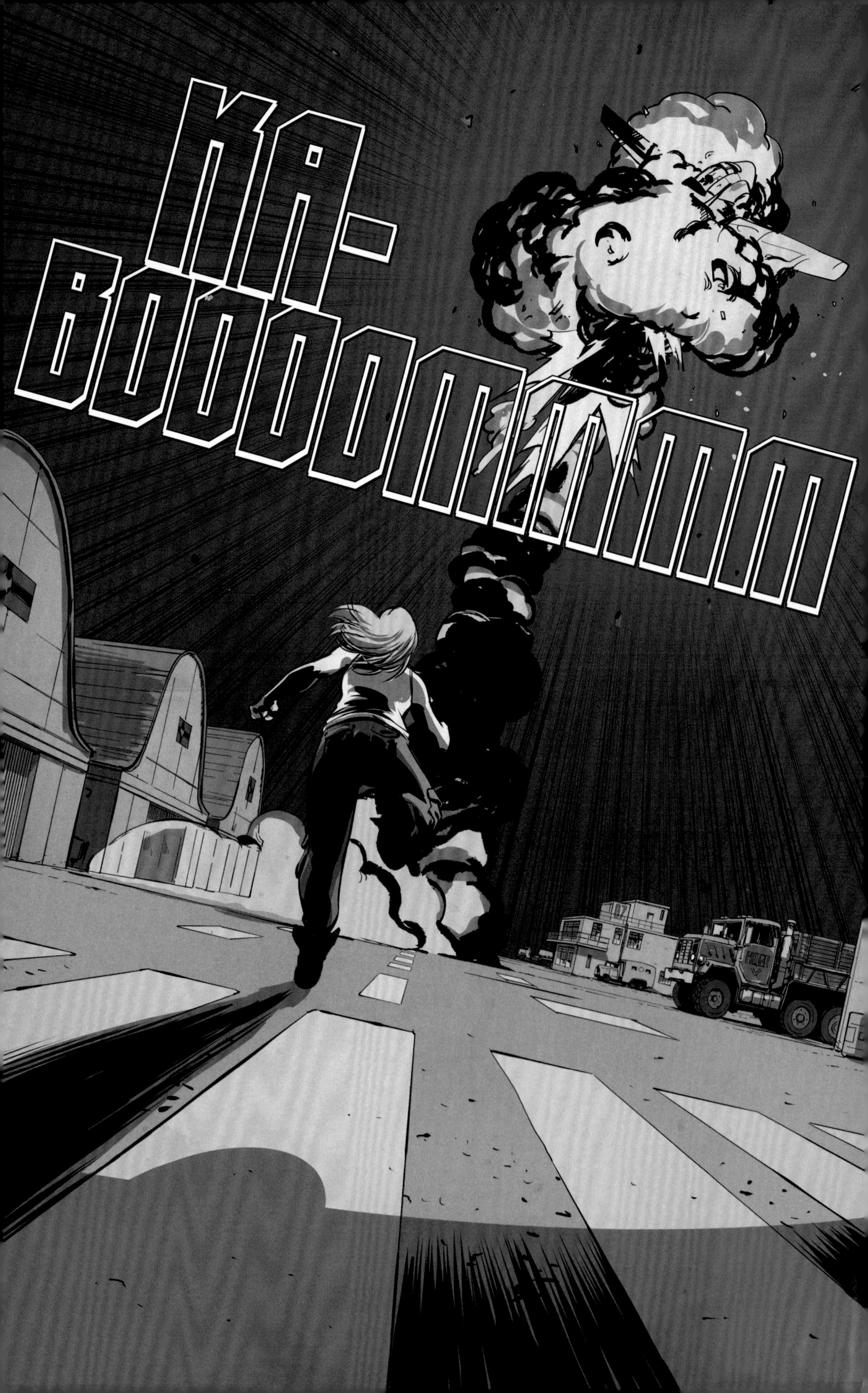
KA-
BOOOOMMMM

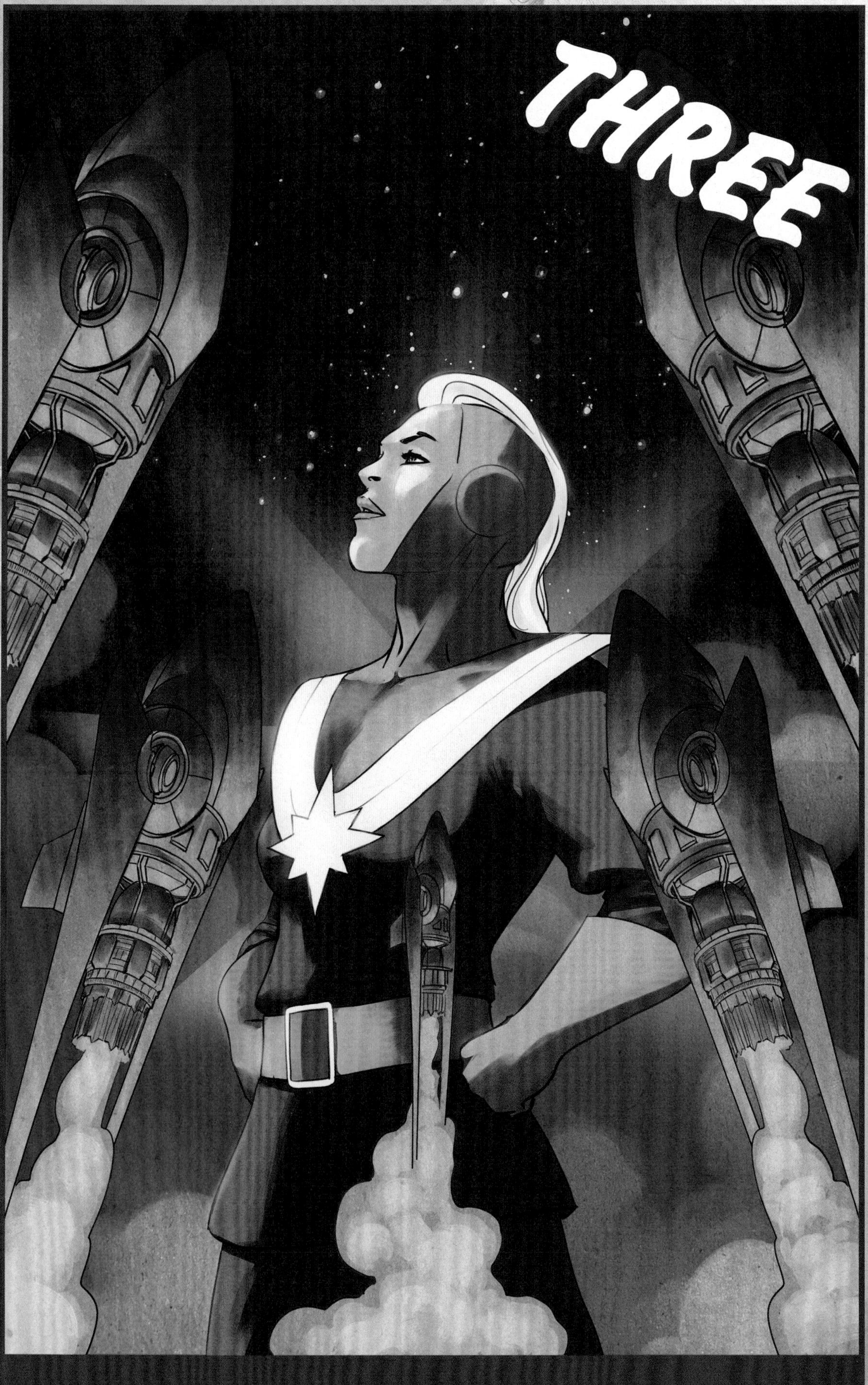
THREE

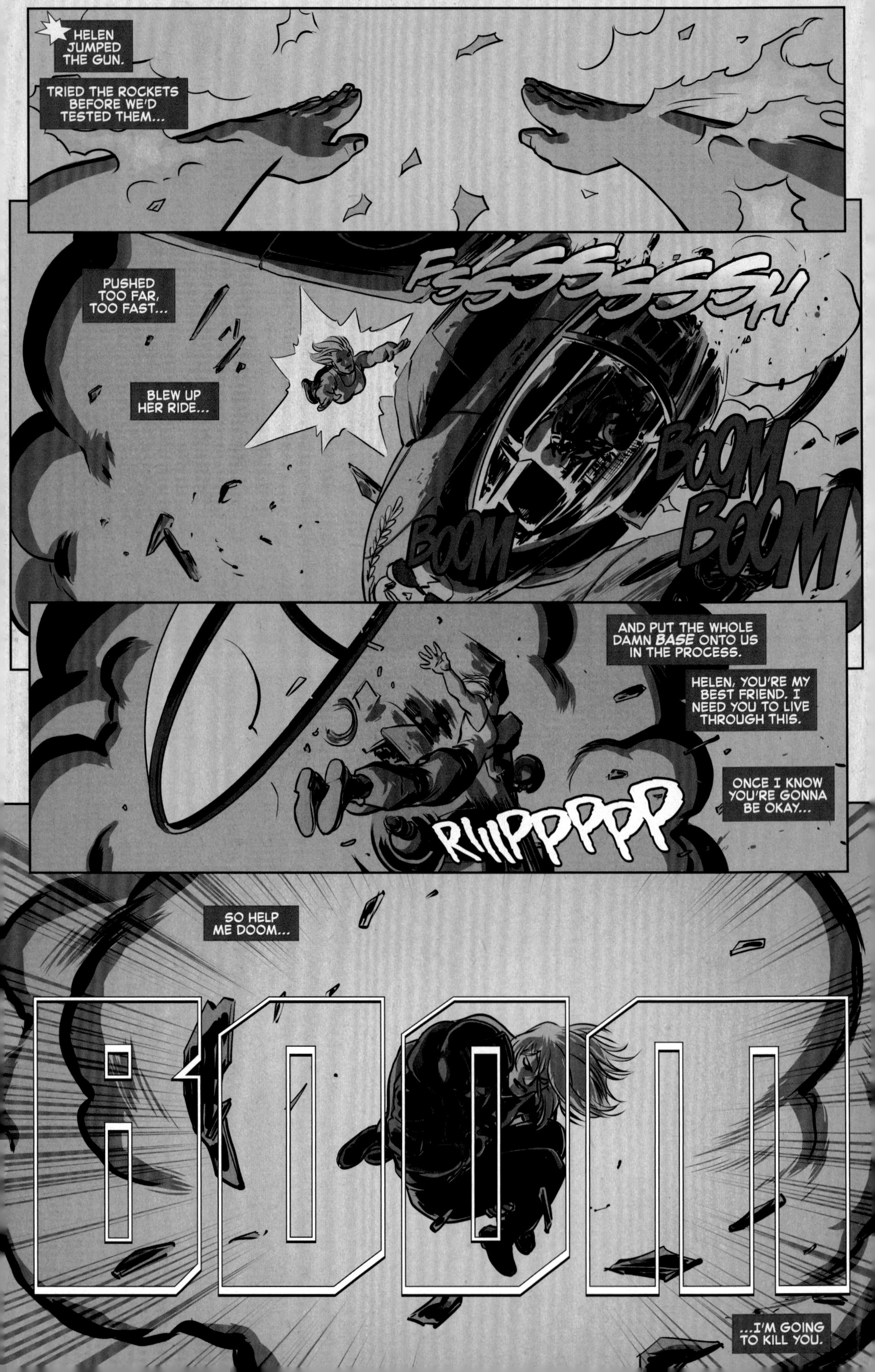
HELEN JUMPED THE GUN.
TRIED THE ROCKETS BEFORE WE'D TESTED THEM...
PUSHED TOO FAR, TOO FAST...
FSSSSSSSSH
BLEW UP HER RIDE...
BOOM
BOOM
BOOM
AND PUT THE WHOLE DAMN BASE ONTO US IN THE PROCESS.
HELEN, YOU'RE MY BEST FRIEND. I NEED YOU TO LIVE THROUGH THIS.
ONCE I KNOW YOU'RE GONNA BE OKAY...
RIIIPPPPP
SO HELP ME DOOM...
BOOM
...I'M GOING TO KILL YOU.

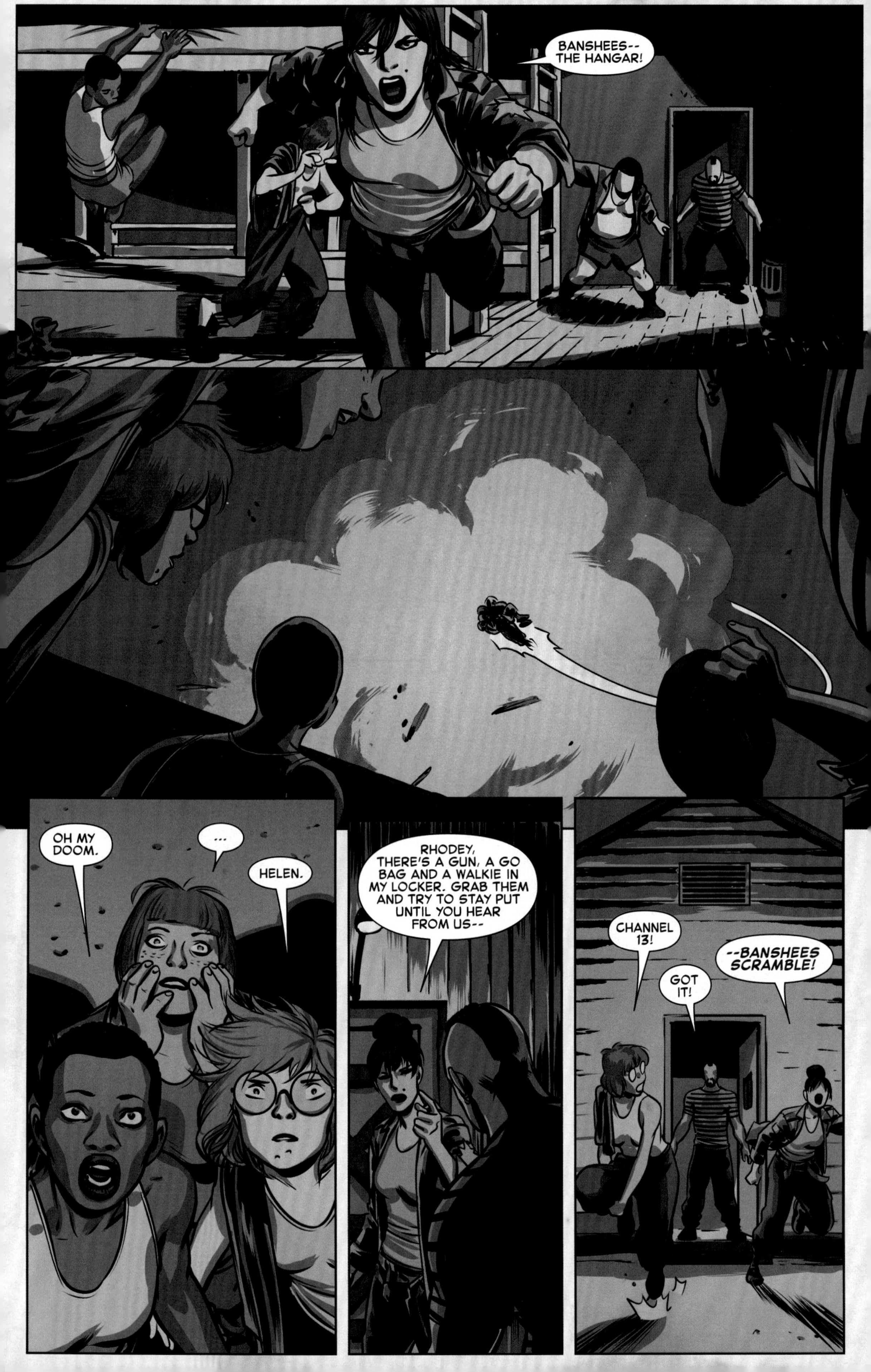
BANSHEES--
THE HANGAR!
OH MY DOOM.
...
HELEN.
RHODEY, THERE'S A GUN, A GO BAG AND A WALKIE IN MY LOCKER. GRAB THEM AND TRY TO STAY PUT UNTIL YOU HEAR FROM US--
CHANNEL 13!
GOT IT!
--BANSHEES SCRAMBLE!

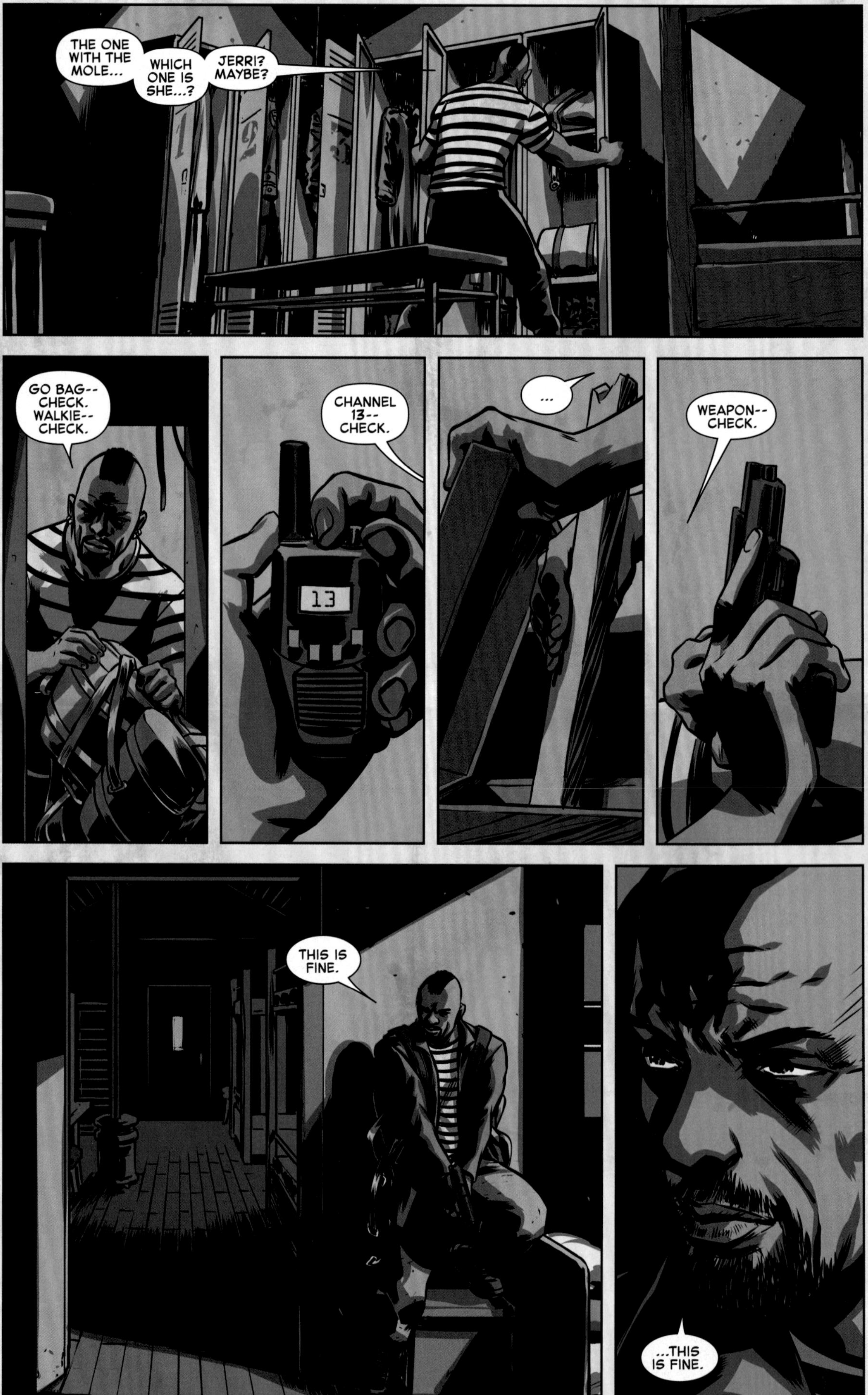
THE ONE WITH THE MOLE...
WHICH ONE IS SHE...?
JERRI? MAYBE?
GO BAG--CHECK. WALKIE--CHECK.
CHANNEL 13--CHECK.
13
...
WEAPON--CHECK.
THIS IS FINE.
...THIS IS FINE.

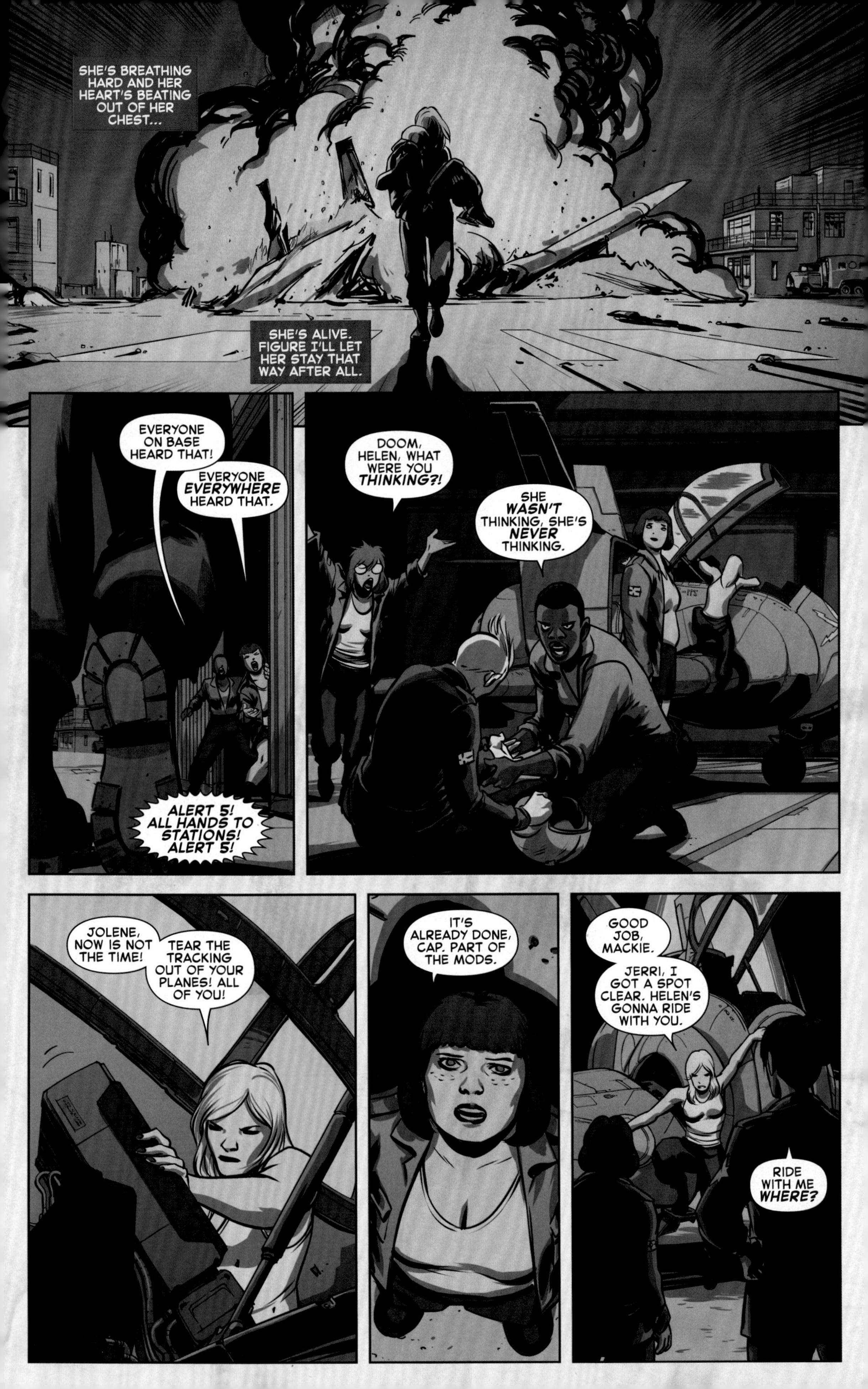
SHE'S BREATHING HARD AND HER HEART'S BEATING OUT OF HER CHEST...
SHE'S ALIVE. FIGURE I'LL LET HER STAY THAT WAY AFTER ALL.
EVERYONE ON BASE HEARD THAT!
EVERYONE *EVERYWHERE* HEARD THAT.
ALERT 5! ALL HANDS TO STATIONS! ALERT 5!
DOOM, HELEN, WHAT WERE YOU *THINKING?!*
SHE *WASN'T* THINKING, SHE'S *NEVER* THINKING.
JOLENE, NOW IS NOT THE TIME!
TEAR THE TRACKING OUT OF YOUR PLANES! ALL OF YOU!
IT'S ALREADY DONE, CAP. PART OF THE MODS.
GOOD JOB, MACKIE.
JERRI, I GOT A SPOT CLEAR. HELEN'S GONNA RIDE WITH YOU.
RIDE WITH ME *WHERE?*

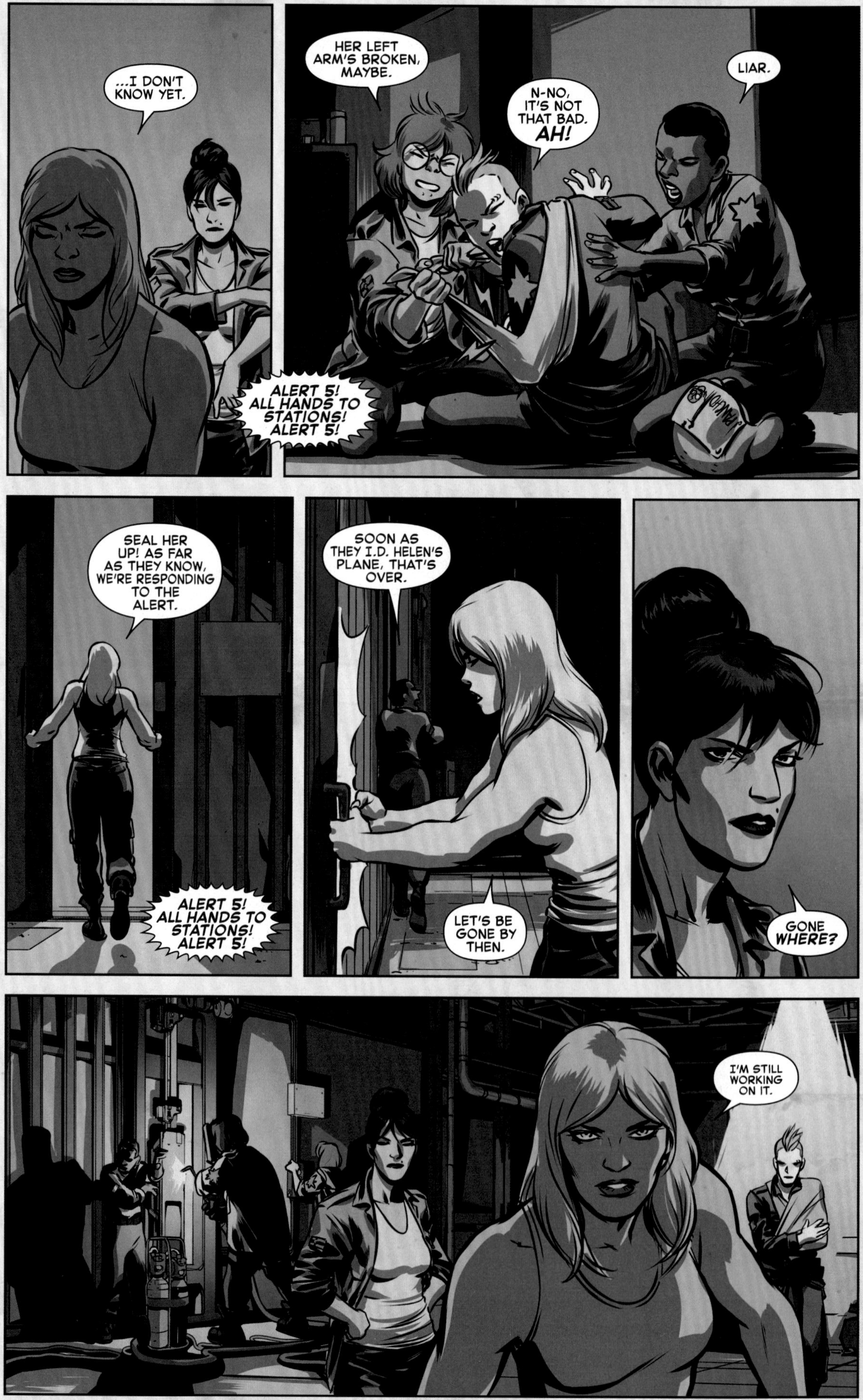
...I DON'T KNOW YET.
HER LEFT ARM'S BROKEN, MAYBE.
N-NO, IT'S NOT THAT BAD. AH!
LIAR.
ALERT 5! ALL HANDS TO STATIONS! ALERT 5!
SEAL HER UP! AS FAR AS THEY KNOW, WE'RE RESPONDING TO THE ALERT.
ALERT 5! ALL HANDS TO STATIONS! ALERT 5!
SOON AS THEY I.D. HELEN'S PLANE, THAT'S OVER.
LET'S BE GONE BY THEN.
GONE WHERE?
I'M STILL WORKING ON IT.

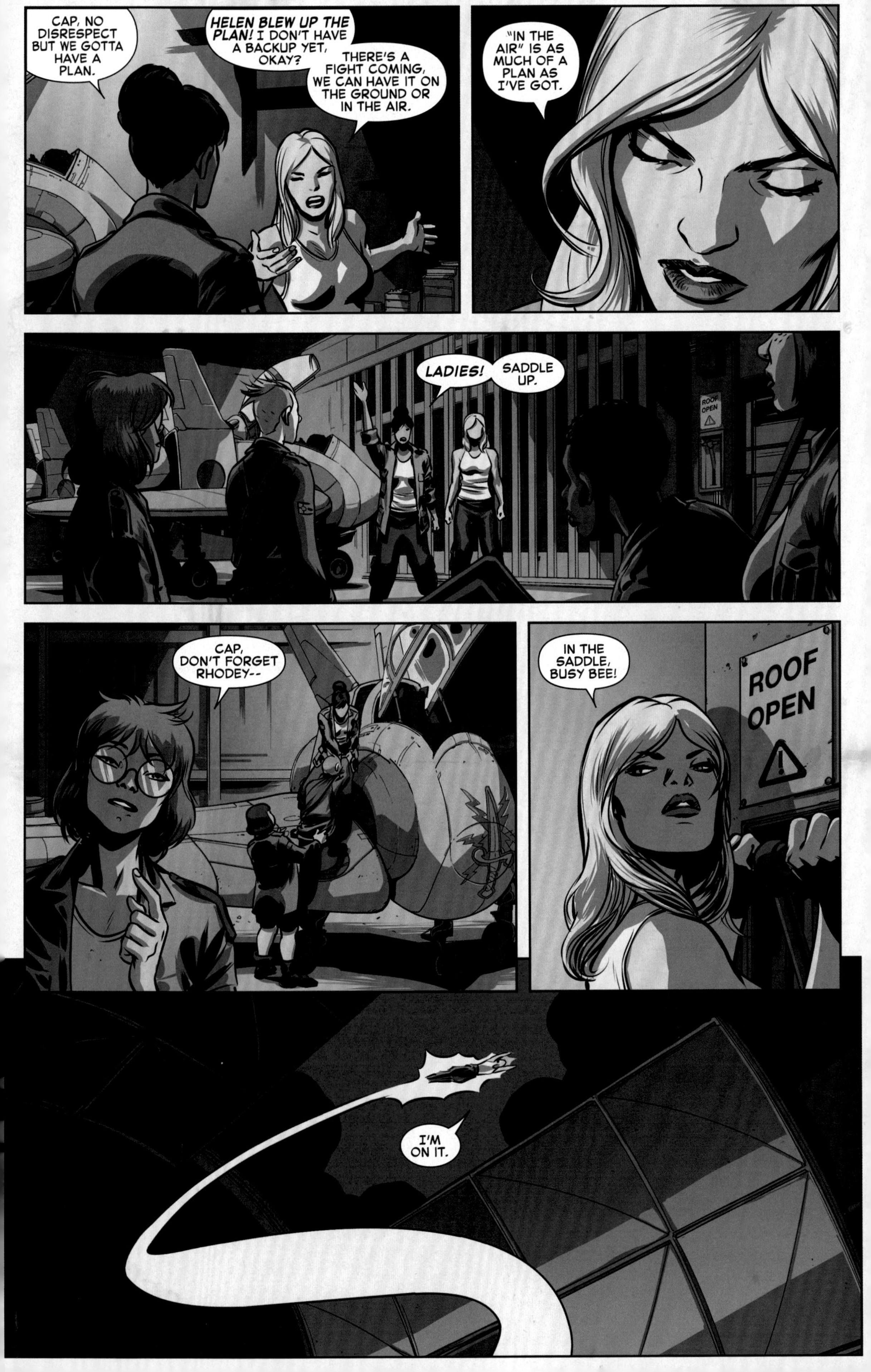

CAP, NO DISRESPECT BUT WE GOTTA HAVE A PLAN.
HELEN BLEW UP THE PLAN! I DON'T HAVE A BACKUP YET, OKAY?
THERE'S A FIGHT COMING, WE CAN HAVE IT ON THE GROUND OR IN THE AIR.
"IN THE AIR" IS AS MUCH OF A PLAN AS I'VE GOT.
LADIES!
SADDLE UP.
ROOF OPEN
CAP, DON'T FORGET RHODEY--
IN THE SADDLE, BUSY BEE!
ROOF OPEN
I'M ON IT.

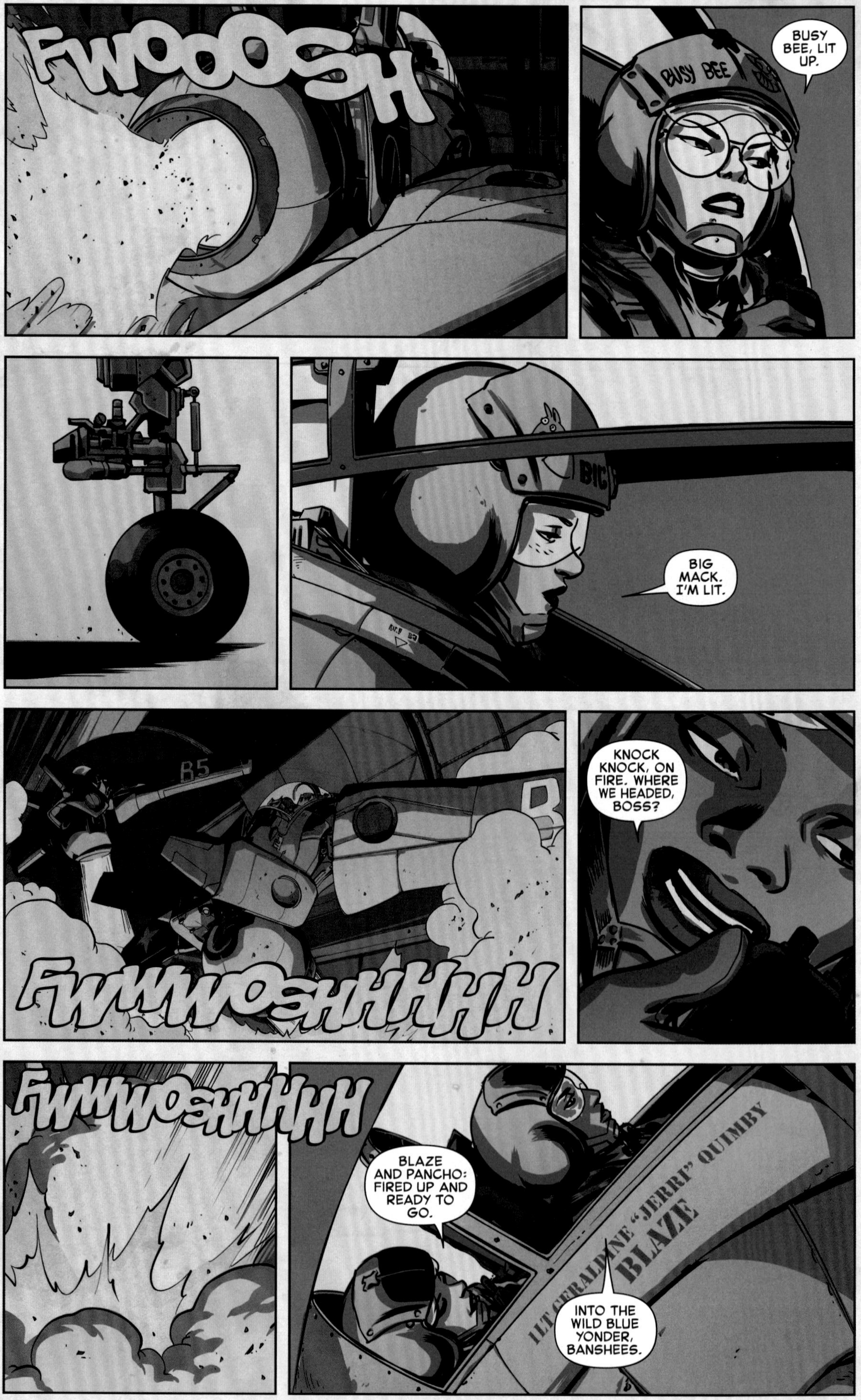
FWOOOSH
BUSY BEE
BUSY BEE, LIT UP.
BIG
BIG MACK. I'M LIT.
B5
FWWWOSHHHHH
KNOCK KNOCK, ON FIRE. WHERE WE HEADED, BOSS?
FWWWOSHHHHH
BLAZE AND PANCHO: FIRED UP AND READY TO GO.
1LT GERALDINE "JERRI" QUIMBY
BLAZE
INTO THE WILD BLUE YONDER, BANSHEES.

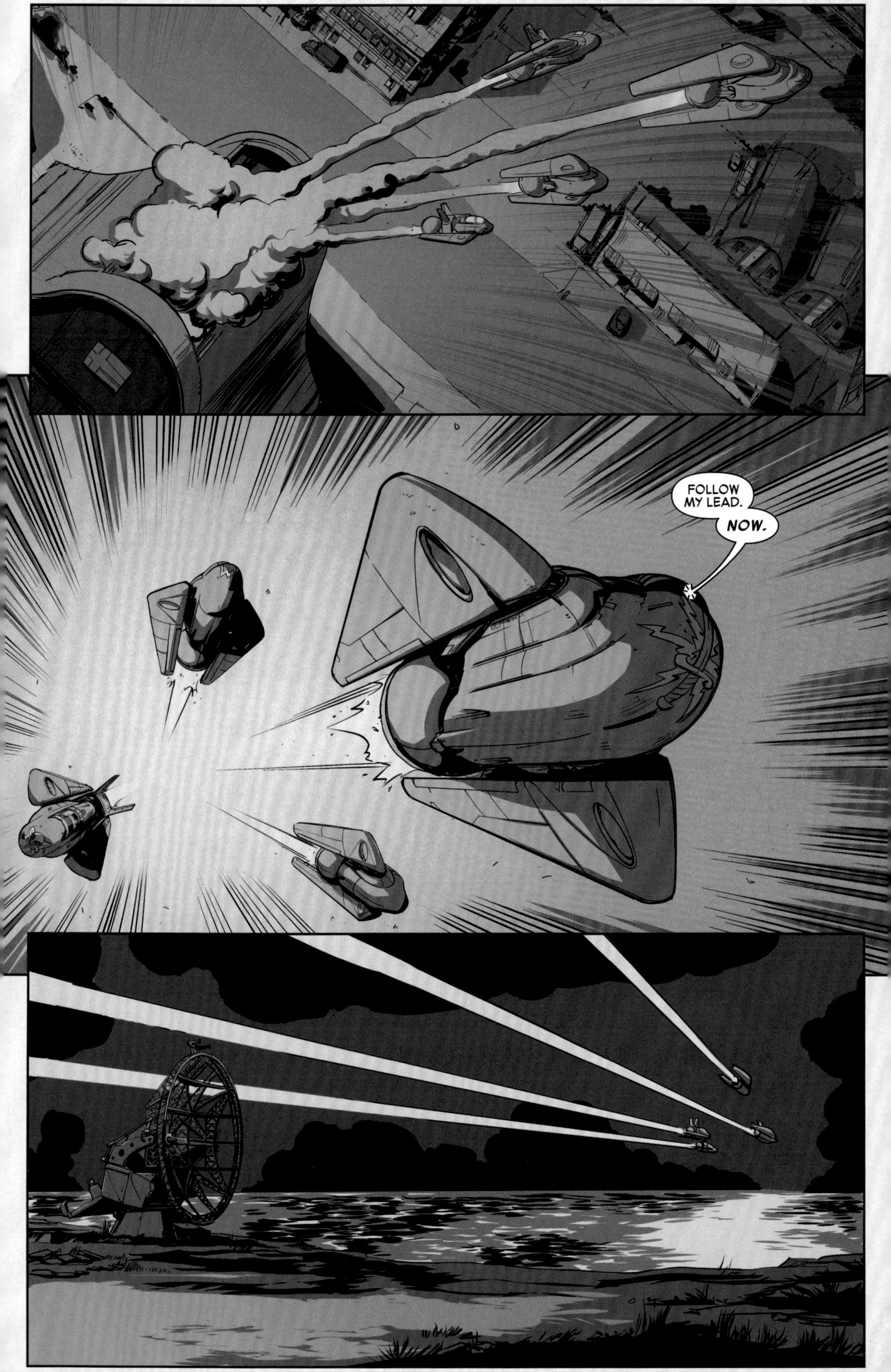
FOLLOW MY LEAD.
NOW.

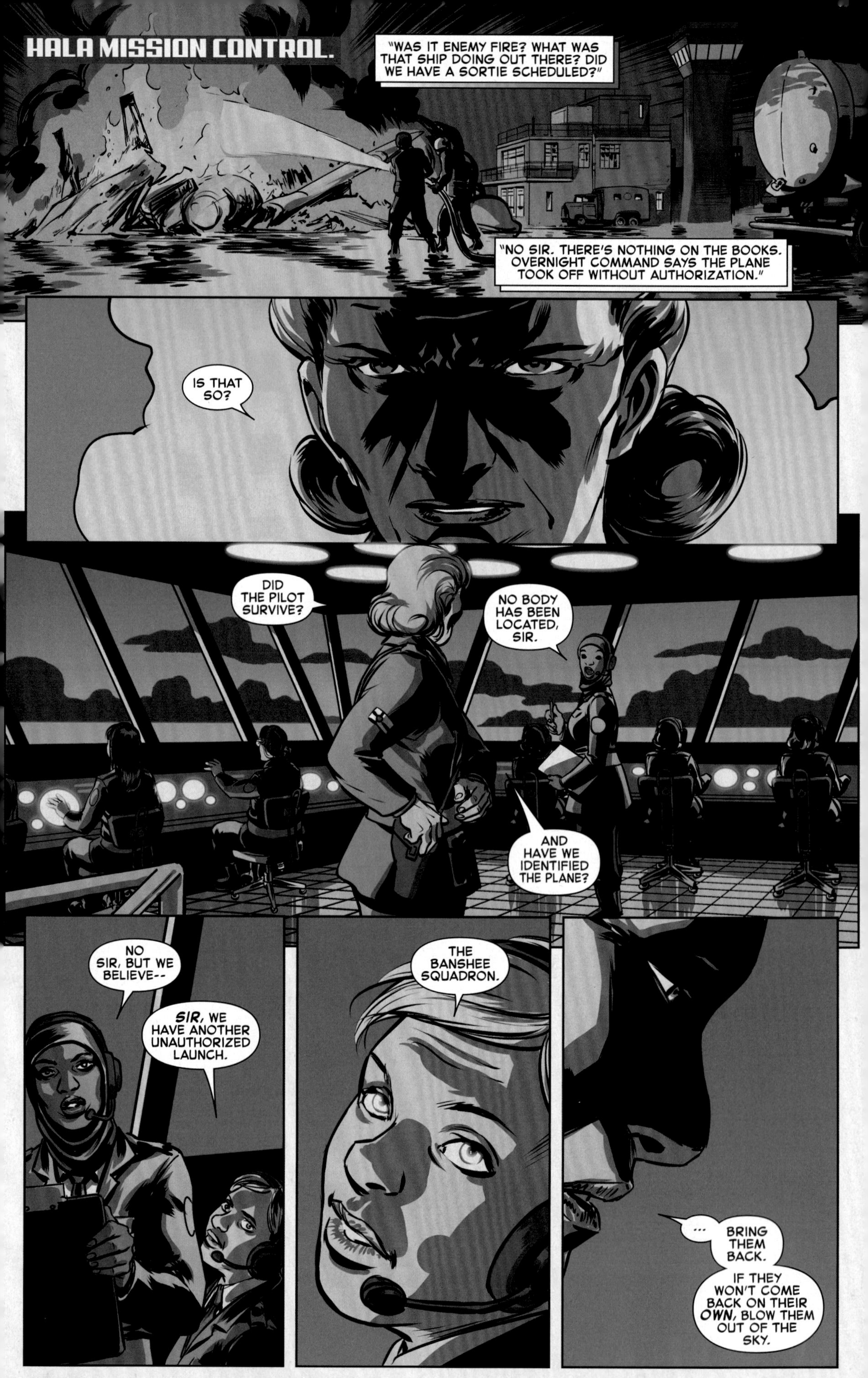
HALA MISSION CONTROL.
"WAS IT ENEMY FIRE? WHAT WAS THAT SHIP DOING OUT THERE? DID WE HAVE A SORTIE SCHEDULED?"
"NO SIR. THERE'S NOTHING ON THE BOOKS. OVERNIGHT COMMAND SAYS THE PLANE TOOK OFF WITHOUT AUTHORIZATION."
IS THAT SO?
DID THE PILOT SURVIVE?
NO BODY HAS BEEN LOCATED, SIR.
AND HAVE WE IDENTIFIED THE PLANE?
NO SIR, BUT WE BELIEVE--
SIR, WE HAVE ANOTHER UNAUTHORIZED LAUNCH.
THE BANSHEE SQUADRON.
... BRING THEM BACK.
IF THEY WON'T COME BACK ON THEIR OWN, BLOW THEM OUT OF THE SKY.

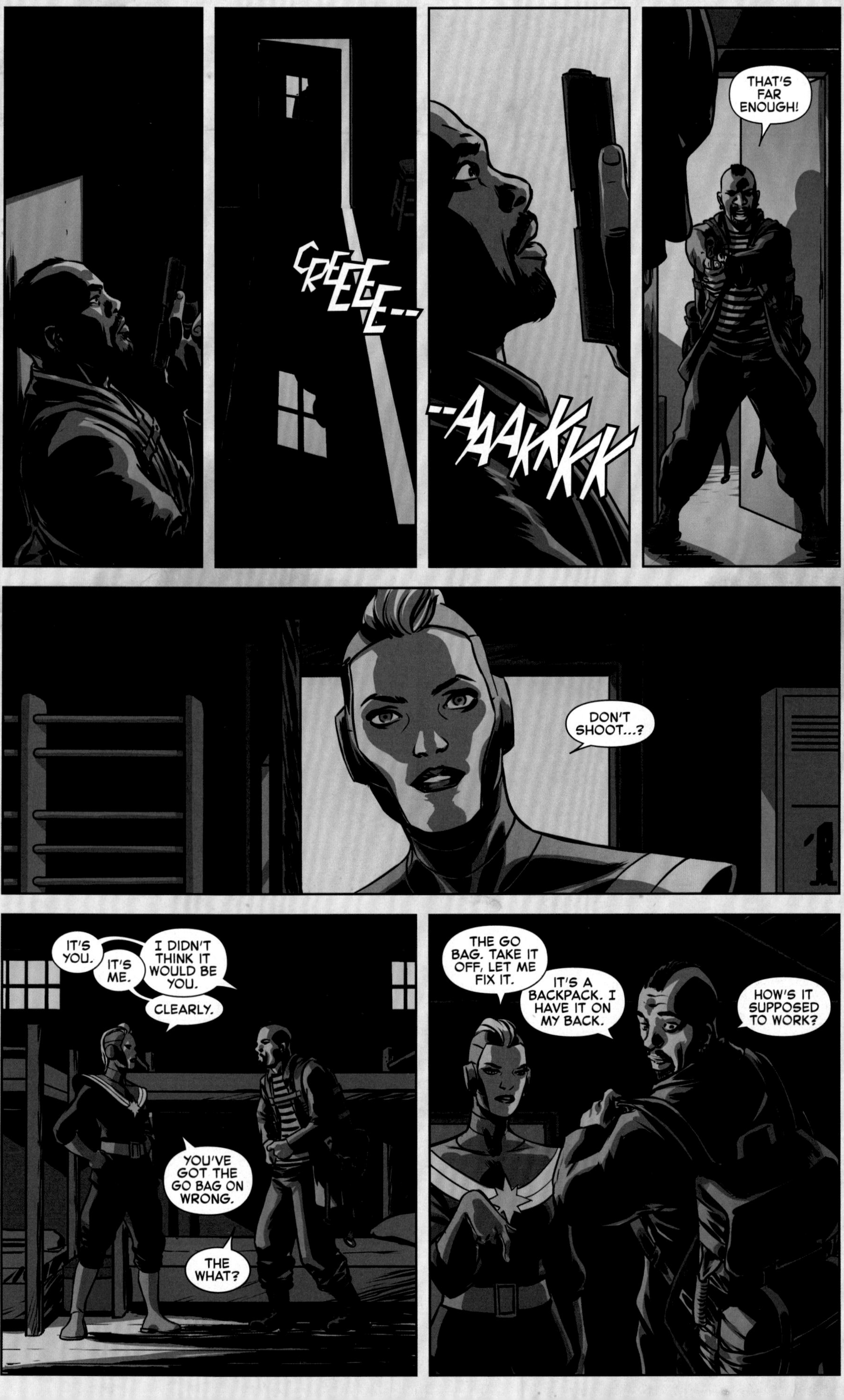
CREEEEE--
--AAAKKKKK
THAT'S FAR ENOUGH!
DON'T SHOOT...?
IT'S YOU.
I DIDN'T THINK IT WOULD BE YOU.
IT'S ME.
CLEARLY.
YOU'VE GOT THE GO BAG ON WRONG.
THE WHAT?
THE GO BAG. TAKE IT OFF, LET ME FIX IT.
IT'S A BACKPACK. I HAVE IT ON MY BACK.
HOW'S IT SUPPOSED TO WORK?

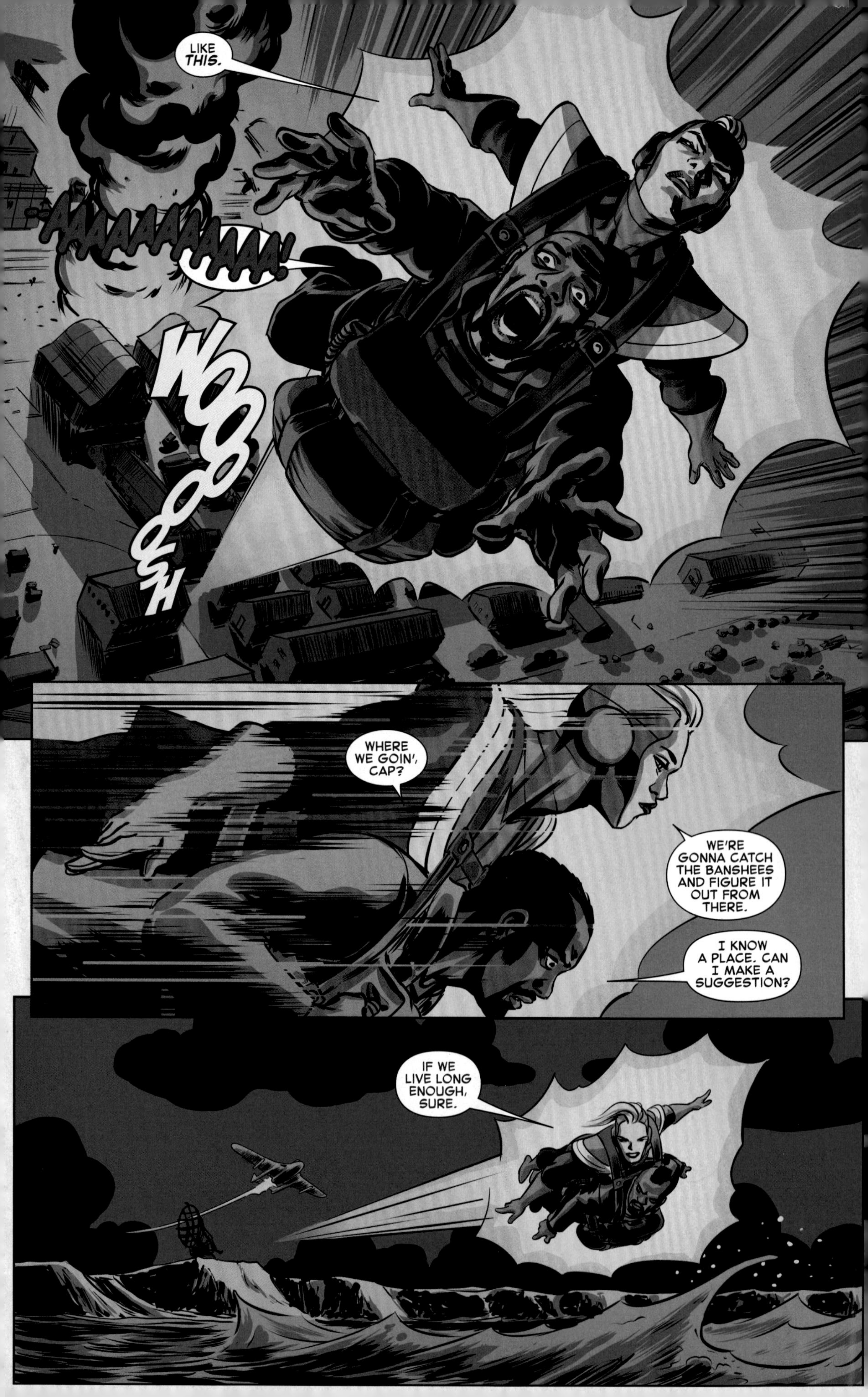
LIKE THIS.
AAAAAAAAAAAA!
WOOOOOOSH
WHERE WE GOIN', CAP?
WE'RE GONNA CATCH THE BANSHEES AND FIGURE IT OUT FROM THERE.
I KNOW A PLACE. CAN I MAKE A SUGGESTION?
IF WE LIVE LONG ENOUGH, SURE.

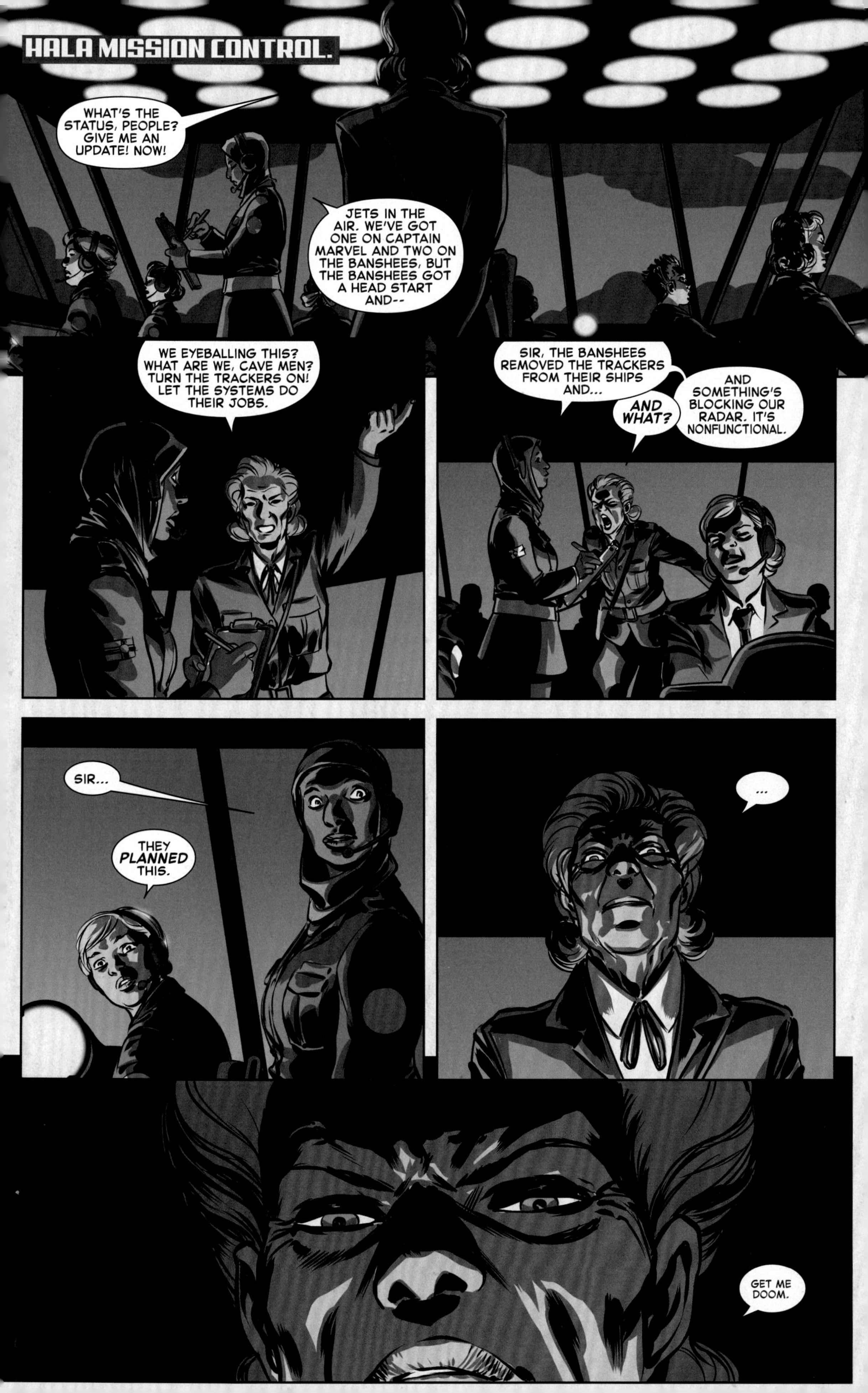
HALA MISSION CONTROL.
WHAT'S THE STATUS, PEOPLE? GIVE ME AN UPDATE! NOW!
JETS IN THE AIR. WE'VE GOT ONE ON CAPTAIN MARVEL AND TWO ON THE BANSHEES, BUT THE BANSHEES GOT A HEAD START AND--
WE EYEBALLING THIS? WHAT ARE WE, CAVE MEN? TURN THE TRACKERS ON! LET THE SYSTEMS DO THEIR JOBS.
SIR, THE BANSHEES REMOVED THE TRACKERS FROM THEIR SHIPS AND...
AND WHAT?
AND SOMETHING'S BLOCKING OUR RADAR. IT'S NONFUNCTIONAL.
SIR...
THEY PLANNED THIS.
...
GET ME DOOM.

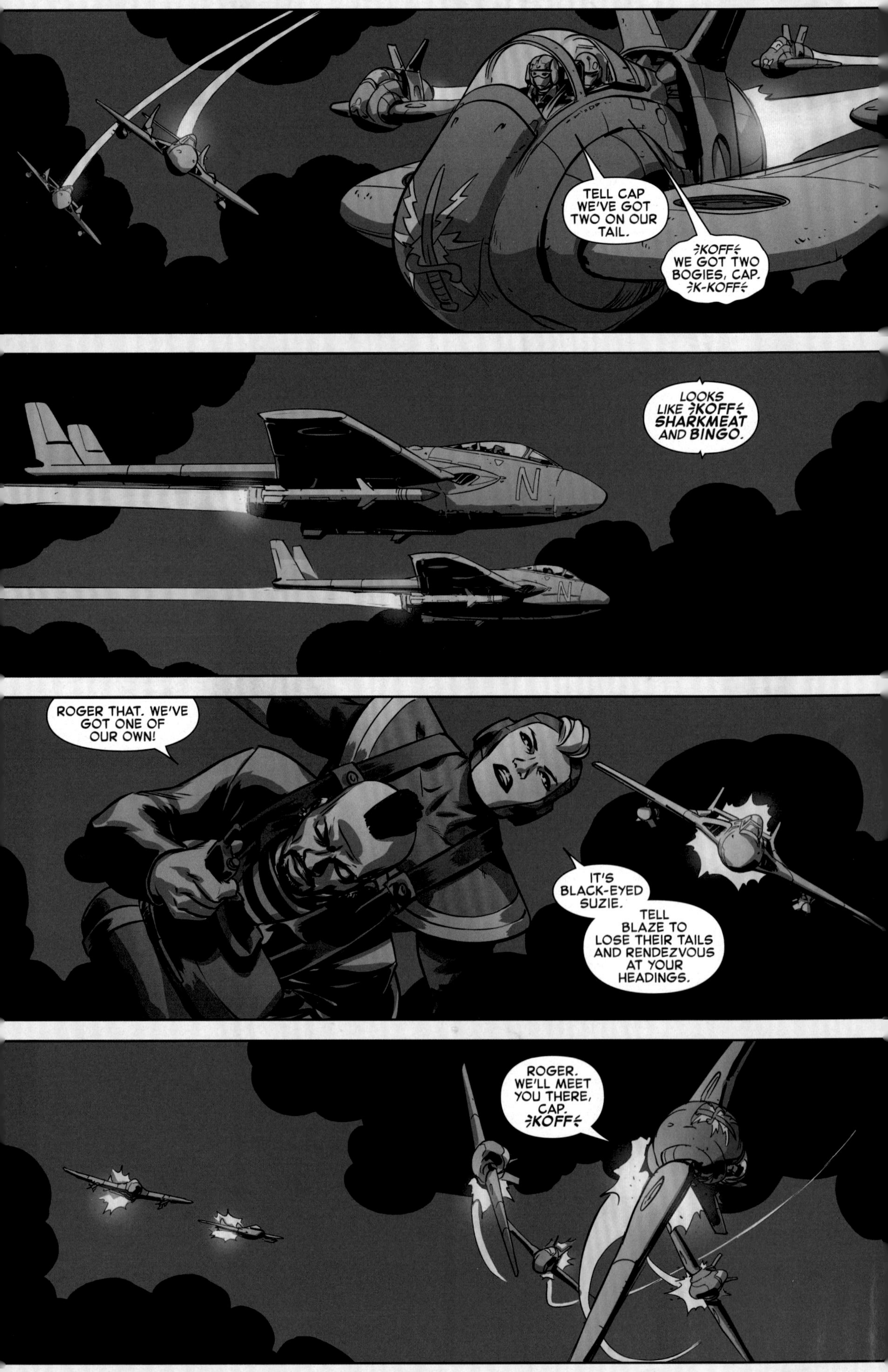
TELL CAP WE'VE GOT TWO ON OUR TAIL.
⊰KOFF⊱ WE GOT TWO BOGIES, CAP. ⊰K-KOFF⊱
LOOKS LIKE ⊰KOFF⊱ SHARKMEAT AND BINGO.
ROGER THAT. WE'VE GOT ONE OF OUR OWN!
IT'S BLACK-EYED SUZIE.
TELL BLAZE TO LOSE THEIR TAILS AND RENDEZVOUS AT YOUR HEADINGS.
ROGER. WE'LL MEET YOU THERE, CAP. ⊰KOFF⊱

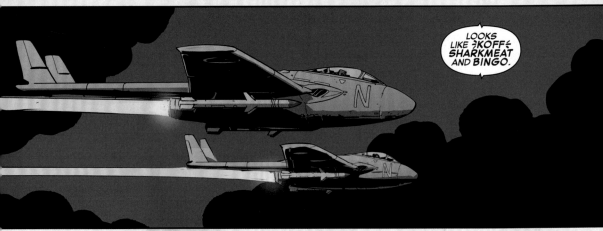

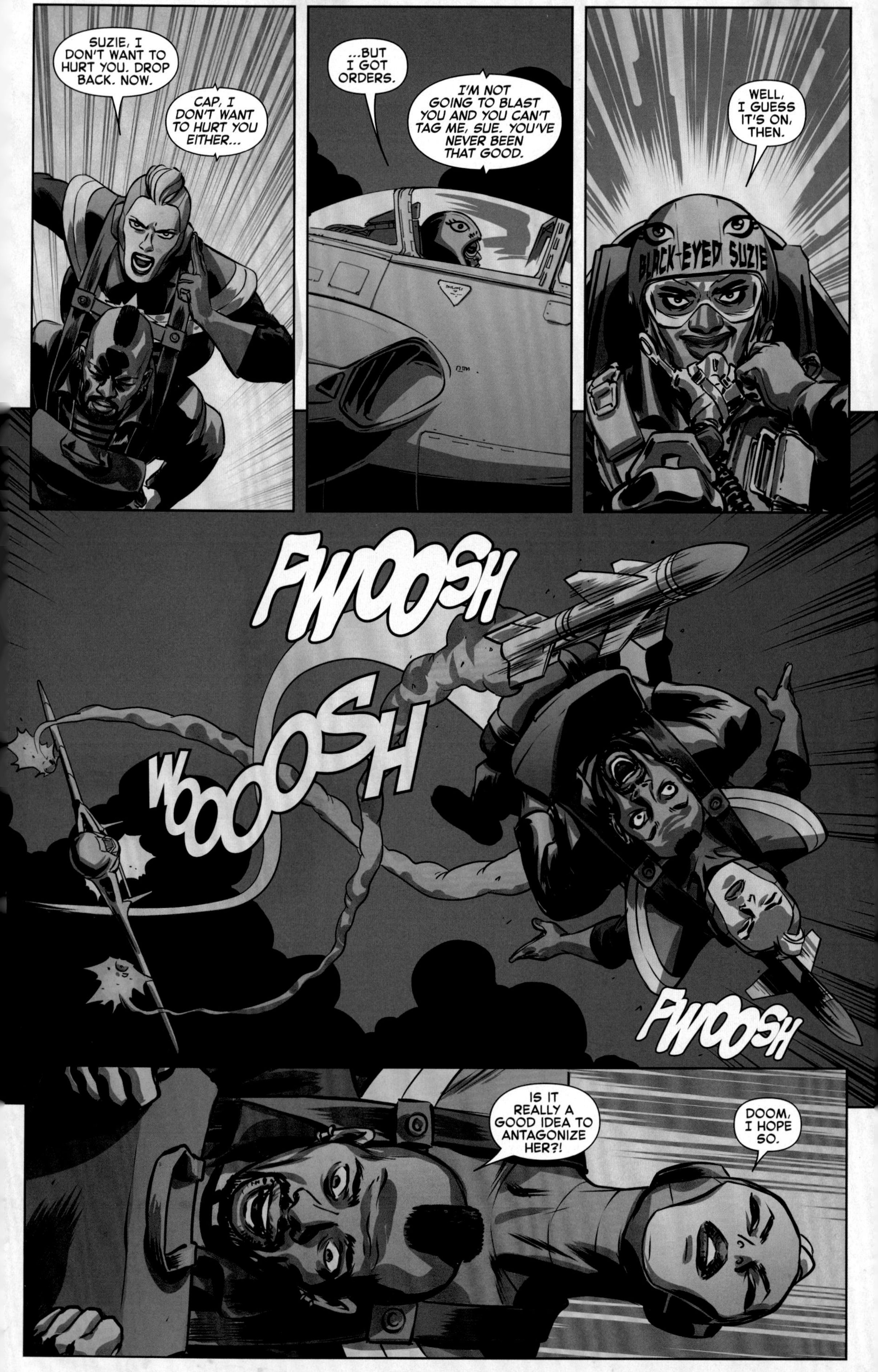
SUZIE, I DON'T WANT TO HURT YOU. DROP BACK. NOW.
CAP, I DON'T WANT TO HURT YOU EITHER...
...BUT I GOT ORDERS.
I'M NOT GOING TO BLAST YOU AND YOU CAN'T TAG ME, SUE. YOU'VE NEVER BEEN THAT GOOD.
WELL, I GUESS IT'S ON, THEN.
BLACK-EYED SUZIE
FWOOSH
WOOOOOSH
FWOOSH
IS IT REALLY A GOOD IDEA TO ANTAGONIZE HER?!
DOOM, I HOPE SO.

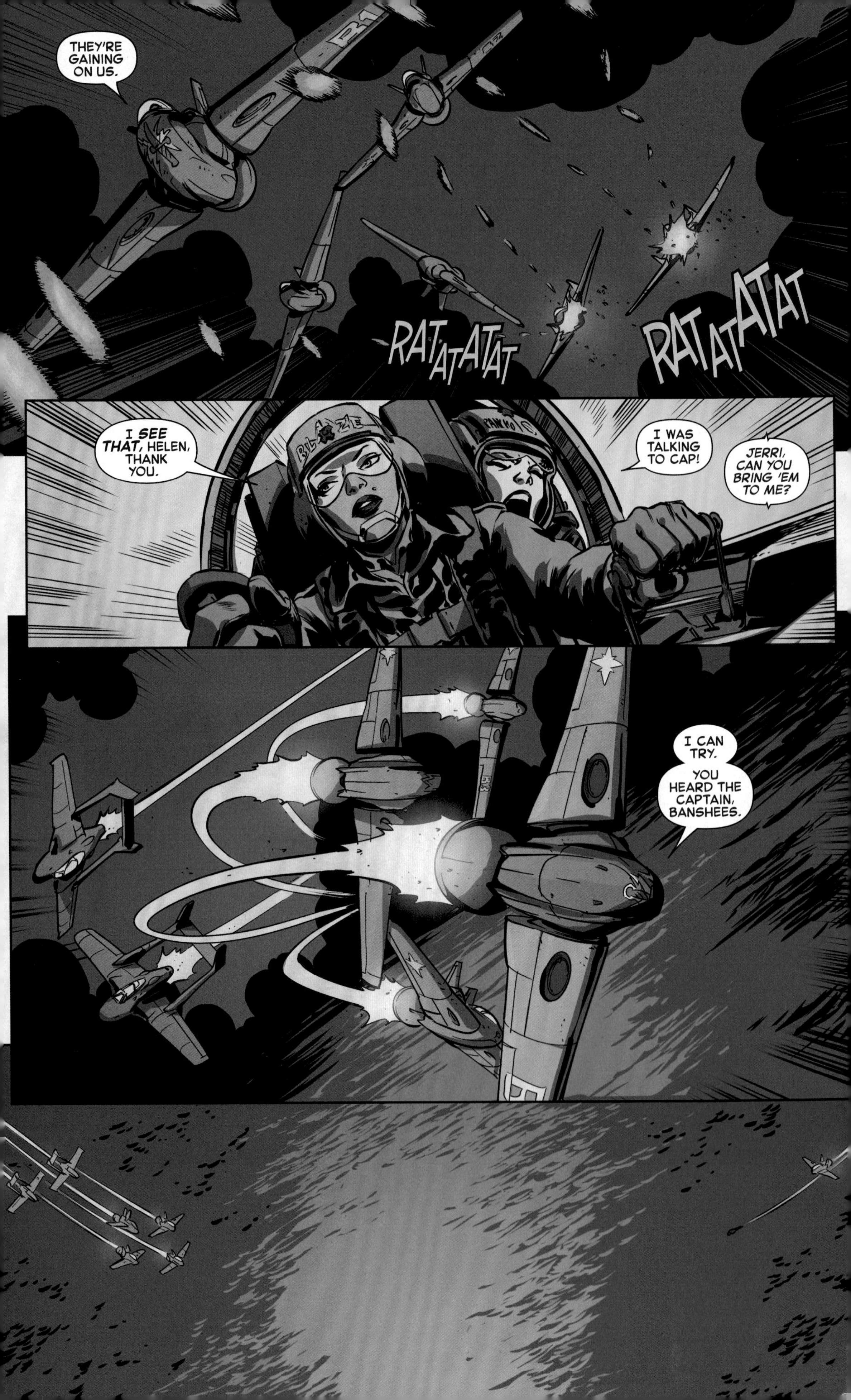
THEY'RE GAINING ON US.
RATATATAT
RATATATAT
I SEE THAT, HELEN, THANK YOU.
I WAS TALKING TO CAP!
JERRI, CAN YOU BRING 'EM TO ME?
I CAN TRY.
YOU HEARD THE CAPTAIN, BANSHEES.

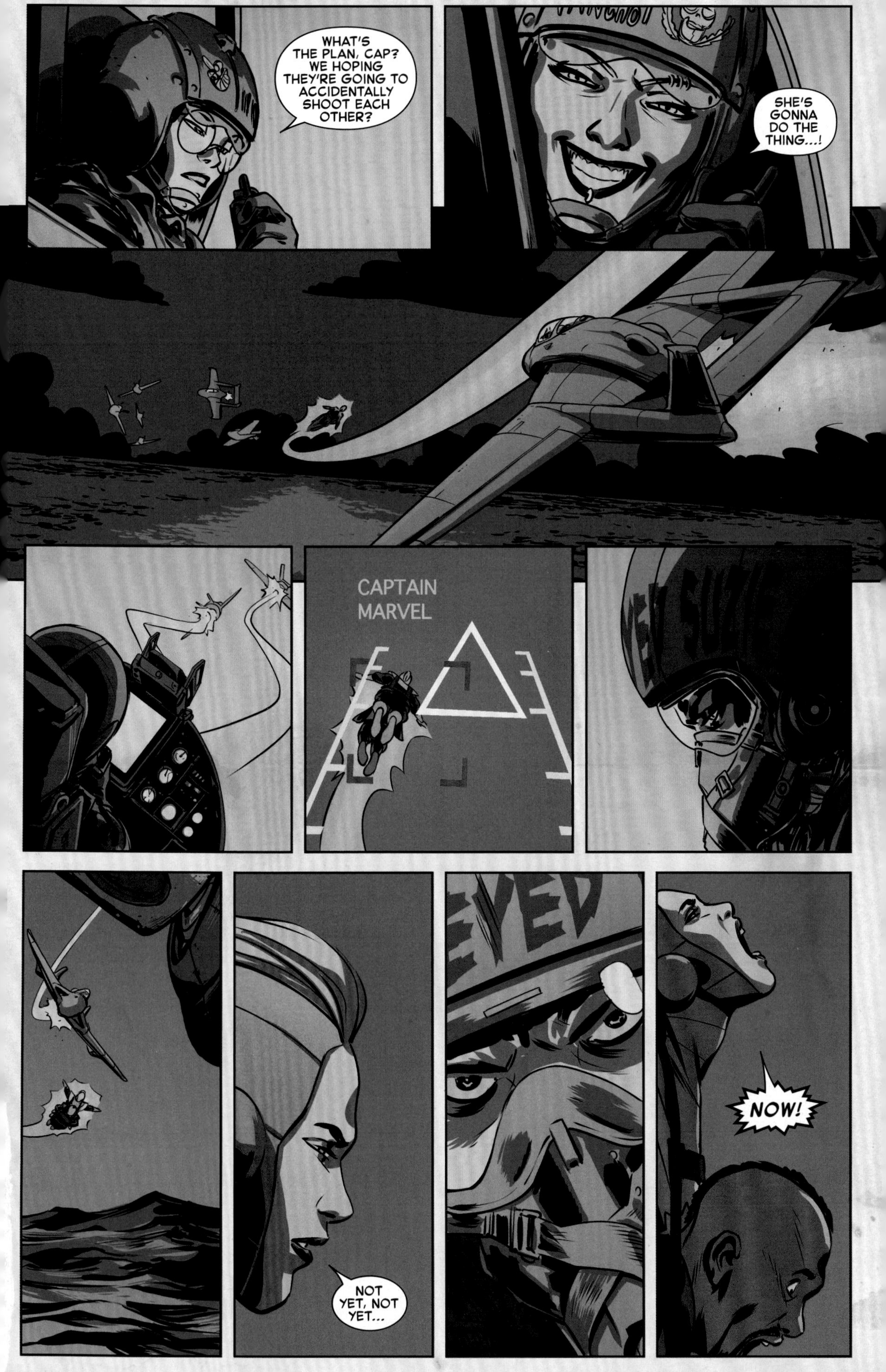
WHAT'S THE PLAN, CAP? WE HOPING THEY'RE GOING TO ACCIDENTALLY SHOOT EACH OTHER?
SHE'S GONNA DO THE THING...!
CAPTAIN MARVEL
NOT YET, NOT YET...
NOW!

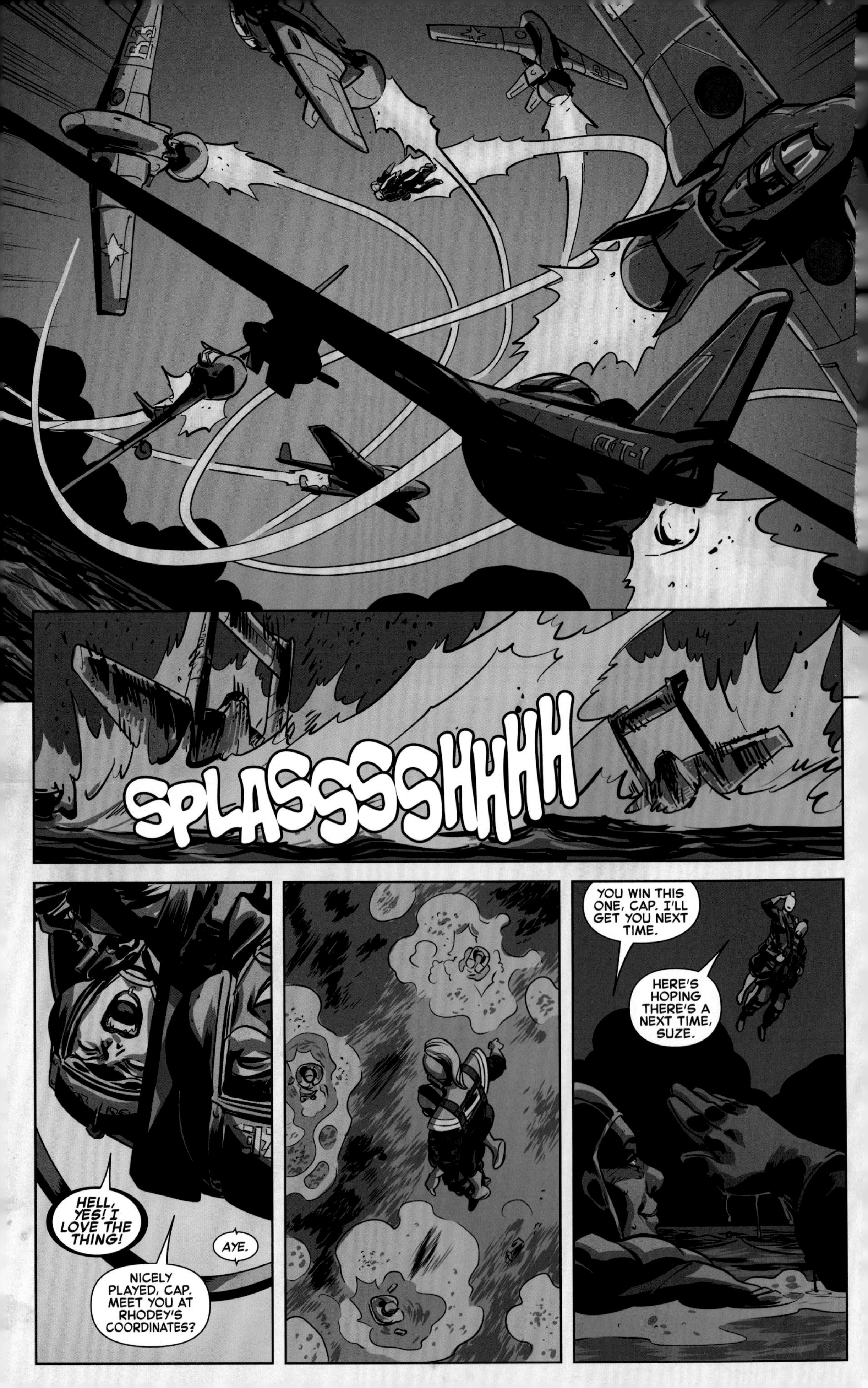

SPLASSSSSHHHH
HELL, YES! I LOVE THE THING!
AYE.
NICELY PLAYED, CAP. MEET YOU AT RHODEY'S COORDINATES?
YOU WIN THIS ONE, CAP. I'LL GET YOU NEXT TIME.
HERE'S HOPING THERE'S A NEXT TIME, SUZE.

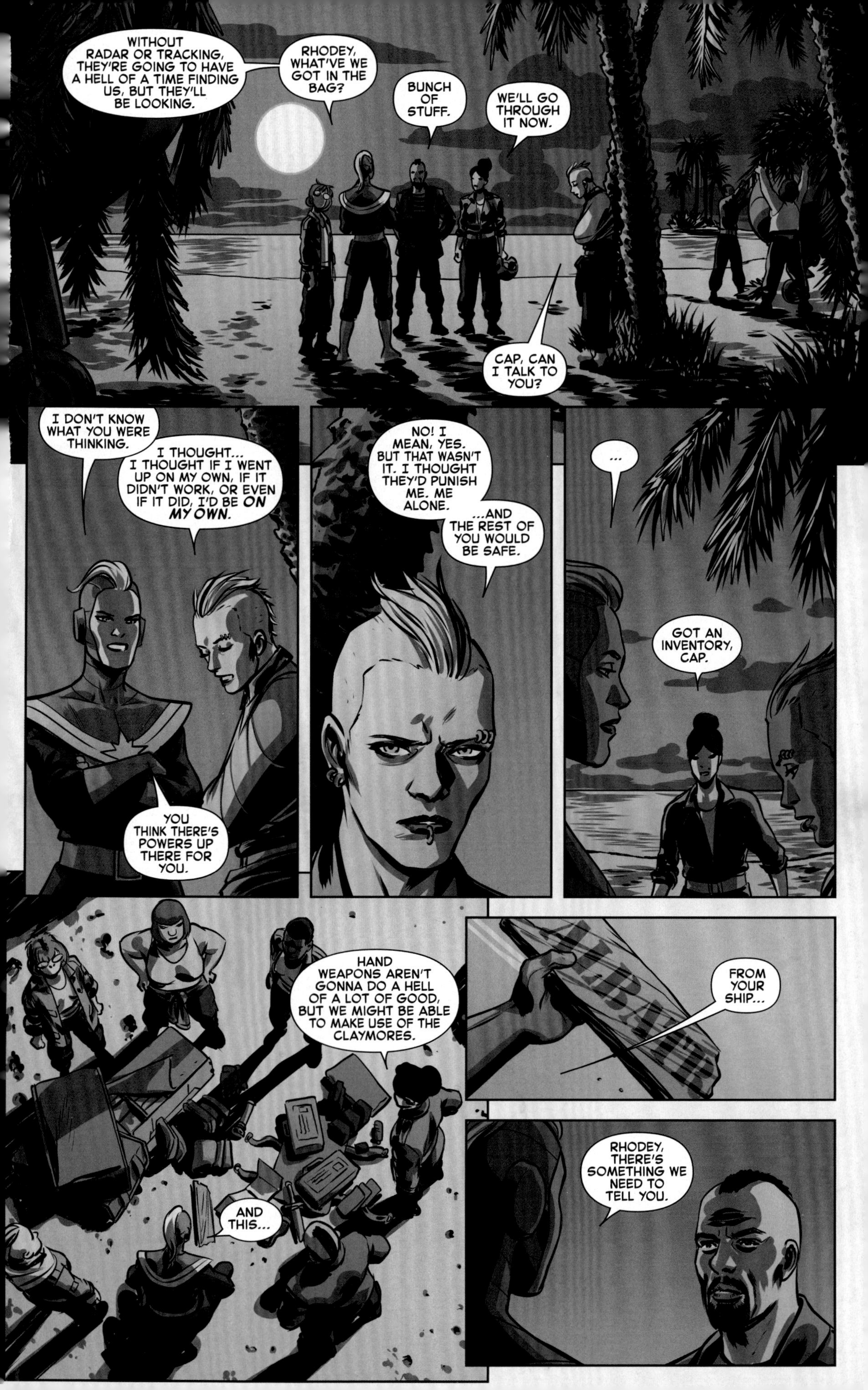
WITHOUT RADAR OR TRACKING, THEY'RE GOING TO HAVE A HELL OF A TIME FINDING US, BUT THEY'LL BE LOOKING.
RHODEY, WHAT'VE WE GOT IN THE BAG?
BUNCH OF STUFF.
WE'LL GO THROUGH IT NOW.
CAP, CAN I TALK TO YOU?
I DON'T KNOW WHAT YOU WERE THINKING.
I THOUGHT... I THOUGHT IF I WENT UP ON MY OWN, IF IT DIDN'T WORK, OR EVEN IF IT DID, I'D BE ON MY OWN.
YOU THINK THERE'S POWERS UP THERE FOR YOU.
NO! I MEAN, YES. BUT THAT WASN'T IT. I THOUGHT THEY'D PUNISH ME. ME ALONE.
...AND THE REST OF YOU WOULD BE SAFE.
...
GOT AN INVENTORY, CAP.
HAND WEAPONS AREN'T GONNA DO A HELL OF A LOT OF GOOD, BUT WE MIGHT BE ABLE TO MAKE USE OF THE CLAYMORES.
AND THIS...
FROM YOUR SHIP...
RHODEY, THERE'S SOMETHING WE NEED TO TELL YOU.

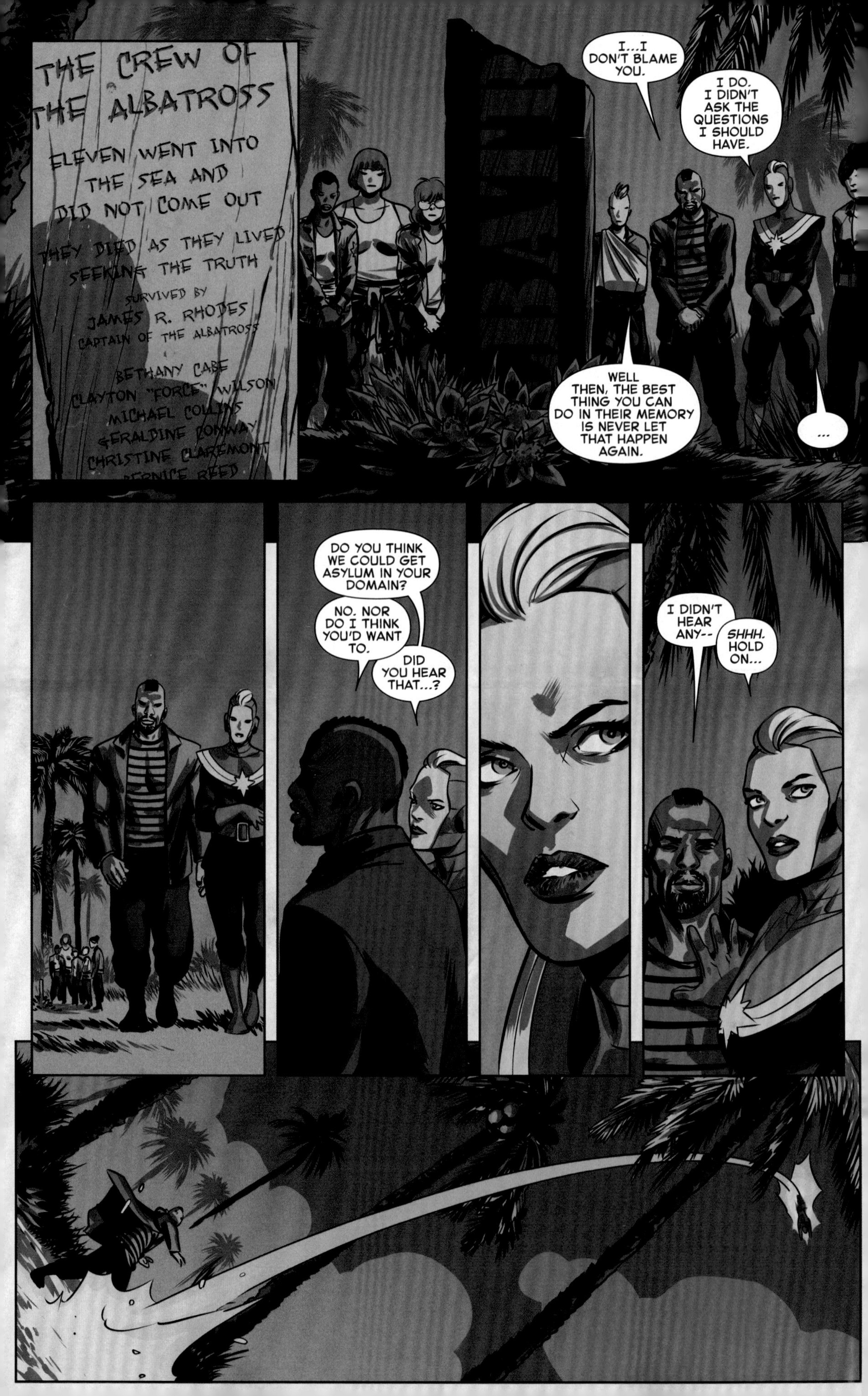
THE CREW OF THE ALBATROSS
ELEVEN WENT INTO THE SEA AND DID NOT COME OUT
THEY DIED AS THEY LIVED SEEKING THE TRUTH
SURVIVED BY
JAMES R. RHODES
CAPTAIN OF THE ALBATROSS
BETHANY CABE
CLAYTON "FORCE" WILSON
MICHAEL COLLINS
GERALDINE CONWAY
CHRISTINE CLAREMONT
I...I DON'T BLAME YOU.
I DO. I DIDN'T ASK THE QUESTIONS I SHOULD HAVE.
WELL THEN, THE BEST THING YOU CAN DO IN THEIR MEMORY IS NEVER LET THAT HAPPEN AGAIN.
...
DO YOU THINK WE COULD GET ASYLUM IN YOUR DOMAIN?
NO. NOR DO I THINK YOU'D WANT TO.
DID YOU HEAR THAT...?
I DIDN'T HEAR ANY--
SHHH. HOLD ON...

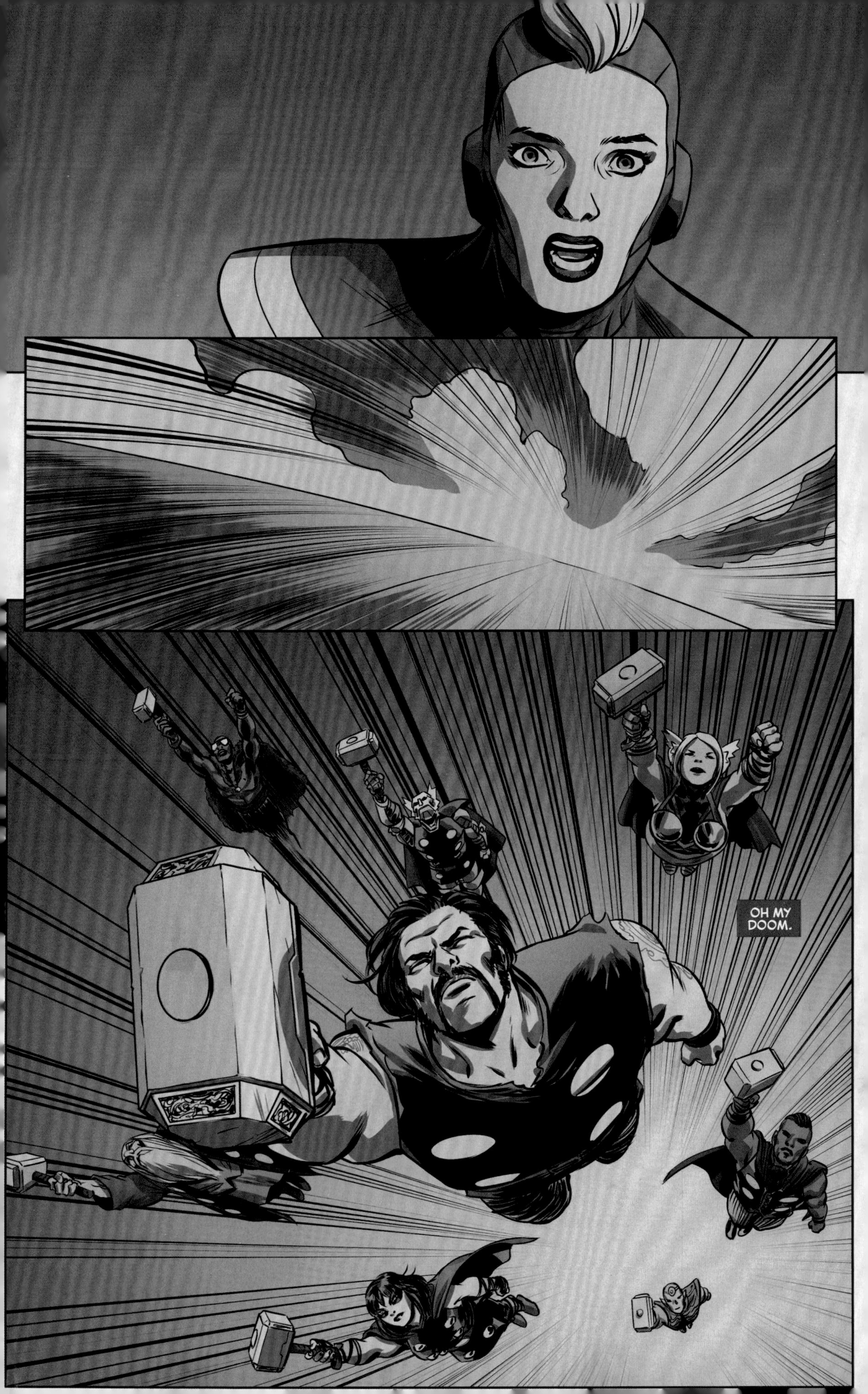
OH MY DOOM.

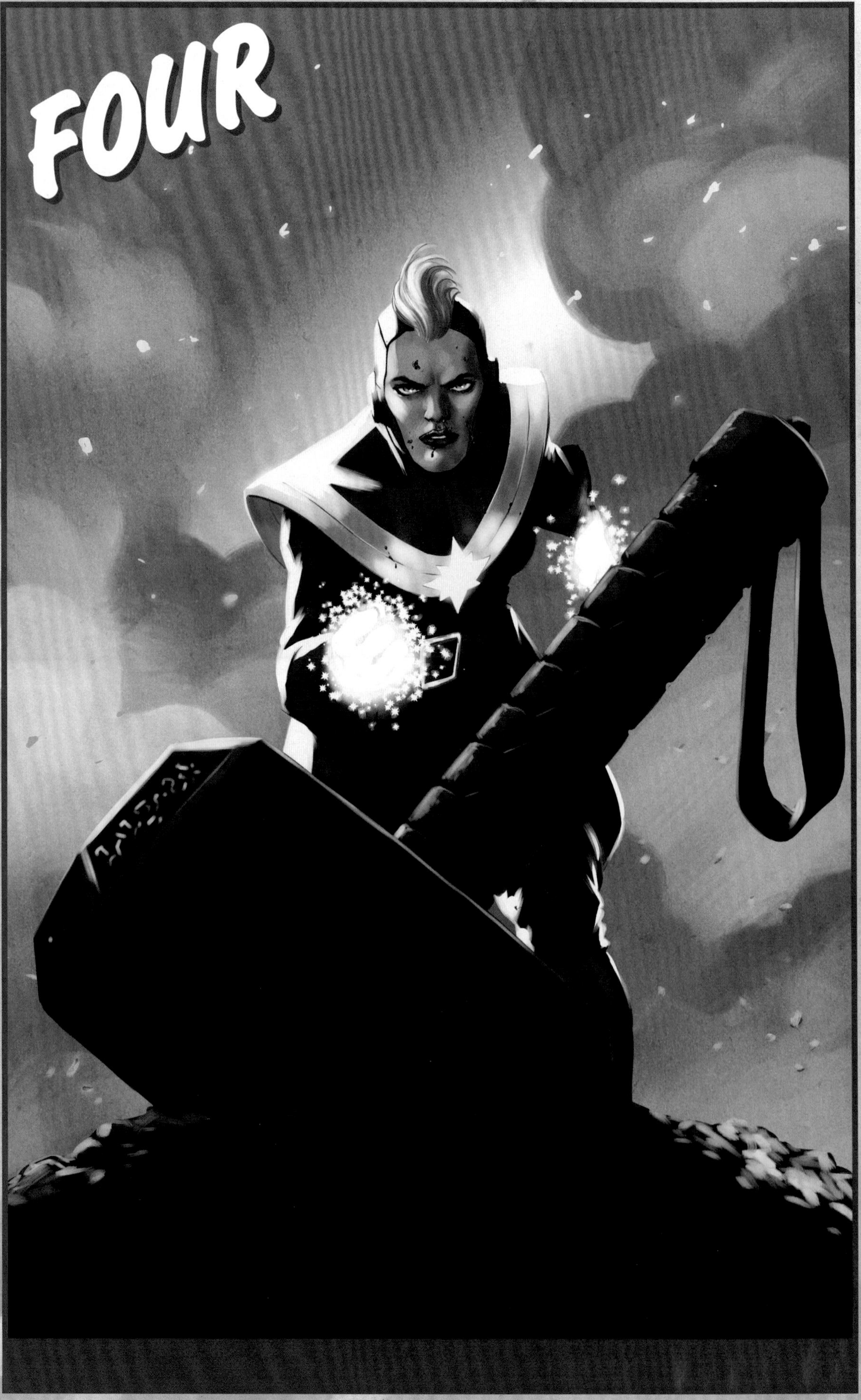
FOUR

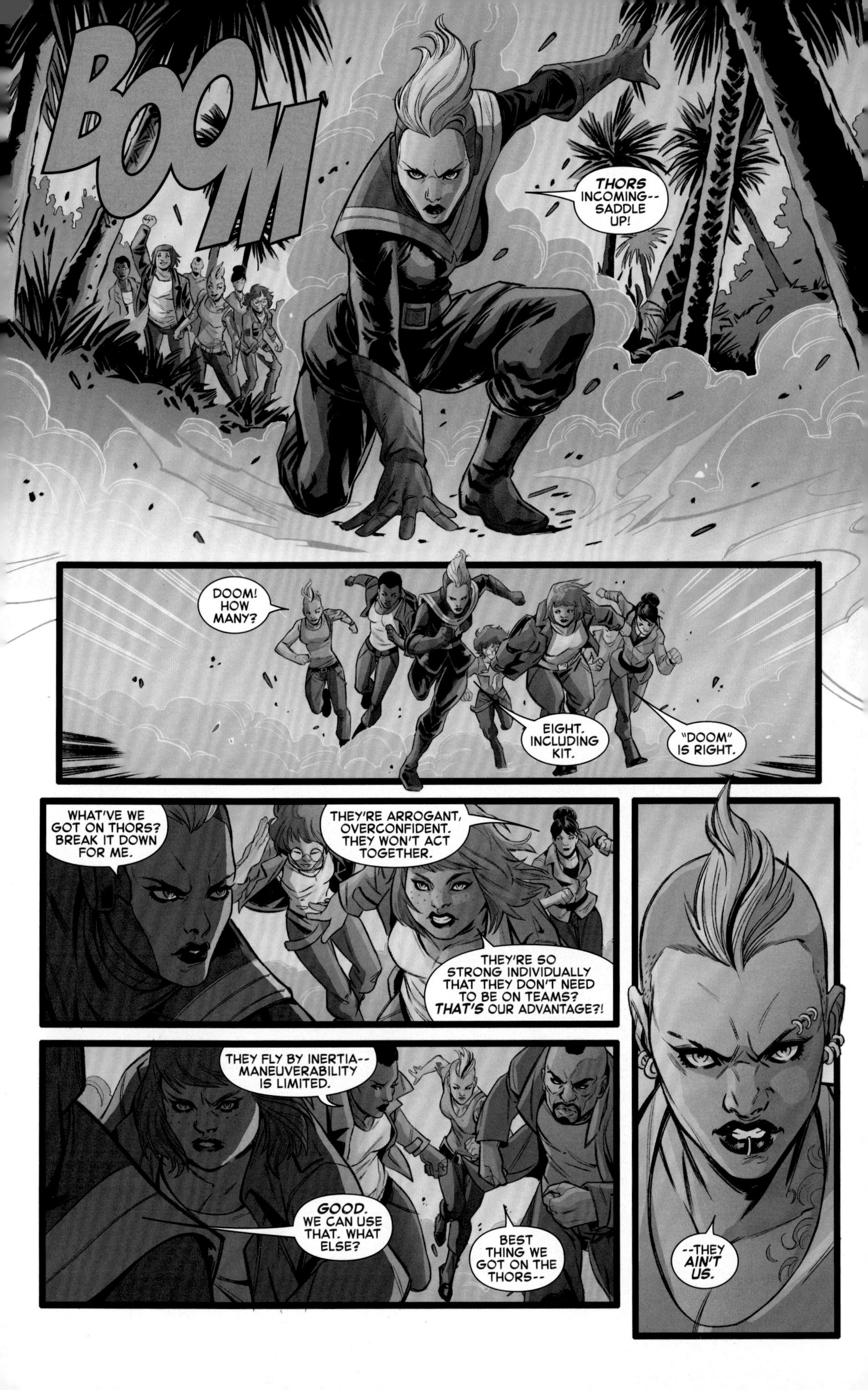
BOOM
THORS INCOMING--SADDLE UP!
DOOM! HOW MANY?
EIGHT. INCLUDING KIT.
"DOOM" IS RIGHT.
WHAT'VE WE GOT ON THORS? BREAK IT DOWN FOR ME.
THEY'RE ARROGANT, OVERCONFIDENT. THEY WON'T ACT TOGETHER.
THEY'RE SO STRONG INDIVIDUALLY THAT THEY DON'T NEED TO BE ON TEAMS? THAT'S OUR ADVANTAGE?!
THEY FLY BY INERTIA--MANEUVERABILITY IS LIMITED.
GOOD. WE CAN USE THAT. WHAT ELSE?
BEST THING WE GOT ON THE THORS--
--THEY AIN'T US.

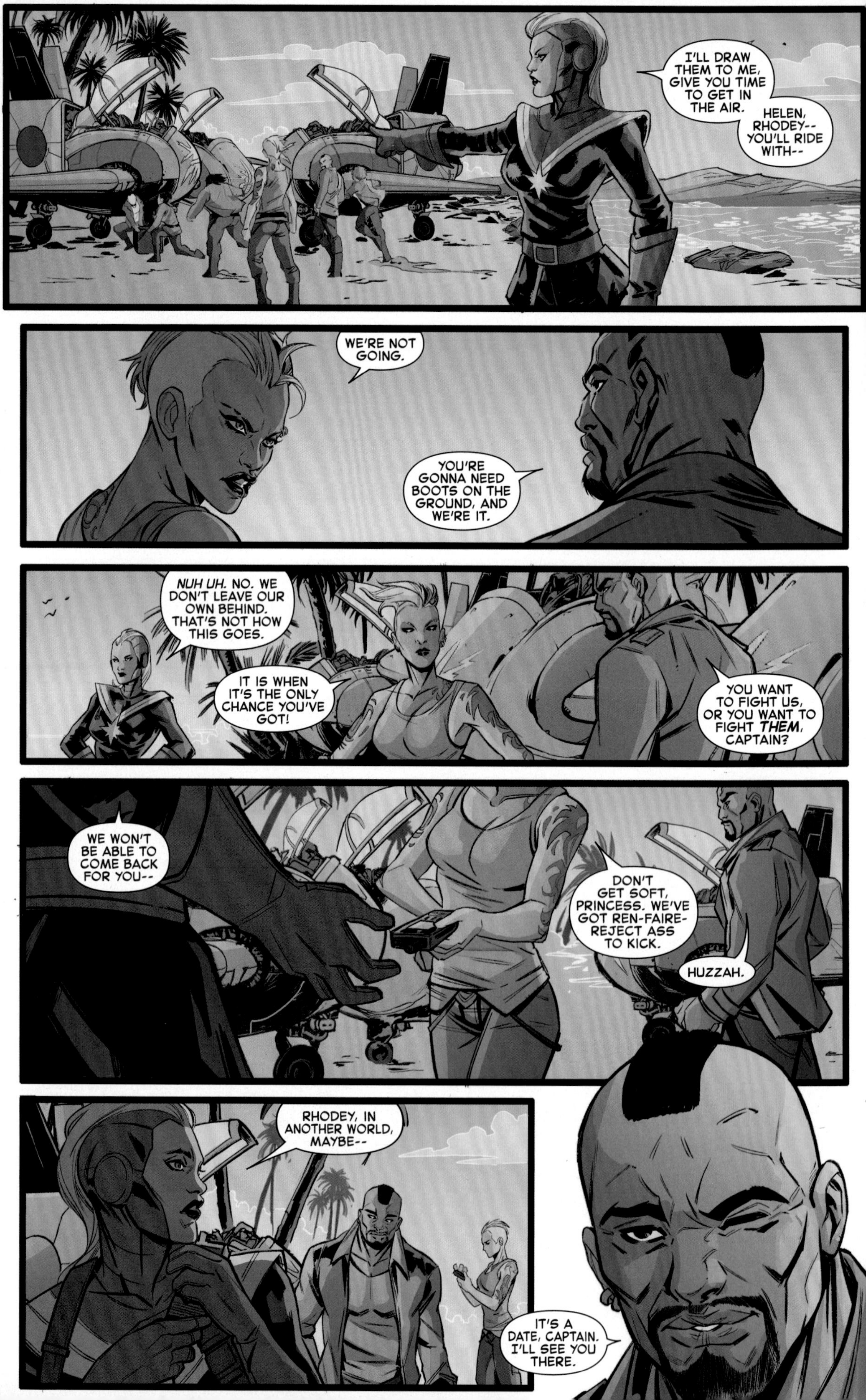

I'LL DRAW THEM TO ME, GIVE YOU TIME TO GET IN THE AIR.
HELEN, RHODEY-- YOU'LL RIDE WITH--
WE'RE NOT GOING.
YOU'RE GONNA NEED BOOTS ON THE GROUND, AND WE'RE IT.
NUH UH. NO. WE DON'T LEAVE OUR OWN BEHIND. THAT'S NOT HOW THIS GOES.
IT IS WHEN IT'S THE ONLY CHANCE YOU'VE GOT!
YOU WANT TO FIGHT US, OR YOU WANT TO FIGHT *THEM*, CAPTAIN?
WE WON'T BE ABLE TO COME BACK FOR YOU--
DON'T GET SOFT, PRINCESS. WE'VE GOT REN-FAIRE-REJECT ASS TO KICK.
HUZZAH.
RHODEY, IN ANOTHER WORLD, MAYBE--
IT'S A DATE, CAPTAIN. I'LL SEE YOU THERE.

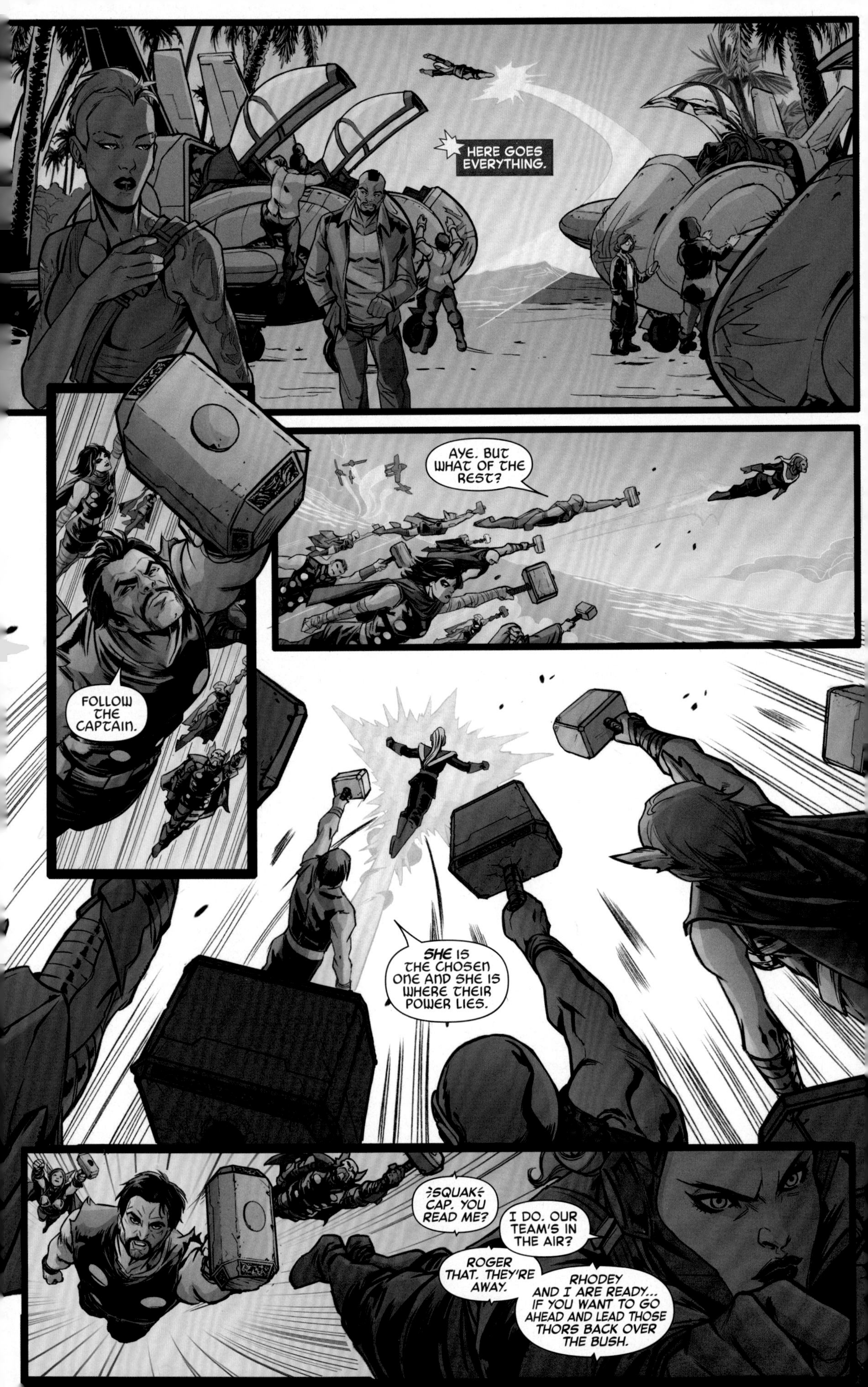
HERE GOES EVERYTHING.
FOLLOW THE CAPTAIN.
AYE. BUT WHAT OF THE REST?
SHE IS THE CHOSEN ONE AND SHE IS WHERE THEIR POWER LIES.
⚡SQUAK⚡ CAP. YOU READ ME?
I DO. OUR TEAM'S IN THE AIR?
ROGER THAT. THEY'RE AWAY.
RHODEY AND I ARE READY... IF YOU WANT TO GO AHEAD AND LEAD THOSE THORS BACK OVER THE BUSH.

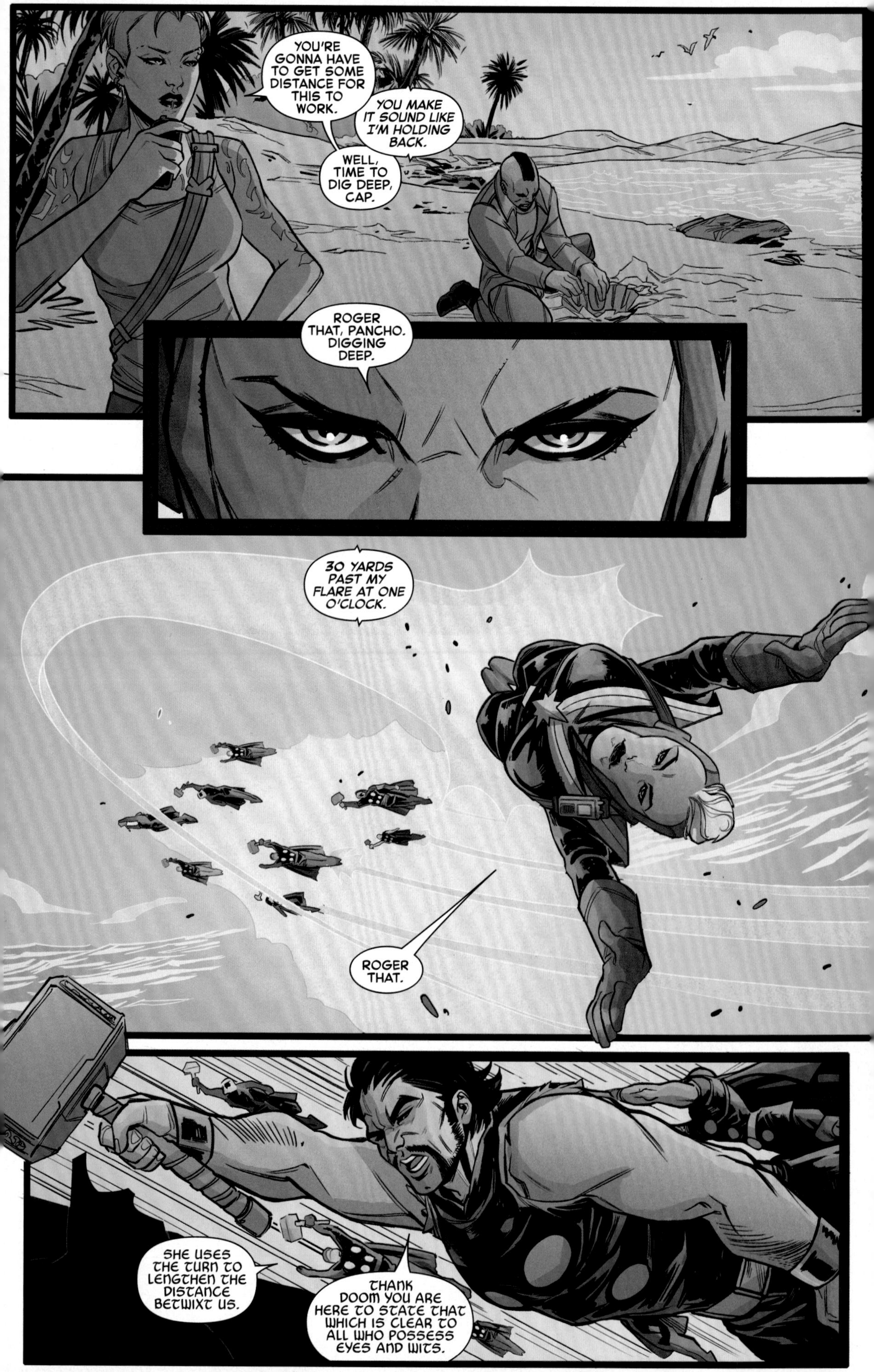
YOU'RE GONNA HAVE TO GET SOME DISTANCE FOR THIS TO WORK.
YOU MAKE IT SOUND LIKE I'M HOLDING BACK.
WELL, TIME TO DIG DEEP, CAP.
ROGER THAT, PANCHO. DIGGING DEEP.
30 YARDS PAST MY FLARE AT ONE O'CLOCK.
ROGER THAT.
SHE USES THE TURN TO LENGTHEN THE DISTANCE BETWIXT US.
THANK DOOM YOU ARE HERE TO STATE THAT WHICH IS CLEAR TO ALL WHO POSSESS EYES AND WITS.

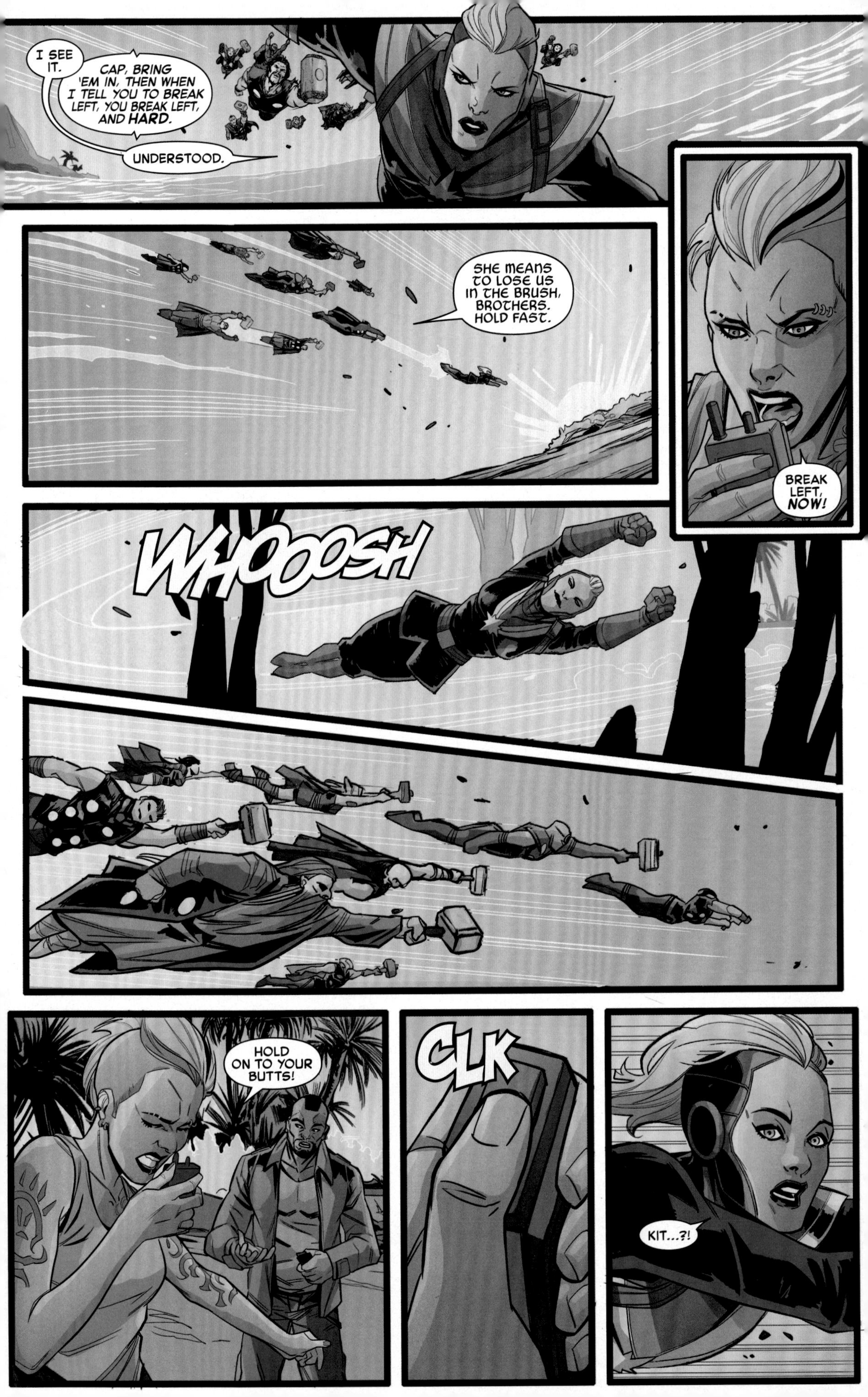
I SEE IT.
CAP, BRING 'EM IN, THEN WHEN I TELL YOU TO BREAK LEFT, YOU BREAK LEFT, AND HARD.
UNDERSTOOD.
SHE MEANS TO LOSE US IN THE BRUSH, BROTHERS. HOLD FAST.
BREAK LEFT, NOW!
WHOOOSH
HOLD ON TO YOUR BUTTS!
CLK
KIT...?!

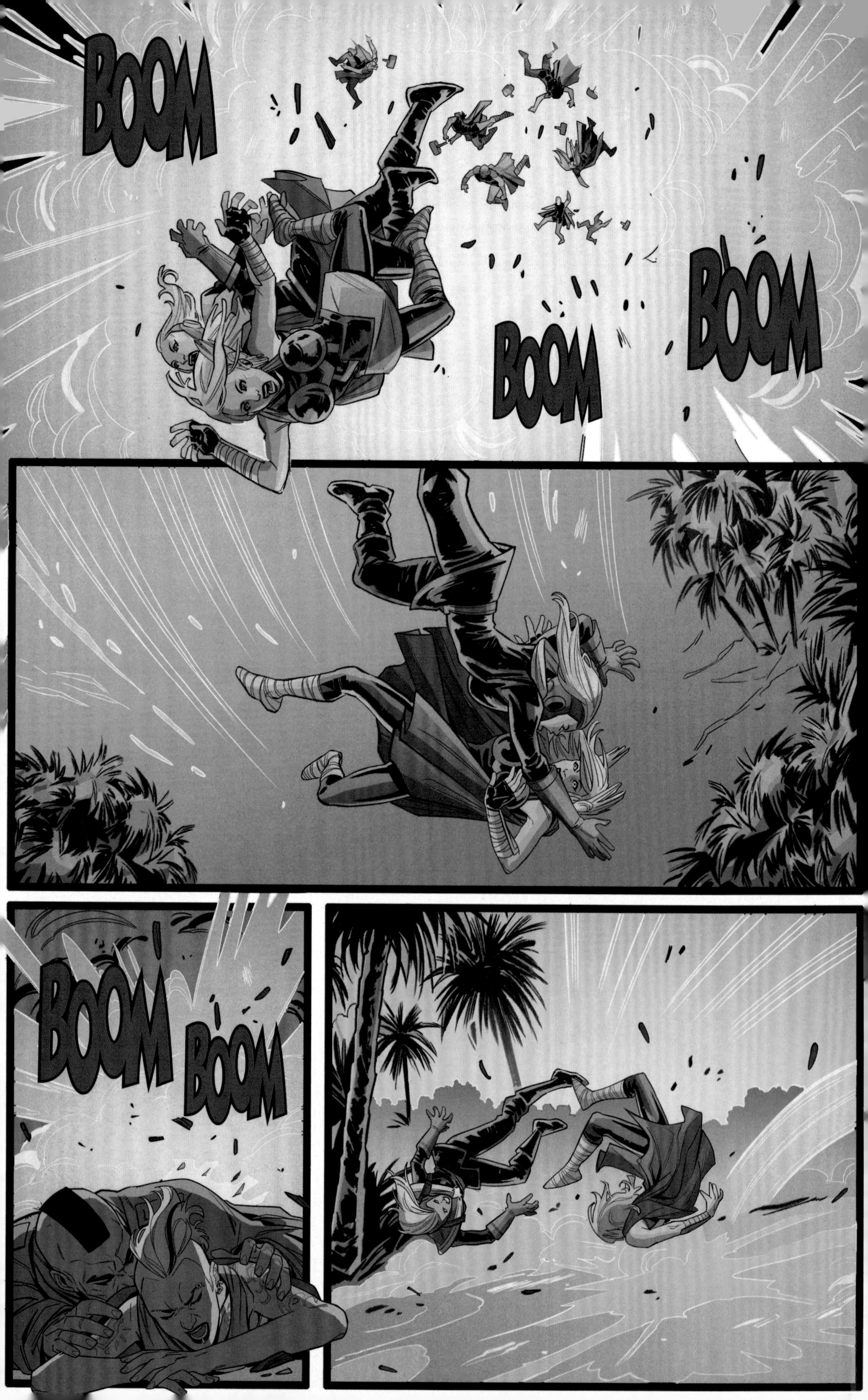
BOOM
BOOM
BOOM
BOOM
BOOM

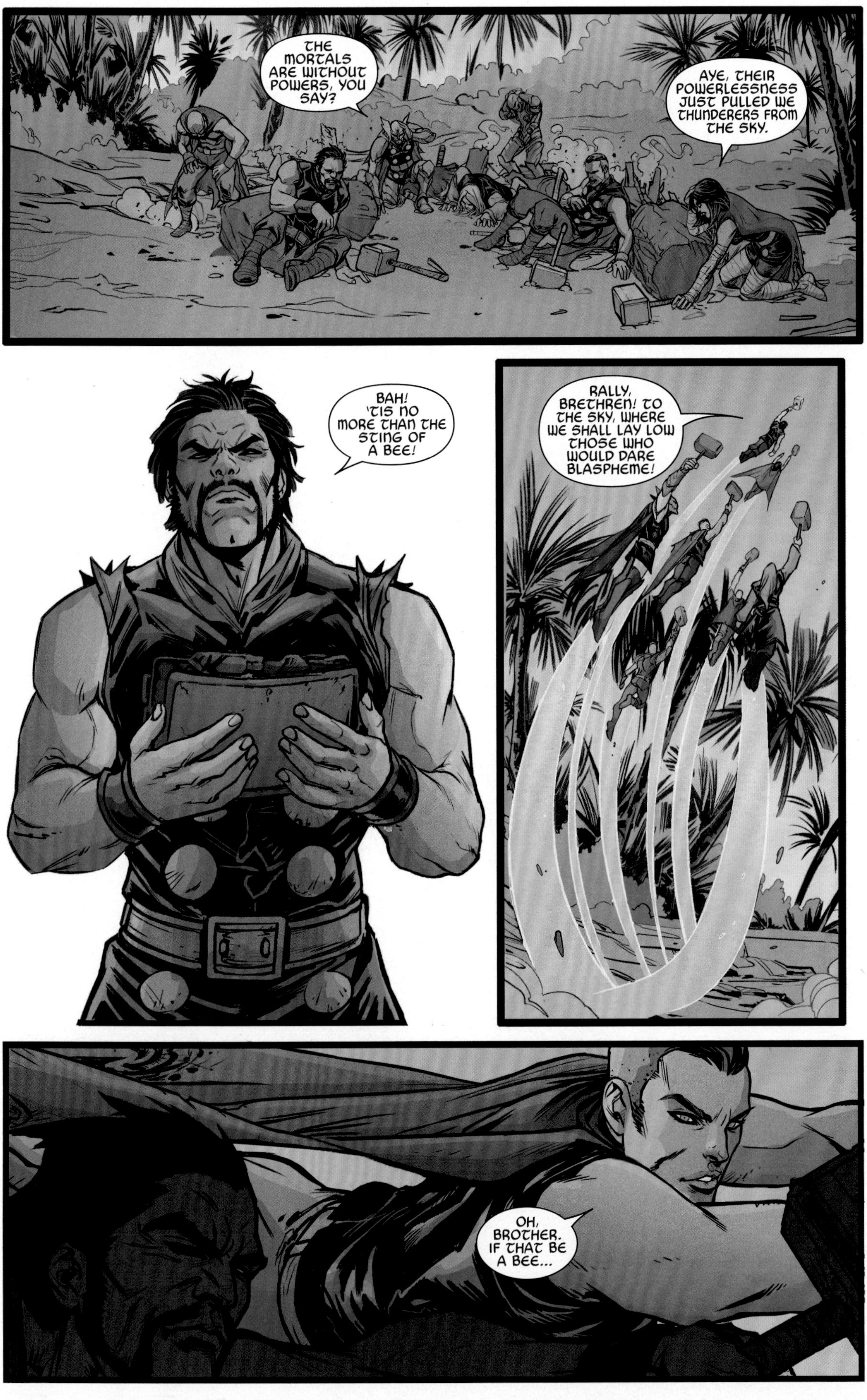
THE MORTALS ARE WITHOUT POWERS, YOU SAY?
AYE, THEIR POWERLESSNESS JUST PULLED WE THUNDERERS FROM THE SKY.
BAH! 'TIS NO MORE THAN THE STING OF A BEE!
RALLY, BRETHREN! TO THE SKY, WHERE WE SHALL LAY LOW THOSE WHO WOULD DARE BLASPHEME!
OH, BROTHER. IF THAT BE A BEE...

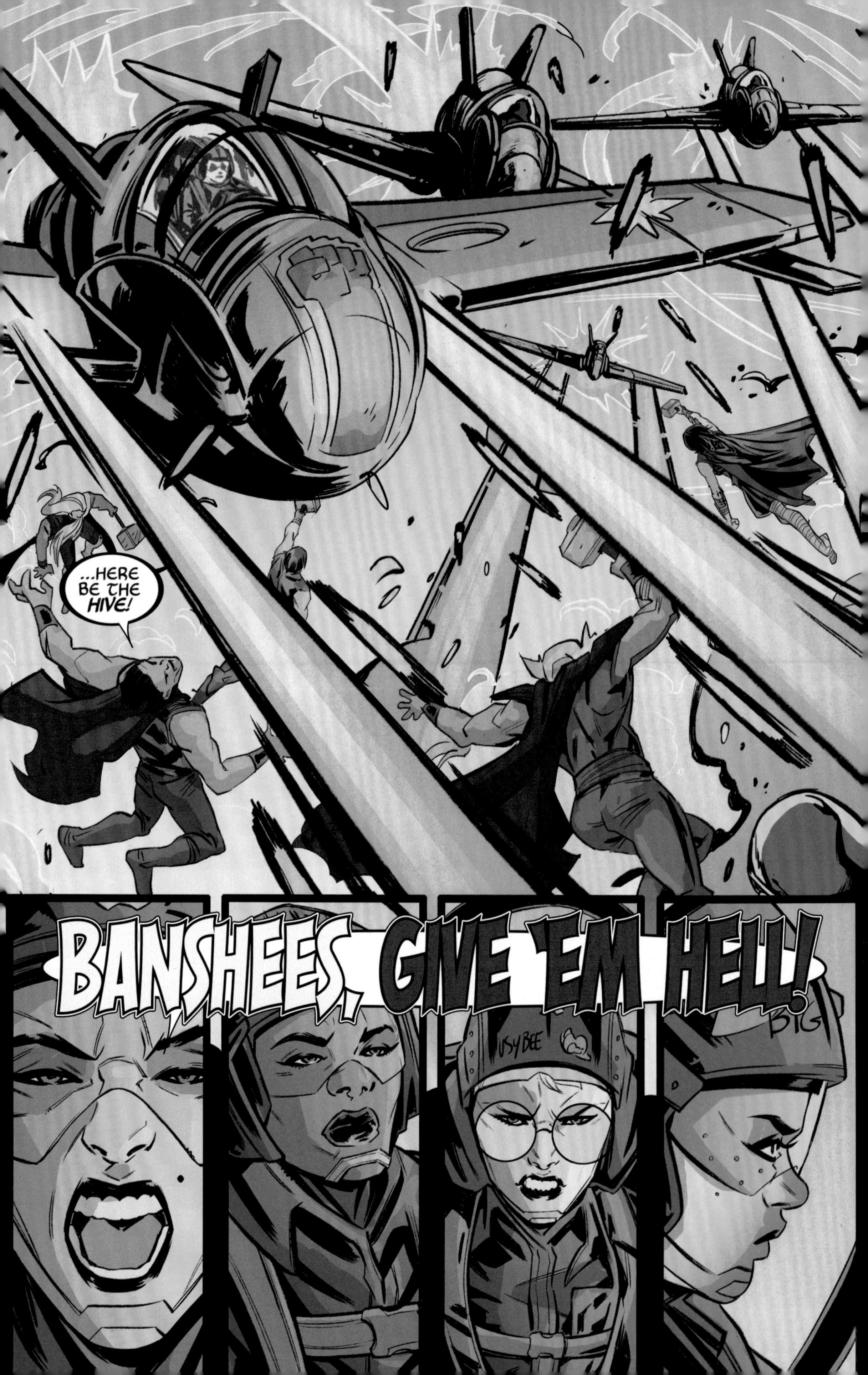
...HERE BE THE HIVE!
BANSHEES, GIVE 'EM HELL!

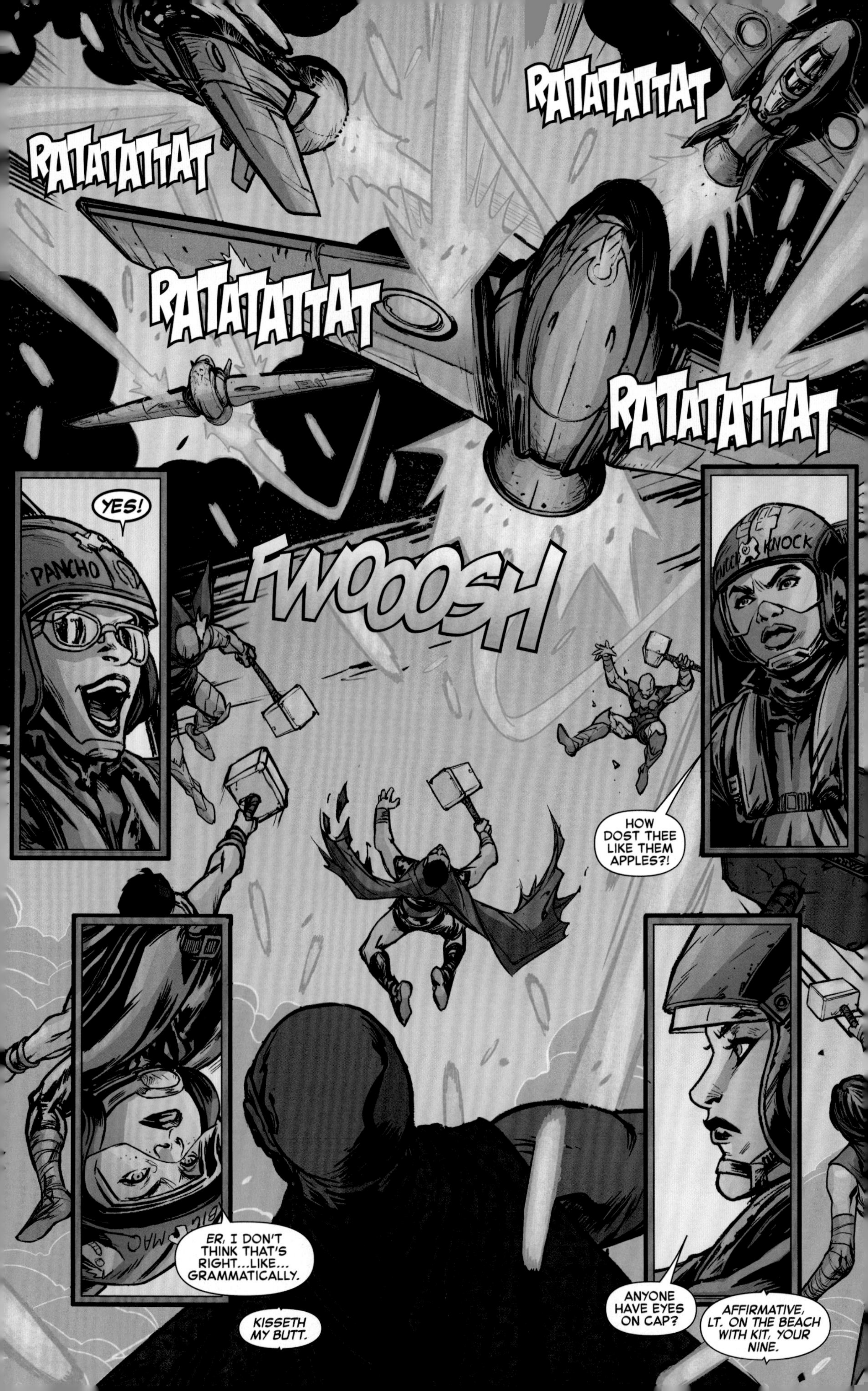
RATATATTAT
RATATATTAT
RATATATTAT
RATATATTAT
YES!
PANCHO
KNOCK KNOCK
FWOOOSH
HOW DOST THEE LIKE THEM APPLES?!
BIG MAC
ER, I DON'T THINK THAT'S RIGHT...LIKE... GRAMMATICALLY.
KISSETH MY BUTT.
ANYONE HAVE EYES ON CAP?
AFFIRMATIVE, LT. ON THE BEACH WITH KIT, YOUR NINE.

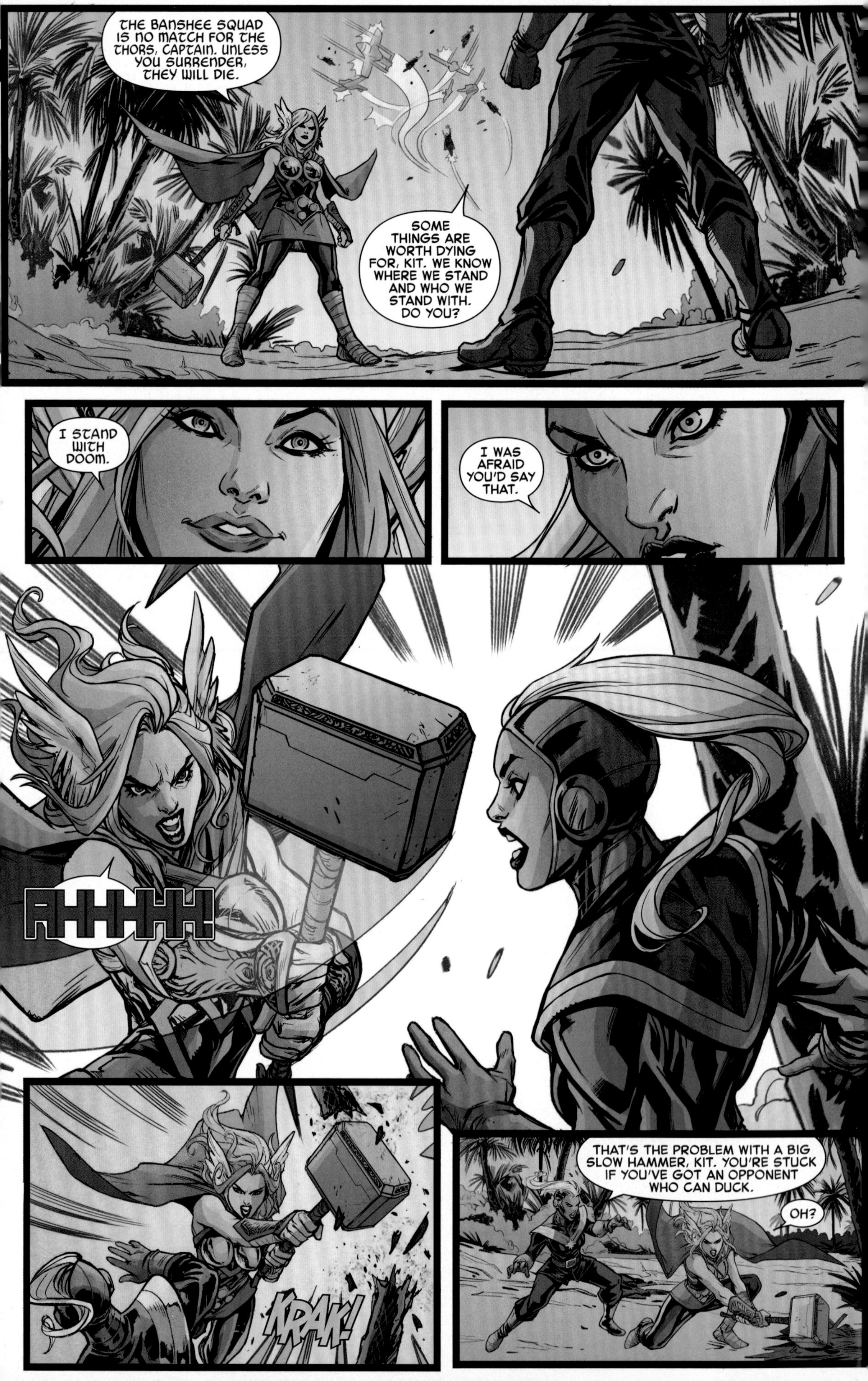
THE BANSHEE SQUAD IS NO MATCH FOR THE THORS, CAPTAIN. UNLESS YOU SURRENDER, THEY WILL DIE.
SOME THINGS ARE WORTH DYING FOR, KIT. WE KNOW WHERE WE STAND AND WHO WE STAND WITH. DO YOU?
I STAND WITH DOOM.
I WAS AFRAID YOU'D SAY THAT.
AHHHHH!
KRAK!
THAT'S THE PROBLEM WITH A BIG SLOW HAMMER, KIT. YOU'RE STUCK IF YOU'VE GOT AN OPPONENT WHO CAN DUCK.
OH?

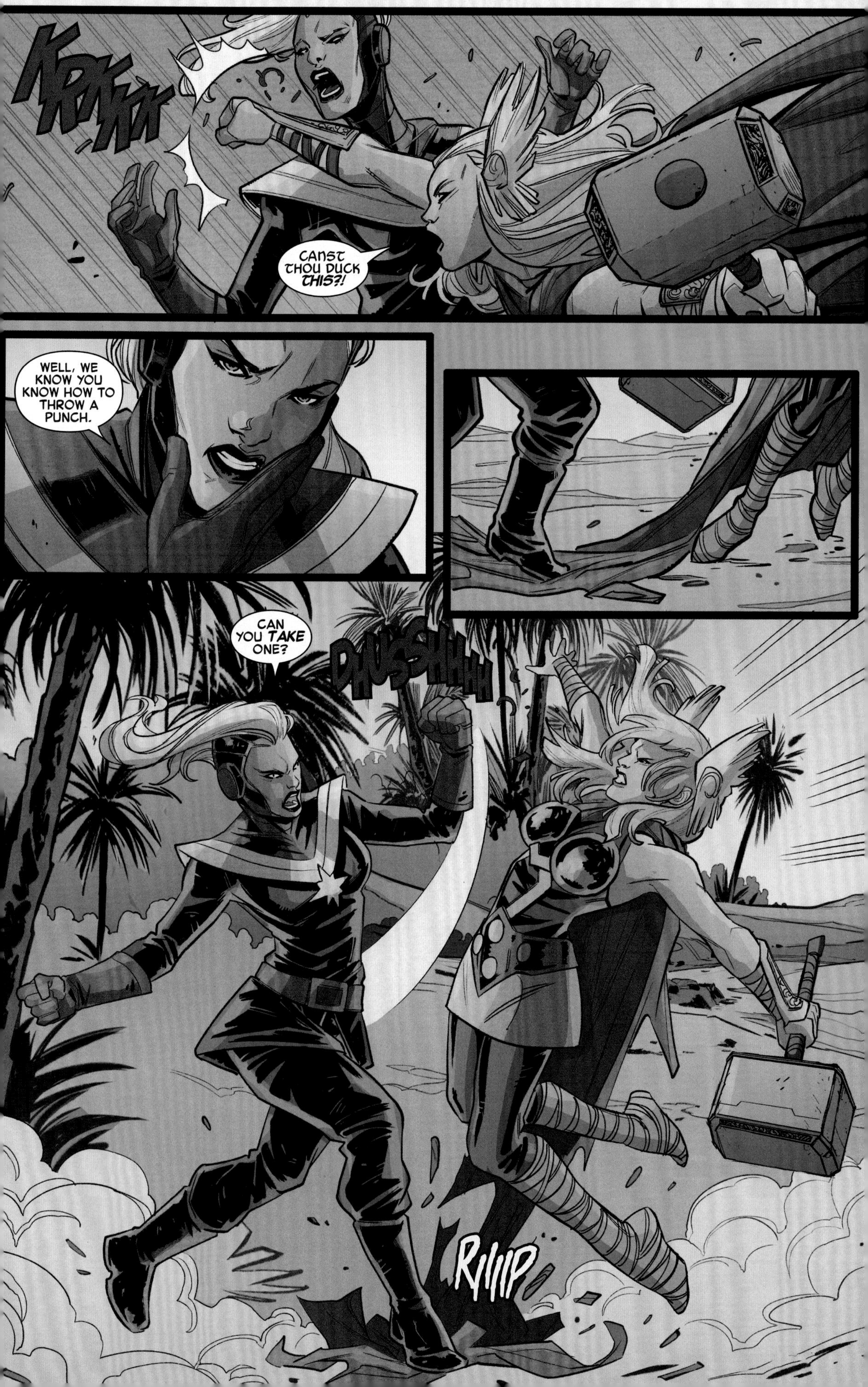
KRAKKK
CANST THOU DUCK THIS?!
WELL, WE KNOW YOU KNOW HOW TO THROW A PUNCH.
CAN YOU TAKE ONE?
DHUSSHHHH
RIIIIP

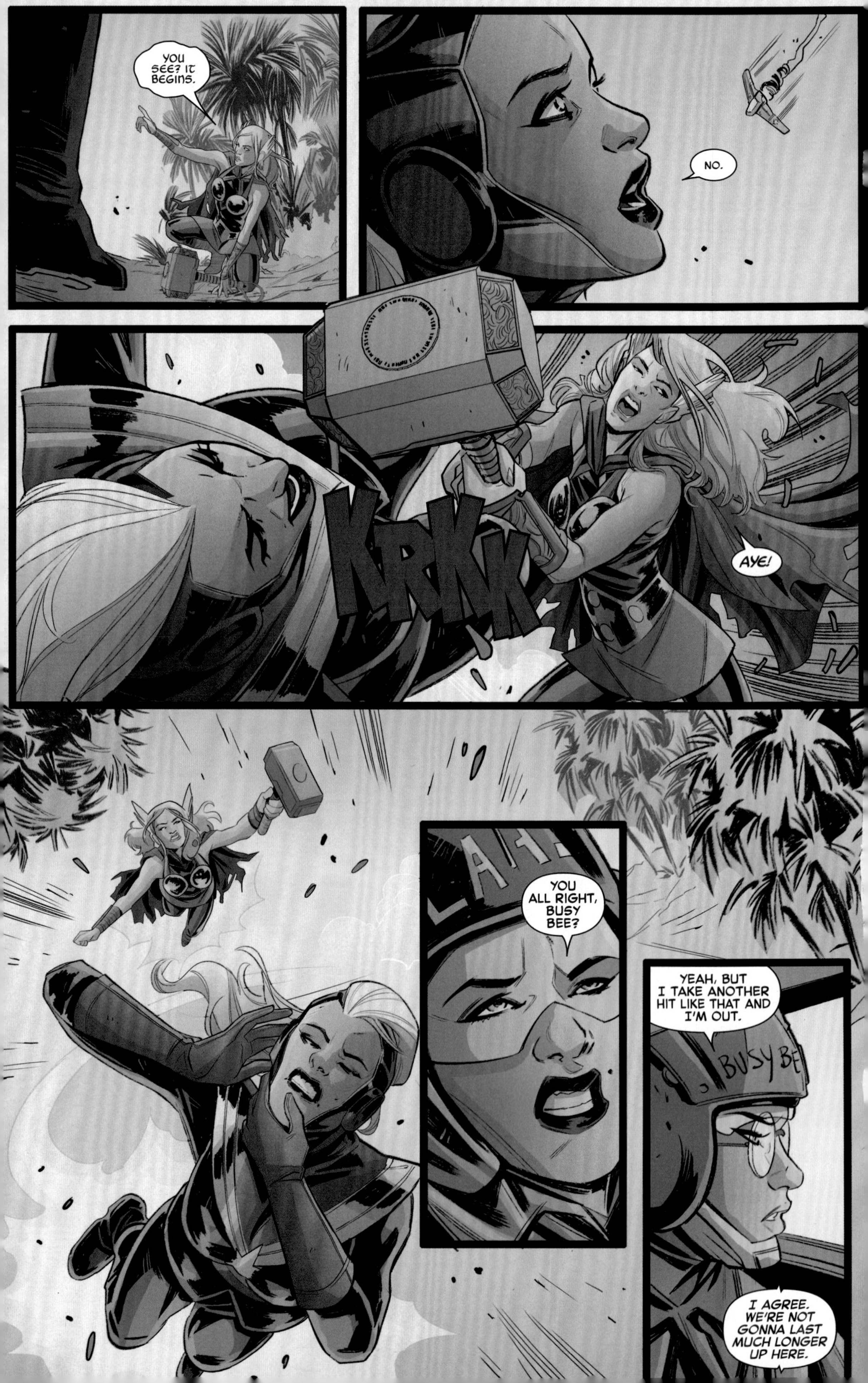
YOU SEE? IT BEGINS.
NO.
KRKK
AYE!
YOU ALL RIGHT, BUSY BEE?
YEAH, BUT I TAKE ANOTHER HIT LIKE THAT AND I'M OUT.
BUSY BE
I AGREE. WE'RE NOT GONNA LAST MUCH LONGER UP HERE.

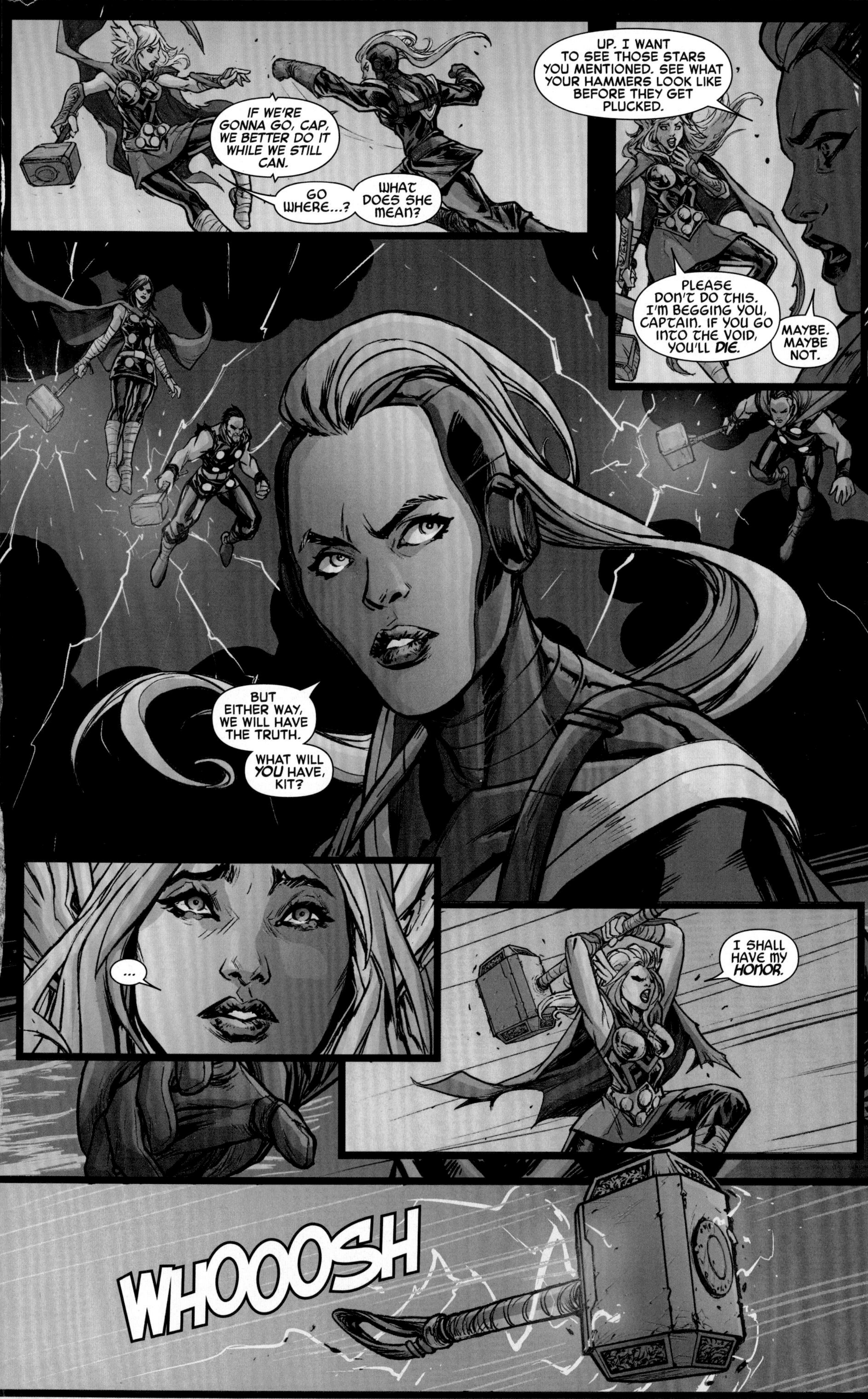
IF WE'RE GONNA GO, CAP, WE BETTER DO IT WHILE WE STILL CAN.
GO WHERE...?
WHAT DOES SHE MEAN?
UP. I WANT TO SEE THOSE STARS YOU MENTIONED. SEE WHAT YOUR HAMMERS LOOK LIKE BEFORE THEY GET PLUCKED.
PLEASE DON'T DO THIS. I'M BEGGING YOU, CAPTAIN. IF YOU GO INTO THE VOID, YOU'LL DIE.
MAYBE. MAYBE NOT.
BUT EITHER WAY, WE WILL HAVE THE TRUTH.
WHAT WILL YOU HAVE, KIT?
...
I SHALL HAVE MY HONOR.
WHOOOSH

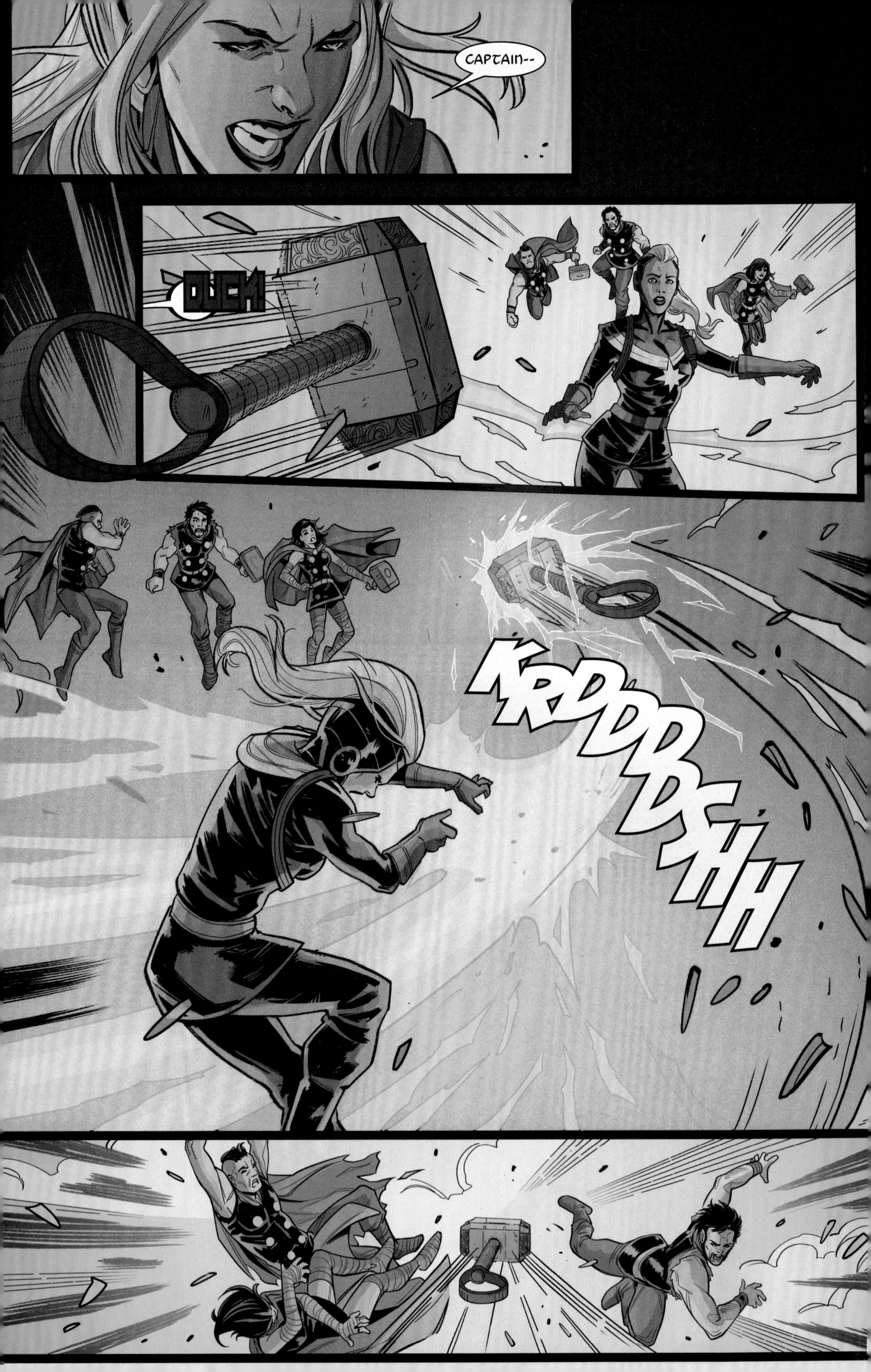
CAPTAIN--
DUCK!
KRDDDSHH

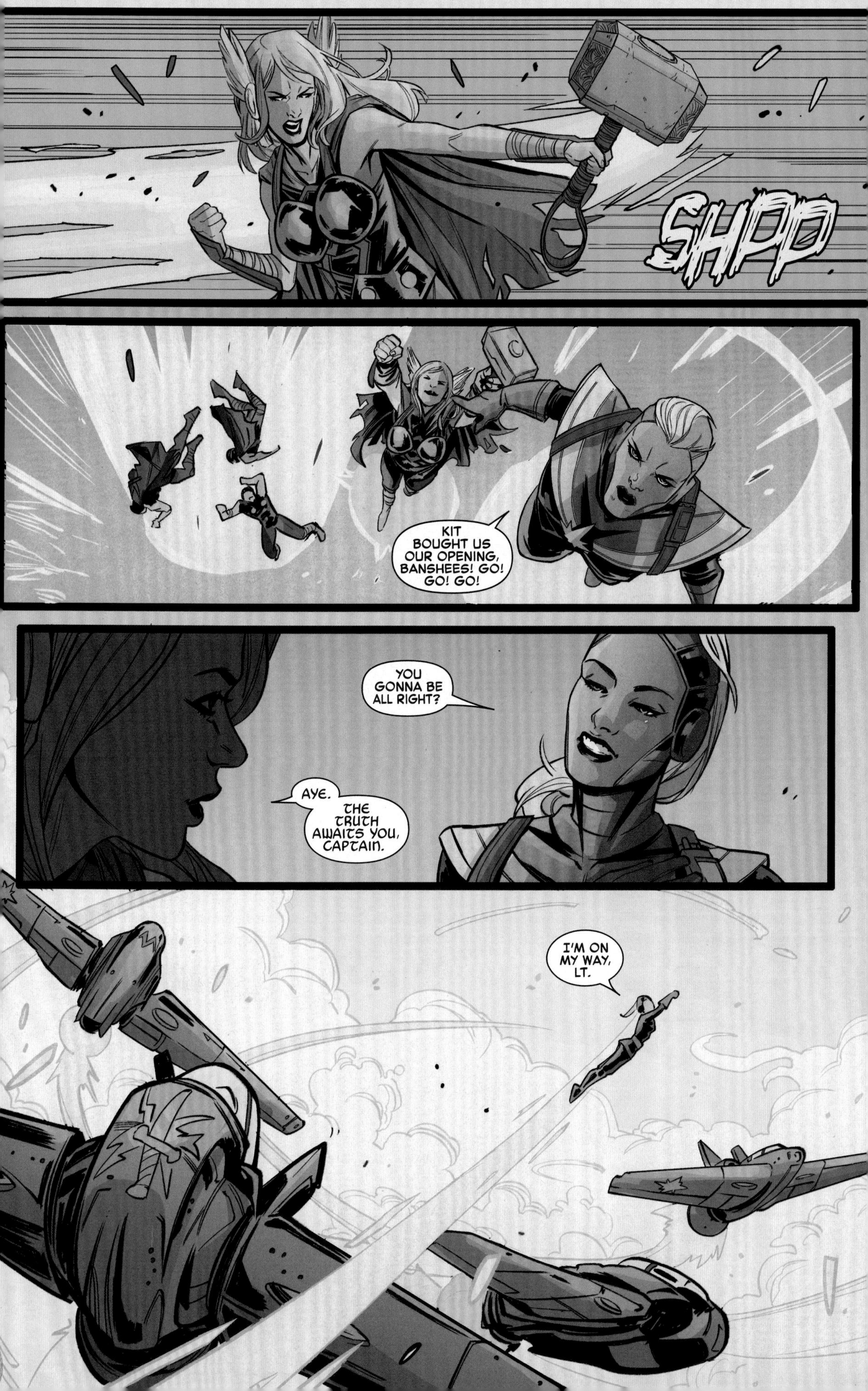
SHPP
KIT BOUGHT US OUR OPENING, BANSHEES! GO! GO! GO!
YOU GONNA BE ALL RIGHT?
AYE.
THE TRUTH AWAITS YOU, CAPTAIN.
I'M ON MY WAY, LT.

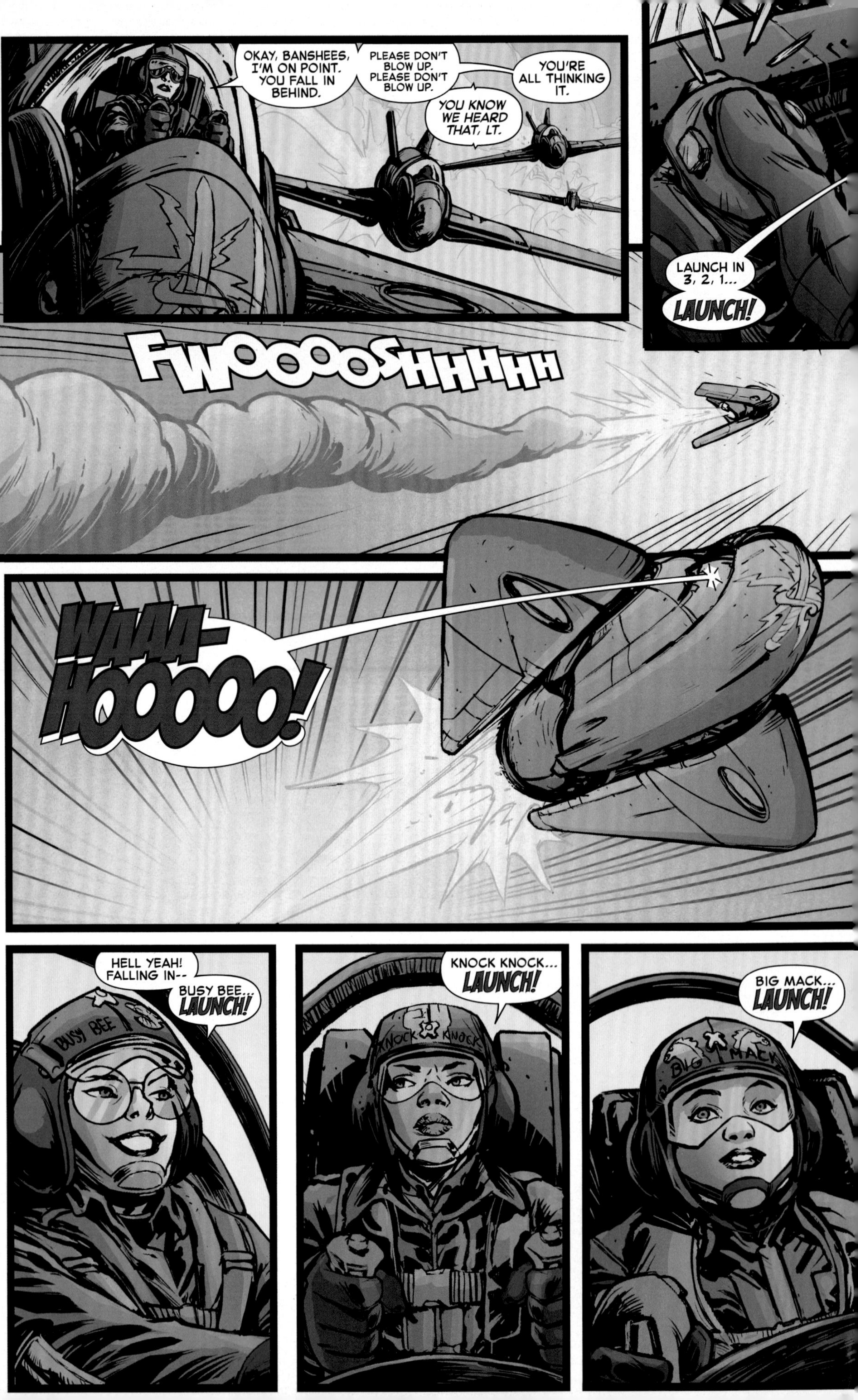
OKAY, BANSHEES, I'M ON POINT. YOU FALL IN BEHIND.
PLEASE DON'T BLOW UP. PLEASE DON'T BLOW UP.
YOU'RE ALL THINKING IT.
YOU KNOW WE HEARD THAT, LT.
LAUNCH IN 3, 2, 1...
LAUNCH!
FWOOOOSHHHHH
WAAA-HOOOOO!
HELL YEAH! FALLING IN--
BUSY BEE... LAUNCH!
BUSY BEE
KNOCK KNOCK... LAUNCH!
KNOCK KNOCK
BIG MACK... LAUNCH!
BIG MACK

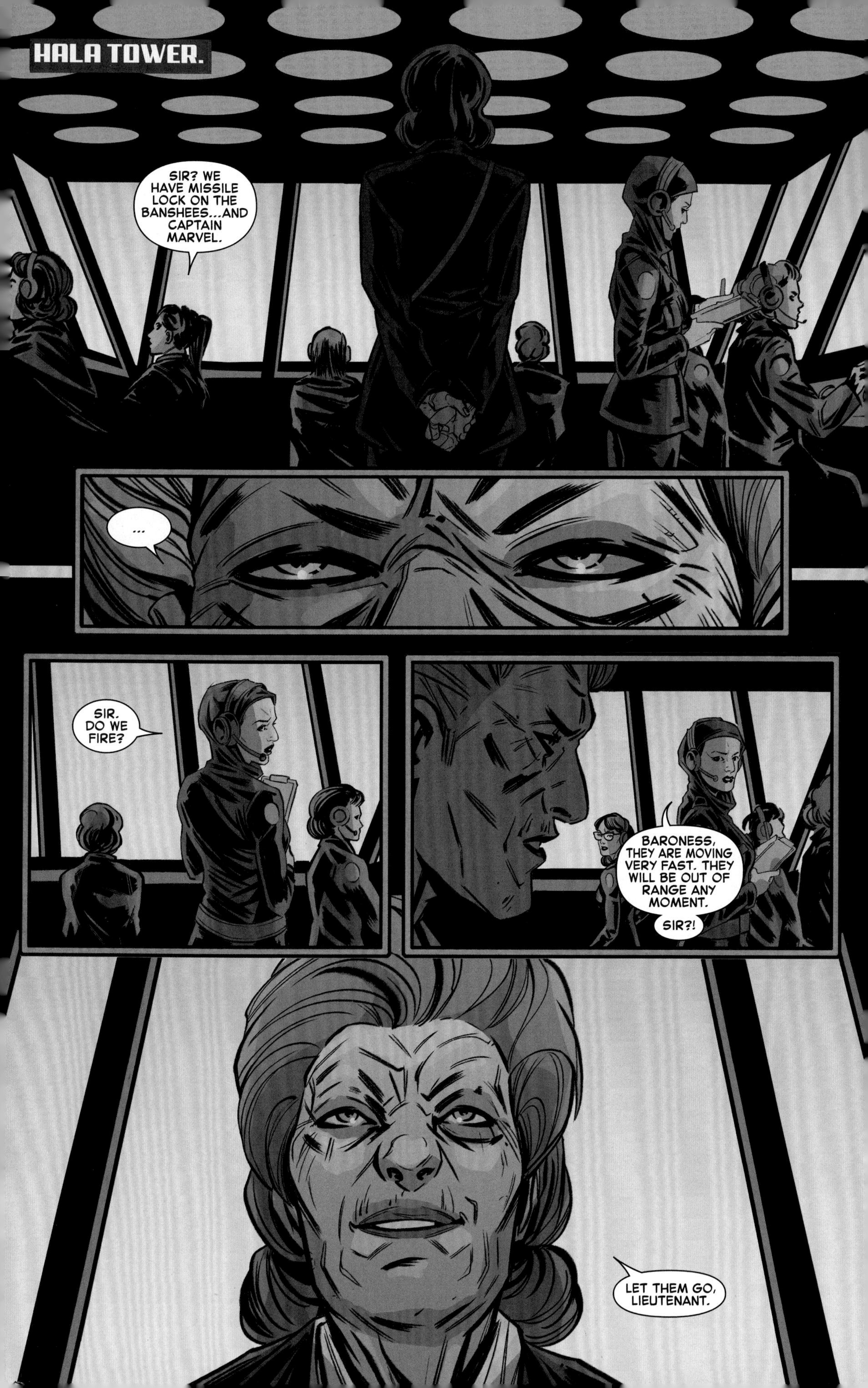
HALA TOWER.
SIR? WE HAVE MISSILE LOCK ON THE BANSHEES...AND CAPTAIN MARVEL.
...
SIR. DO WE FIRE?
BARONESS, THEY ARE MOVING VERY FAST. THEY WILL BE OUT OF RANGE ANY MOMENT.
SIR?!
LET THEM GO, LIEUTENANT.

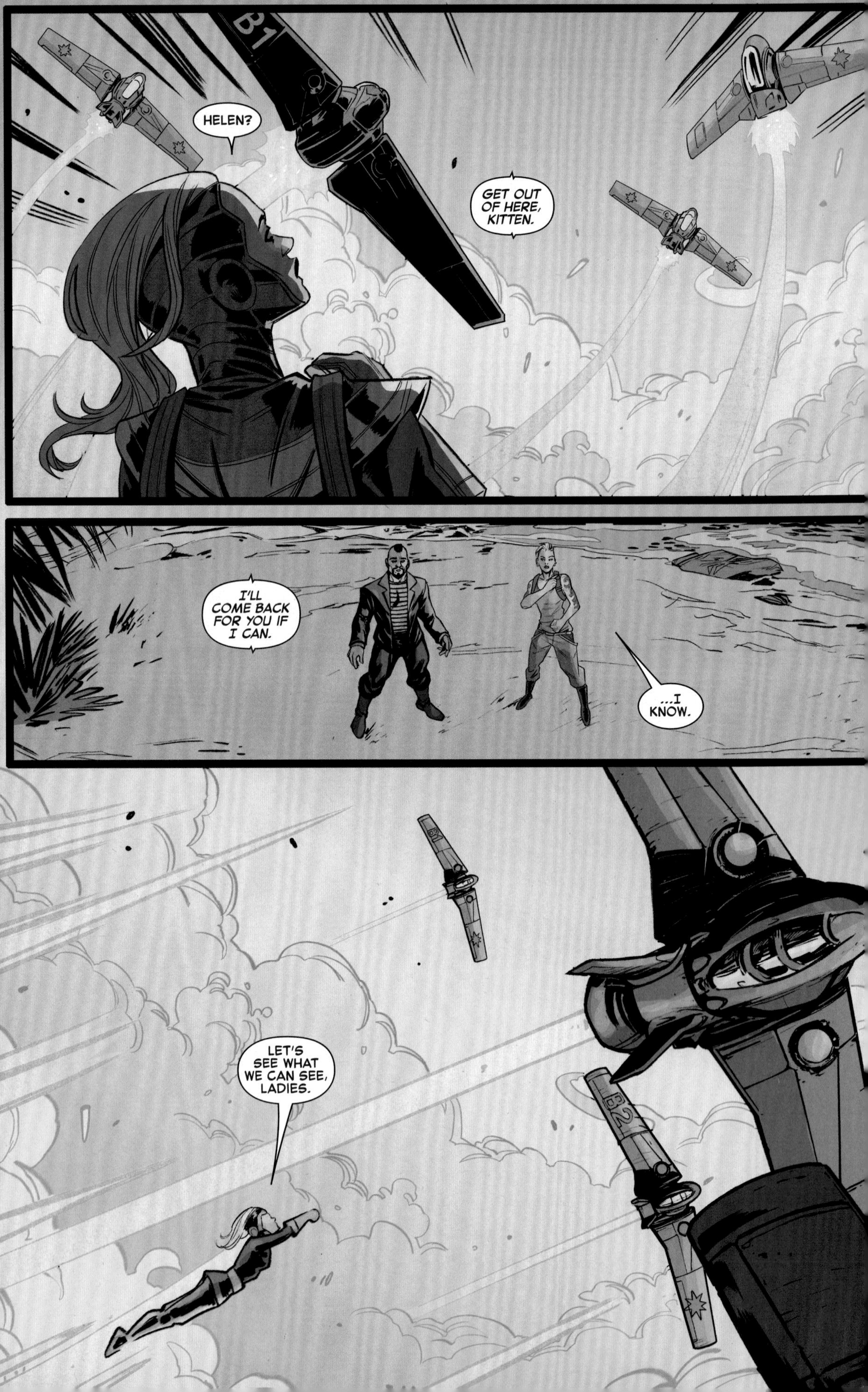
HELEN?
GET OUT OF HERE, KITTEN.
I'LL COME BACK FOR YOU IF I CAN.
...I KNOW.
LET'S SEE WHAT WE CAN SEE, LADIES.

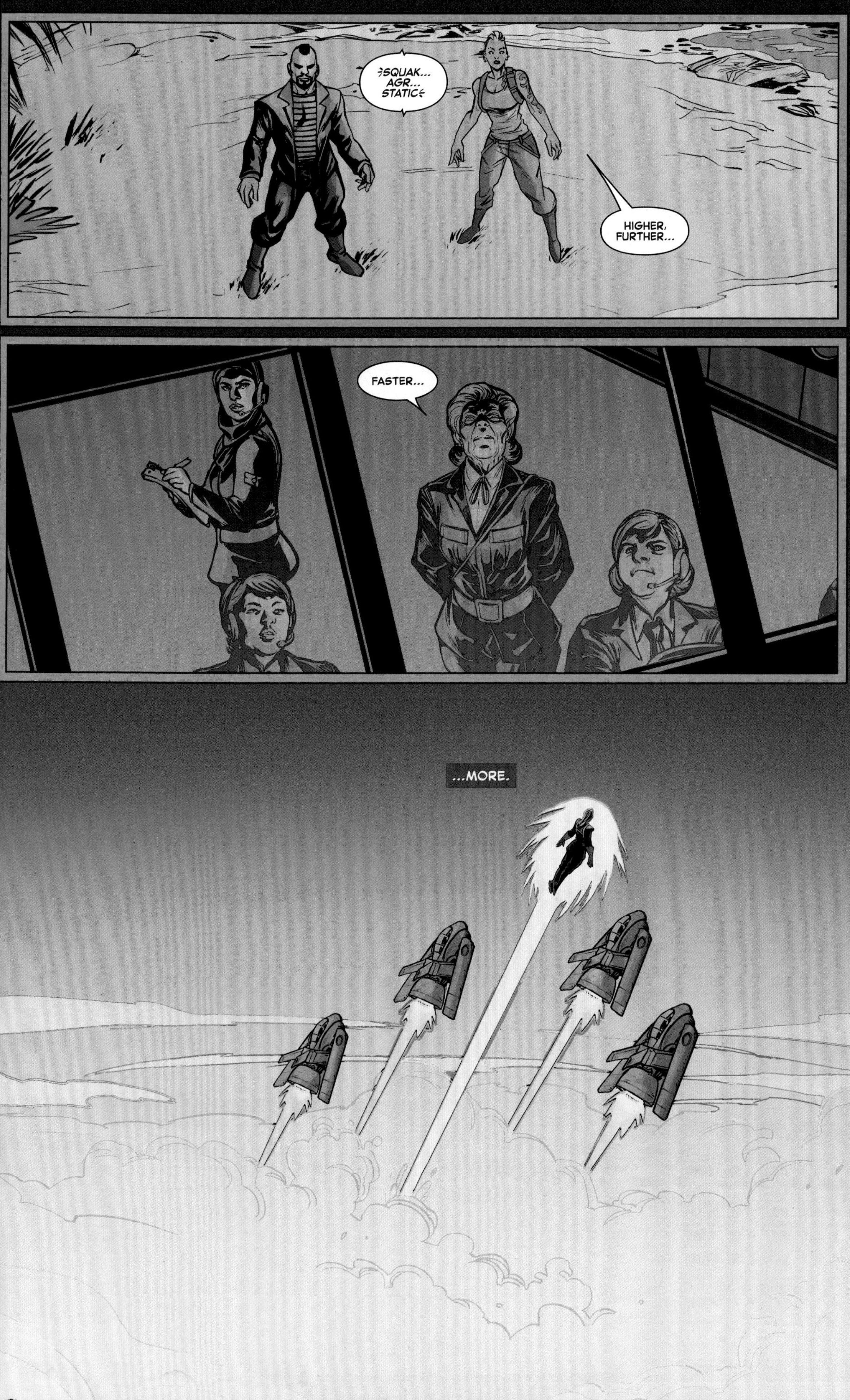

SQUAK... AGR... STATIC
HIGHER, FURTHER...
FASTER...
...MORE.

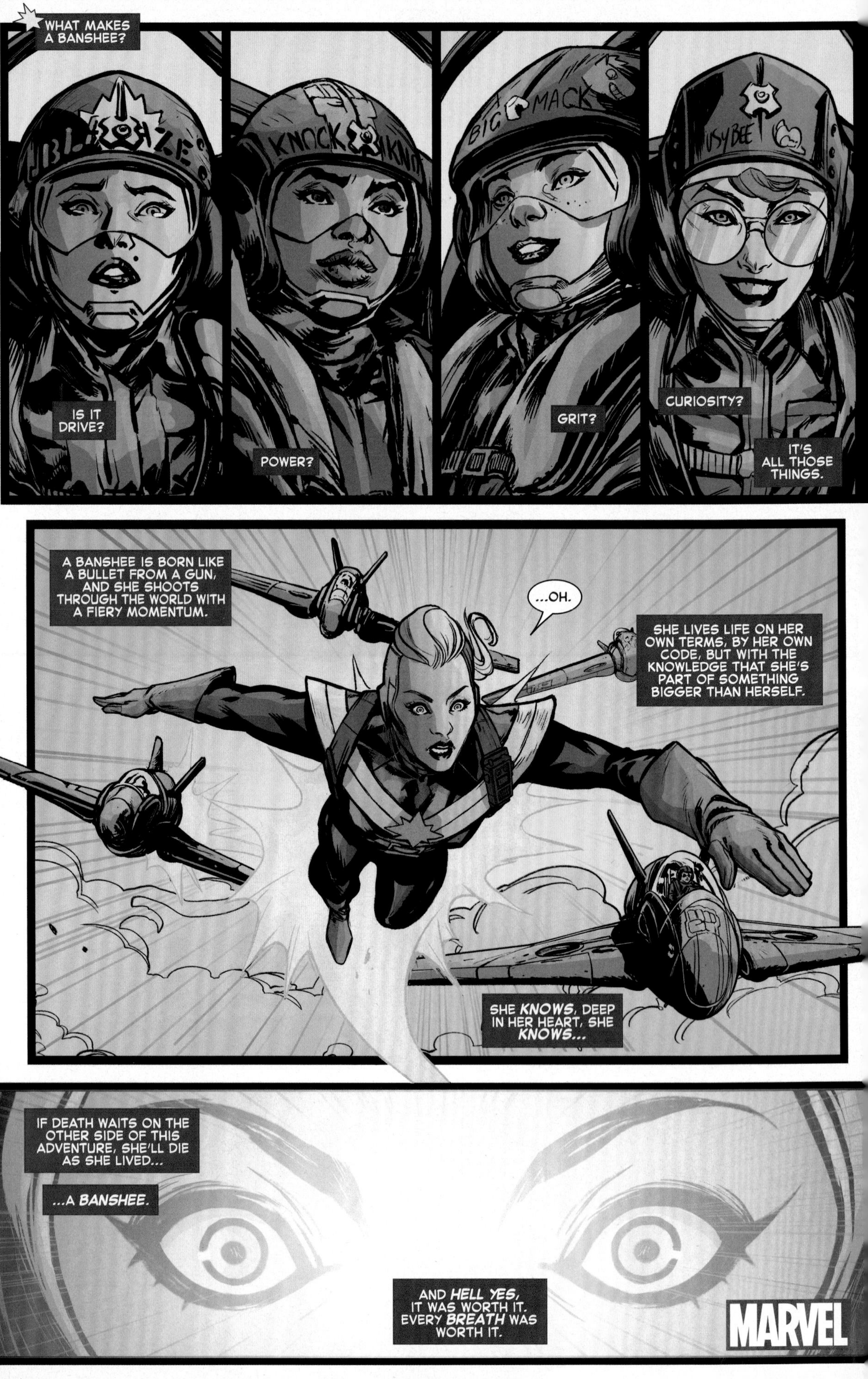
WHAT MAKES A BANSHEE?
IS IT DRIVE?
POWER?
GRIT?
CURIOSITY?
IT'S ALL THOSE THINGS.
A BANSHEE IS BORN LIKE A BULLET FROM A GUN, AND SHE SHOOTS THROUGH THE WORLD WITH A FIERY MOMENTUM.
...OH.
SHE LIVES LIFE ON HER OWN TERMS, BY HER OWN CODE, BUT WITH THE KNOWLEDGE THAT SHE'S PART OF SOMETHING BIGGER THAN HERSELF.
SHE *KNOWS*, DEEP IN HER HEART, SHE *KNOWS*...
IF DEATH WAITS ON THE OTHER SIDE OF THIS ADVENTURE, SHE'LL DIE AS SHE LIVED...
...A *BANSHEE*.
AND *HELL YES*, IT WAS WORTH IT. EVERY *BREATH* WAS WORTH IT.
MARVEL

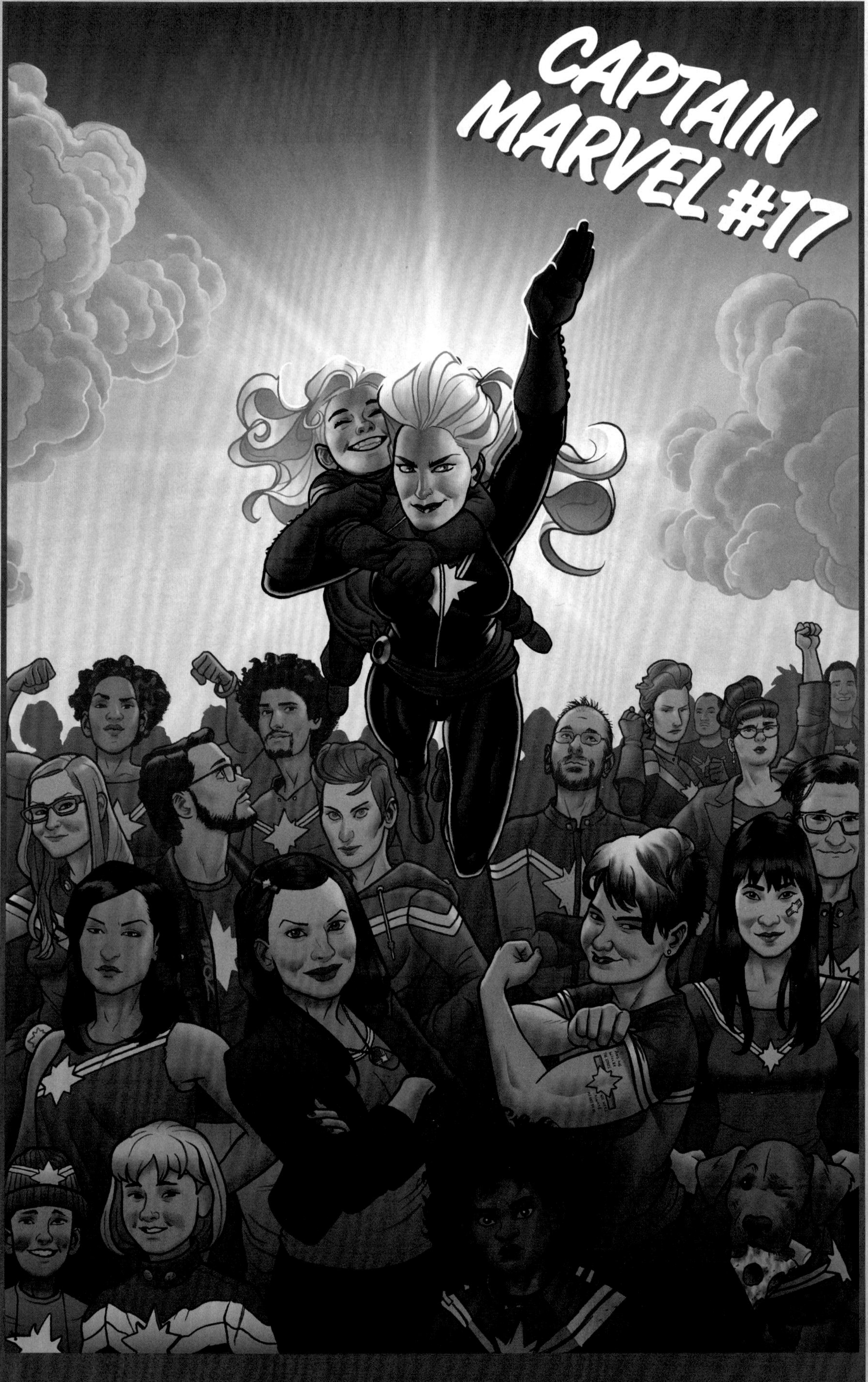
CAPTAIN MARVEL #17

When former U.S. Air Force pilot, Carol Danvers was caught in the explosion of an alien device called the Psyche-Magnitron, she was transformed into one of the world's most powerful super beings. She now uses her abilities to protect her planet and fight for justice as an Avenger. She is Earth's Mightiest Hero...she is...

CAPTAIN MARVEL

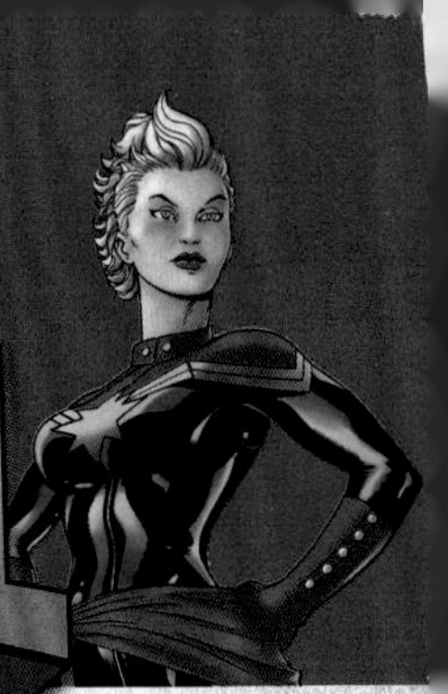

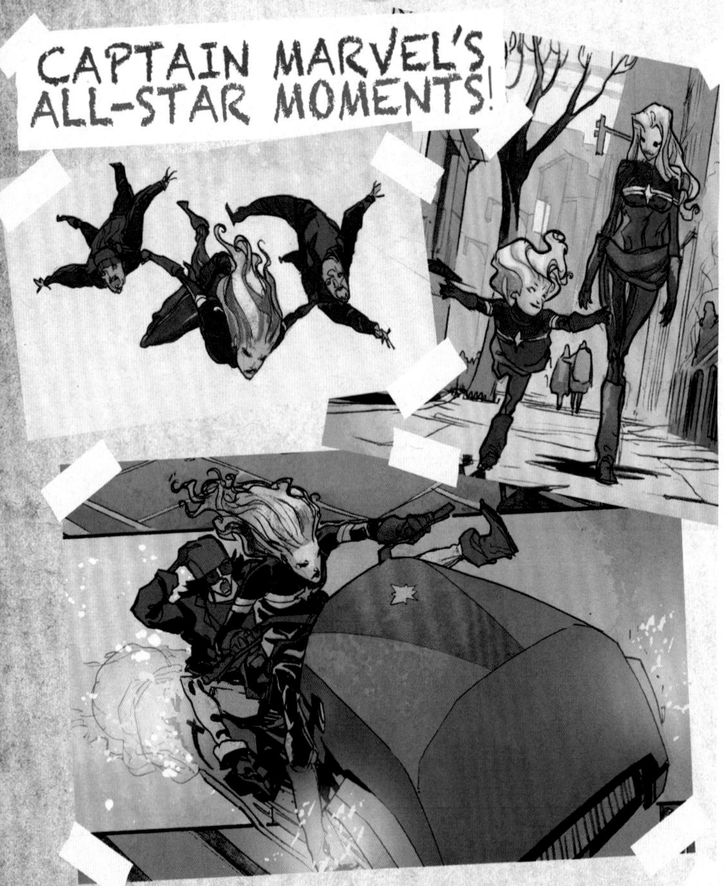

CAPTAIN MARVEL'S ALL-STAR MOMENTS!

KIT'S TO-DO LIST

- TEA PARTY WITH MR. SNUFFLES & KITTY BEAR
- CHECK THE LIBRARY FOR BOOKS ON AMNESIA -- MAYBE I'LL FIND INFO TO HELP FIX CAPTAIN MARVEL'S MEMORY!
- SEE IF WE CAN FIND CAPTAIN MARVEL A NEW APARTMENT!
- HELP GILBERT FINISH HIS IRON MAN SUIT!
- SUPER HERO LESSONS!

KELLY SUE DeCONNICK WRITER
FILIPE ANDRADE ARTIST
JORDIE BELLAIRE COLORIST

JOE QUINONES COVER
VC's JOE CARAMAGNA LETTERER
DEVIN LEWIS ASSISTANT EDITOR
SANA AMANAT EDITOR

STEPHEN WACKER SENIOR EDITOR
AXEL ALONSO EDITOR IN CHIEF
JOE QUESADA CHIEF CREATIVE OFFICER
DAN BUCKLEY PUBLISHER
ALAN FINE EXEC. PRODUCER

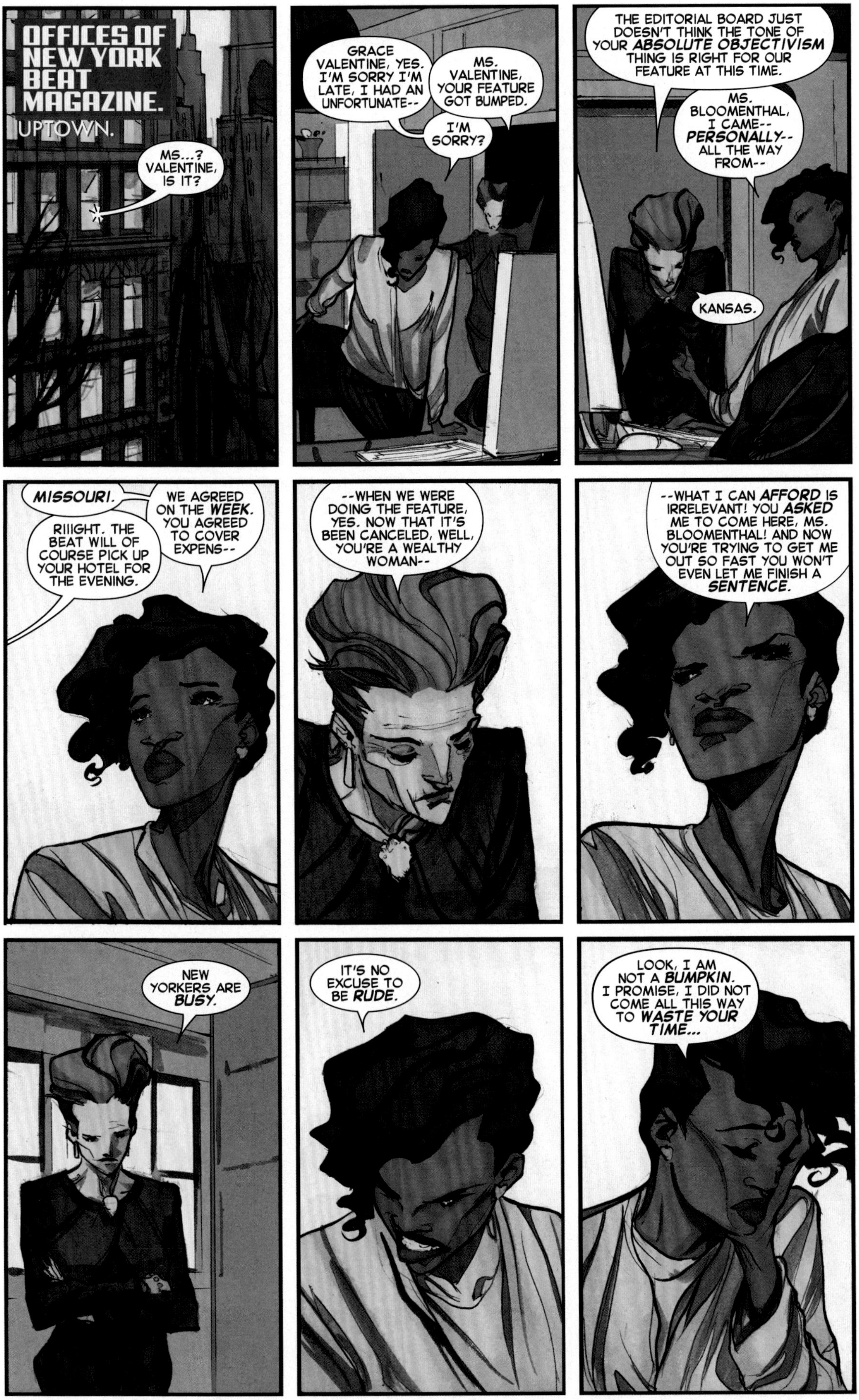
OFFICES OF NEW YORK BEAT MAGAZINE.
UPTOWN.
MS...? VALENTINE, IS IT?
GRACE VALENTINE, YES. I'M SORRY I'M LATE, I HAD AN UNFORTUNATE--
MS. VALENTINE, YOUR FEATURE GOT BUMPED.
I'M SORRY?
THE EDITORIAL BOARD JUST DOESN'T THINK THE TONE OF YOUR ABSOLUTE OBJECTIVISM THING IS RIGHT FOR OUR FEATURE AT THIS TIME.
MS. BLOOMENTHAL, I CAME-- PERSONALLY-- ALL THE WAY FROM--
KANSAS.
MISSOURI.
WE AGREED ON THE WEEK. YOU AGREED TO COVER EXPENS--
RIIIGHT. THE BEAT WILL OF COURSE PICK UP YOUR HOTEL FOR THE EVENING.
--WHEN WE WERE DOING THE FEATURE, YES. NOW THAT IT'S BEEN CANCELED, WELL, YOU'RE A WEALTHY WOMAN--
--WHAT I CAN AFFORD IS IRRELEVANT! YOU ASKED ME TO COME HERE, MS. BLOOMENTHAL! AND NOW YOU'RE TRYING TO GET ME OUT SO FAST YOU WON'T EVEN LET ME FINISH A SENTENCE.
NEW YORKERS ARE BUSY.
IT'S NO EXCUSE TO BE RUDE.
LOOK, I AM NOT A BUMPKIN. I PROMISE, I DID NOT COME ALL THIS WAY TO WASTE YOUR TIME...

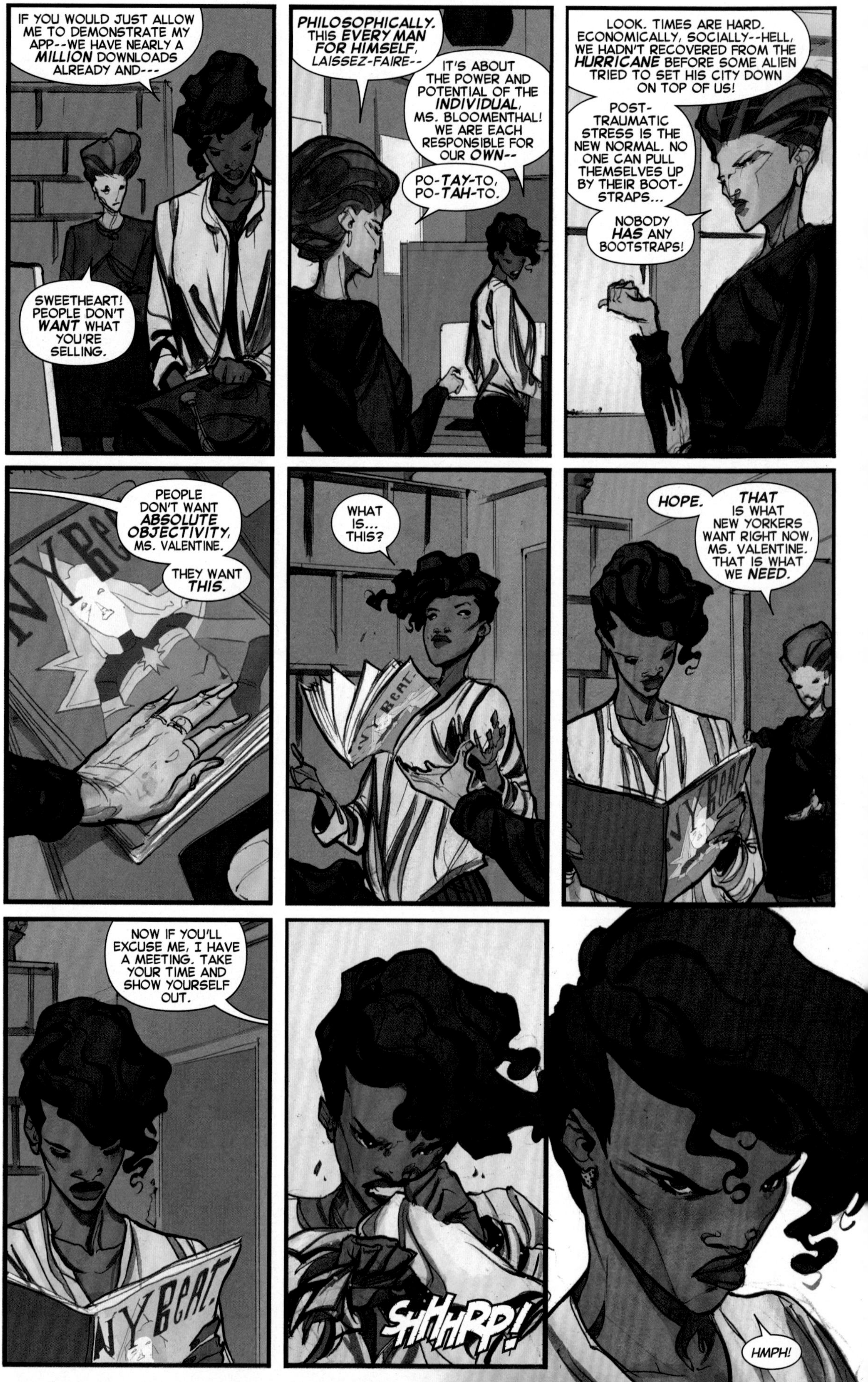

IF YOU WOULD JUST ALLOW ME TO DEMONSTRATE MY APP--WE HAVE NEARLY A MILLION DOWNLOADS ALREADY AND---
SWEETHEART! PEOPLE DON'T WANT WHAT YOU'RE SELLING.
PHILOSOPHICALLY. THIS EVERY MAN FOR HIMSELF, LAISSEZ-FAIRE--
IT'S ABOUT THE POWER AND POTENTIAL OF THE INDIVIDUAL, MS. BLOOMENTHAL! WE ARE EACH RESPONSIBLE FOR OUR OWN--
PO-TAY-TO, PO-TAH-TO.
LOOK. TIMES ARE HARD. ECONOMICALLY, SOCIALLY--HELL, WE HADN'T RECOVERED FROM THE HURRICANE BEFORE SOME ALIEN TRIED TO SET HIS CITY DOWN ON TOP OF US!
POST-TRAUMATIC STRESS IS THE NEW NORMAL. NO ONE CAN PULL THEMSELVES UP BY THEIR BOOT-STRAPS...
NOBODY HAS ANY BOOTSTRAPS!
PEOPLE DON'T WANT ABSOLUTE OBJECTIVITY, MS. VALENTINE.
THEY WANT THIS.
WHAT IS... THIS?
HOPE.
THAT IS WHAT NEW YORKERS WANT RIGHT NOW, MS. VALENTINE. THAT IS WHAT WE NEED.
NOW IF YOU'LL EXCUSE ME, I HAVE A MEETING. TAKE YOUR TIME AND SHOW YOURSELF OUT.
SHHHRP!
HMPH!

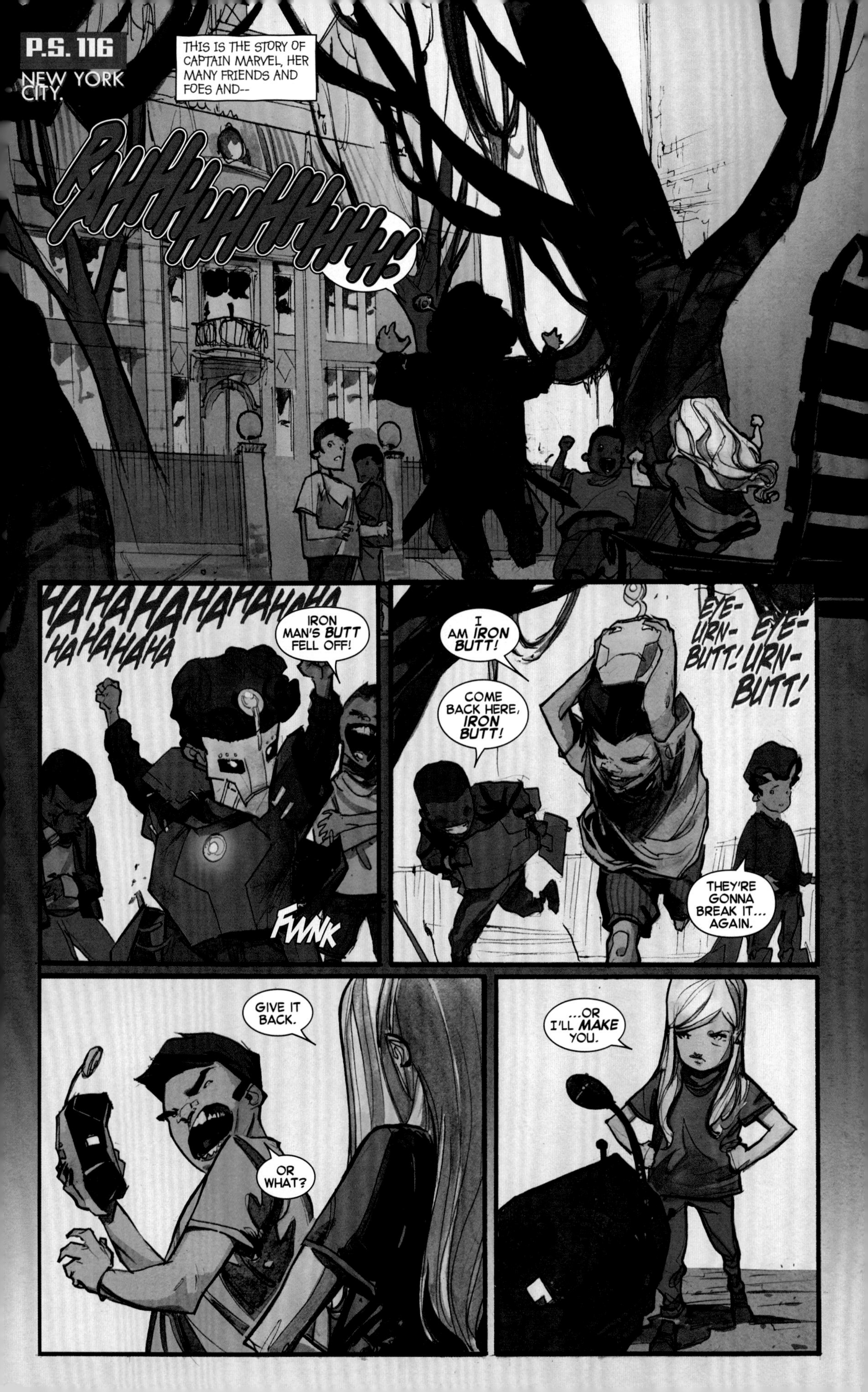

P.S. 116
NEW YORK CITY.
THIS IS THE STORY OF CAPTAIN MARVEL, HER MANY FRIENDS AND FOES AND--
BAHHHHHHHHHHHHH!
HAHAHAHAHAHAHAHAHA HAHAHAHA
IRON MAN'S BUTT FELL OFF!
FWNK
I AM IRON BUTT!
COME BACK HERE, IRON BUTT!
EYE-URN-BUTT! EYE-URN-BUTT!
THEY'RE GONNA BREAK IT... AGAIN.
GIVE IT BACK.
OR WHAT?
...OR I'LL MAKE YOU.

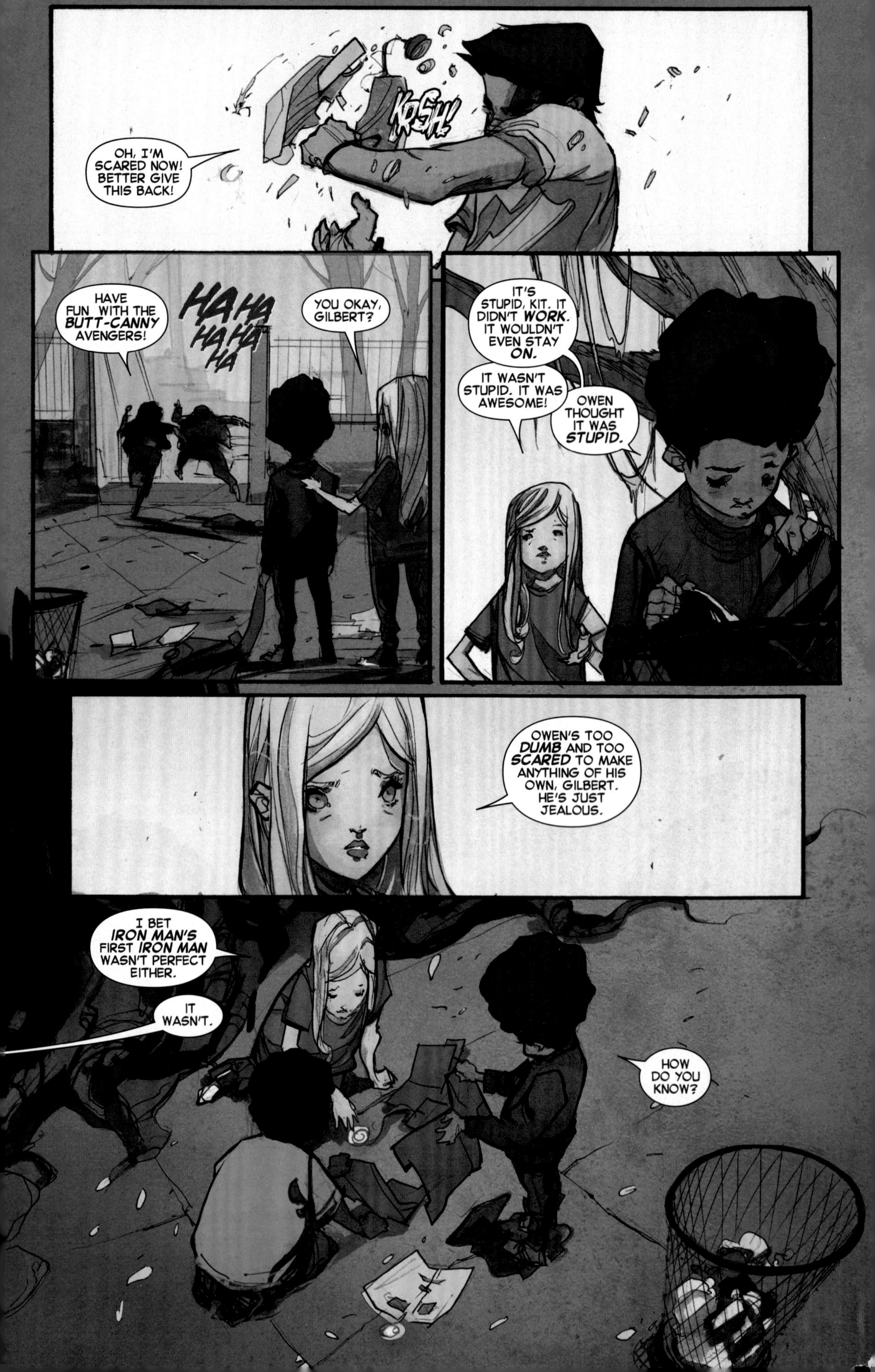
OH, I'M SCARED NOW! BETTER GIVE THIS BACK!
KRSH!
HAVE FUN WITH THE BUTT-CANNY AVENGERS!
HA HA HA HA HA
YOU OKAY, GILBERT?
IT'S STUPID, KIT. IT DIDN'T WORK. IT WOULDN'T EVEN STAY ON.
IT WASN'T STUPID. IT WAS AWESOME!
OWEN THOUGHT IT WAS STUPID.
OWEN'S TOO DUMB AND TOO SCARED TO MAKE ANYTHING OF HIS OWN, GILBERT. HE'S JUST JEALOUS.
I BET IRON MAN'S FIRST IRON MAN WASN'T PERFECT EITHER.
IT WASN'T.
HOW DO YOU KNOW?

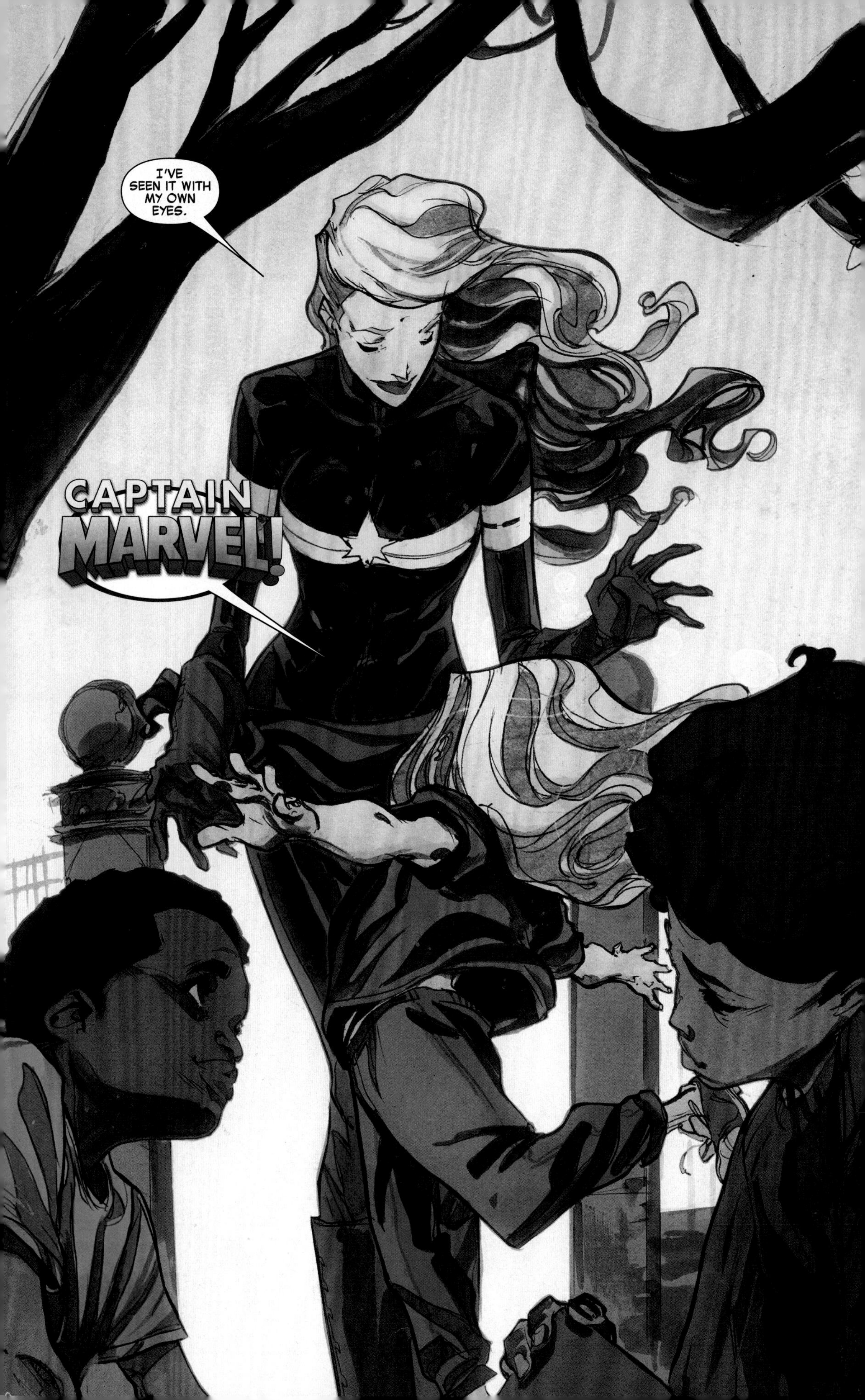
I'VE SEEN IT WITH MY OWN EYES.
CAPTAIN MARVEL!

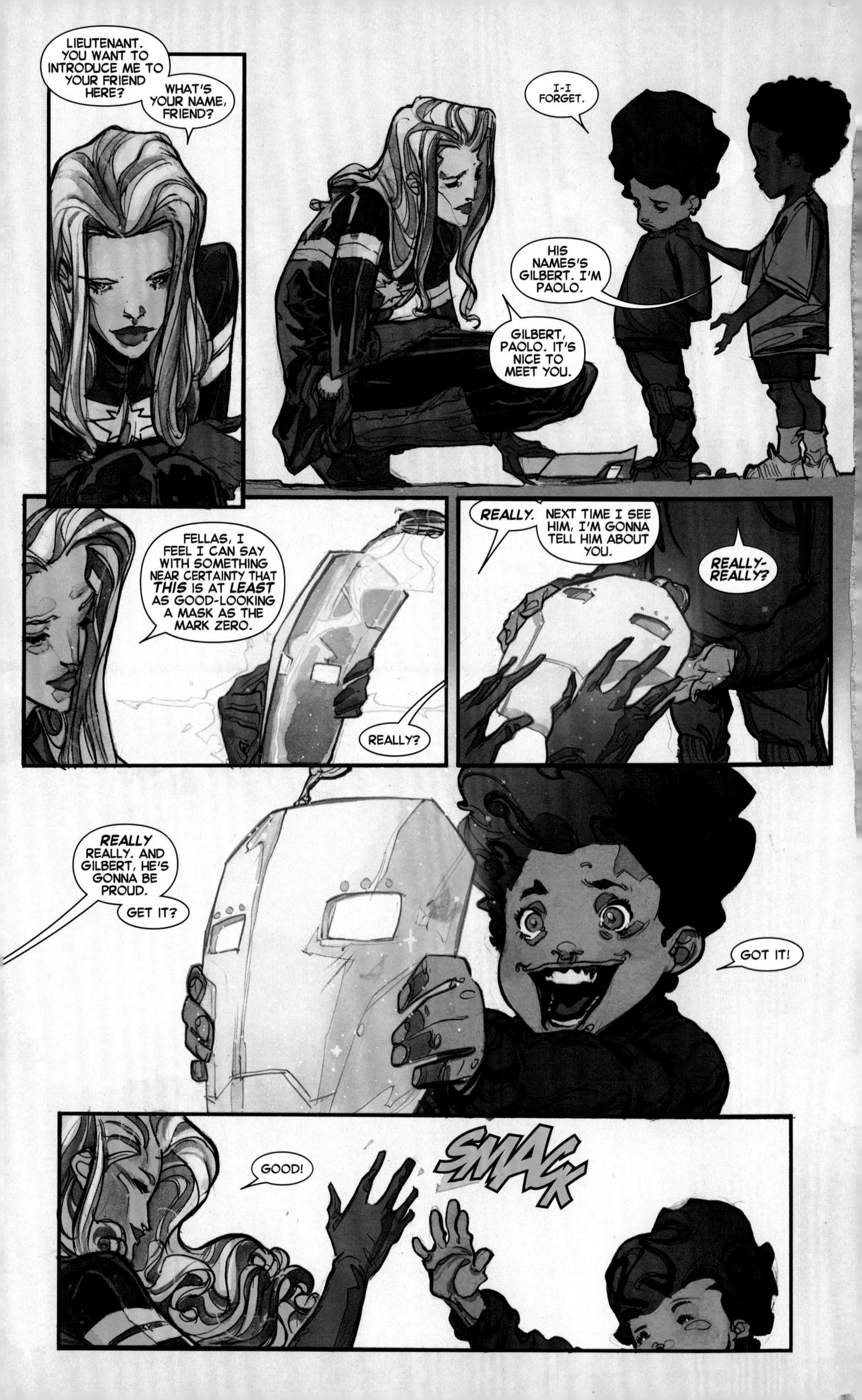
LIEUTENANT. YOU WANT TO INTRODUCE ME TO YOUR FRIEND HERE?
WHAT'S YOUR NAME, FRIEND?
I-I FORGET.
HIS NAMES'S GILBERT. I'M PAOLO.
GILBERT, PAOLO. IT'S NICE TO MEET YOU.
FELLAS, I FEEL I CAN SAY WITH SOMETHING NEAR CERTAINTY THAT THIS IS AT LEAST AS GOOD-LOOKING A MASK AS THE MARK ZERO.
REALLY?
REALLY.
NEXT TIME I SEE HIM, I'M GONNA TELL HIM ABOUT YOU.
REALLY-REALLY?
REALLY REALLY. AND GILBERT, HE'S GONNA BE PROUD.
GET IT?
GOT IT!
GOOD!
SMACK

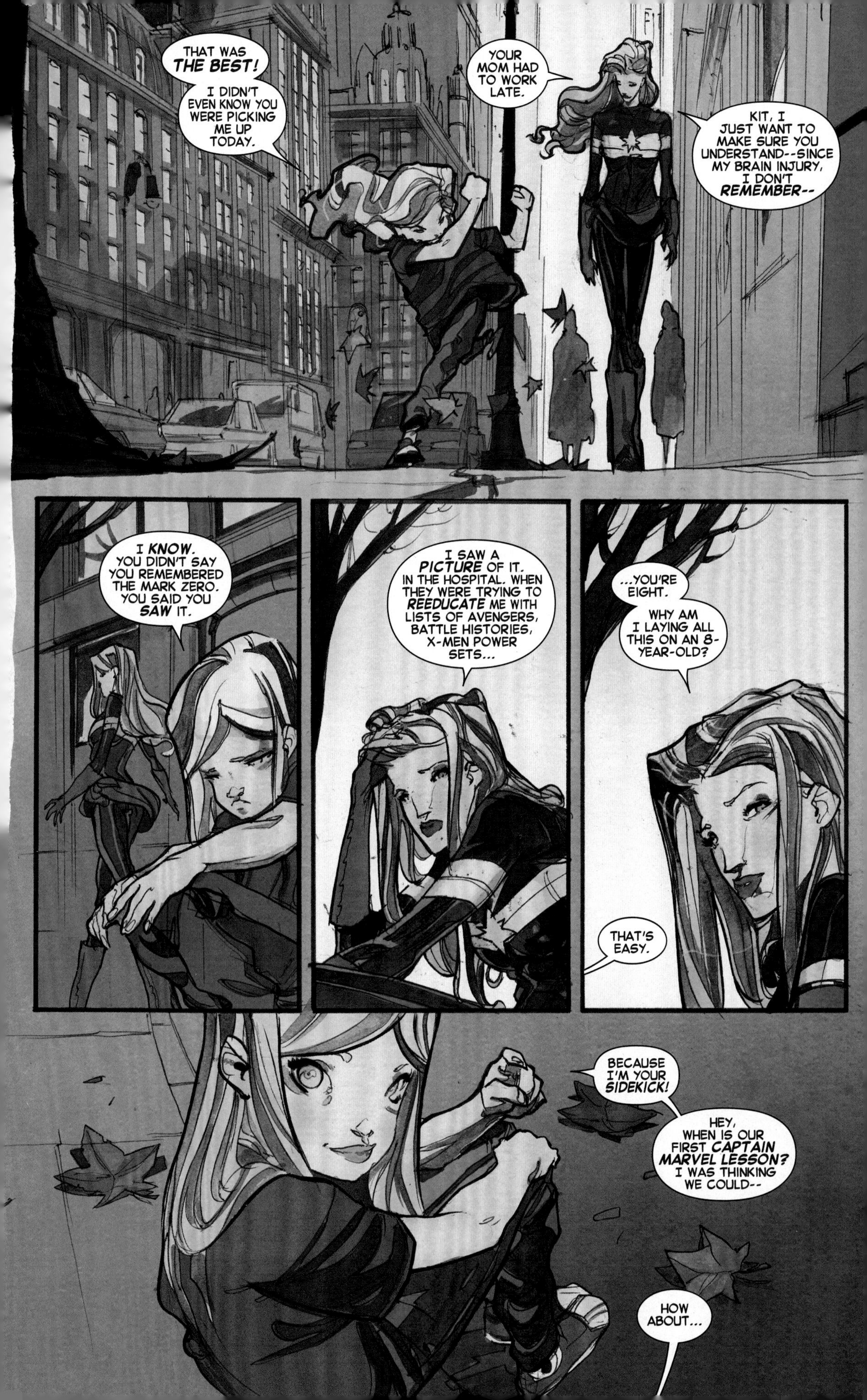

THAT WAS THE BEST!
I DIDN'T EVEN KNOW YOU WERE PICKING ME UP TODAY.
YOUR MOM HAD TO WORK LATE.
KIT, I JUST WANT TO MAKE SURE YOU UNDERSTAND--SINCE MY BRAIN INJURY, I DON'T REMEMBER--
I KNOW. YOU DIDN'T SAY YOU REMEMBERED THE MARK ZERO. YOU SAID YOU SAW IT.
I SAW A PICTURE OF IT. IN THE HOSPITAL. WHEN THEY WERE TRYING TO REEDUCATE ME WITH LISTS OF AVENGERS, BATTLE HISTORIES, X-MEN POWER SETS...
...YOU'RE EIGHT.
WHY AM I LAYING ALL THIS ON AN 8-YEAR-OLD?
THAT'S EASY.
BECAUSE I'M YOUR SIDEKICK!
HEY, WHEN IS OUR FIRST CAPTAIN MARVEL LESSON? I WAS THINKING WE COULD--
HOW ABOUT...

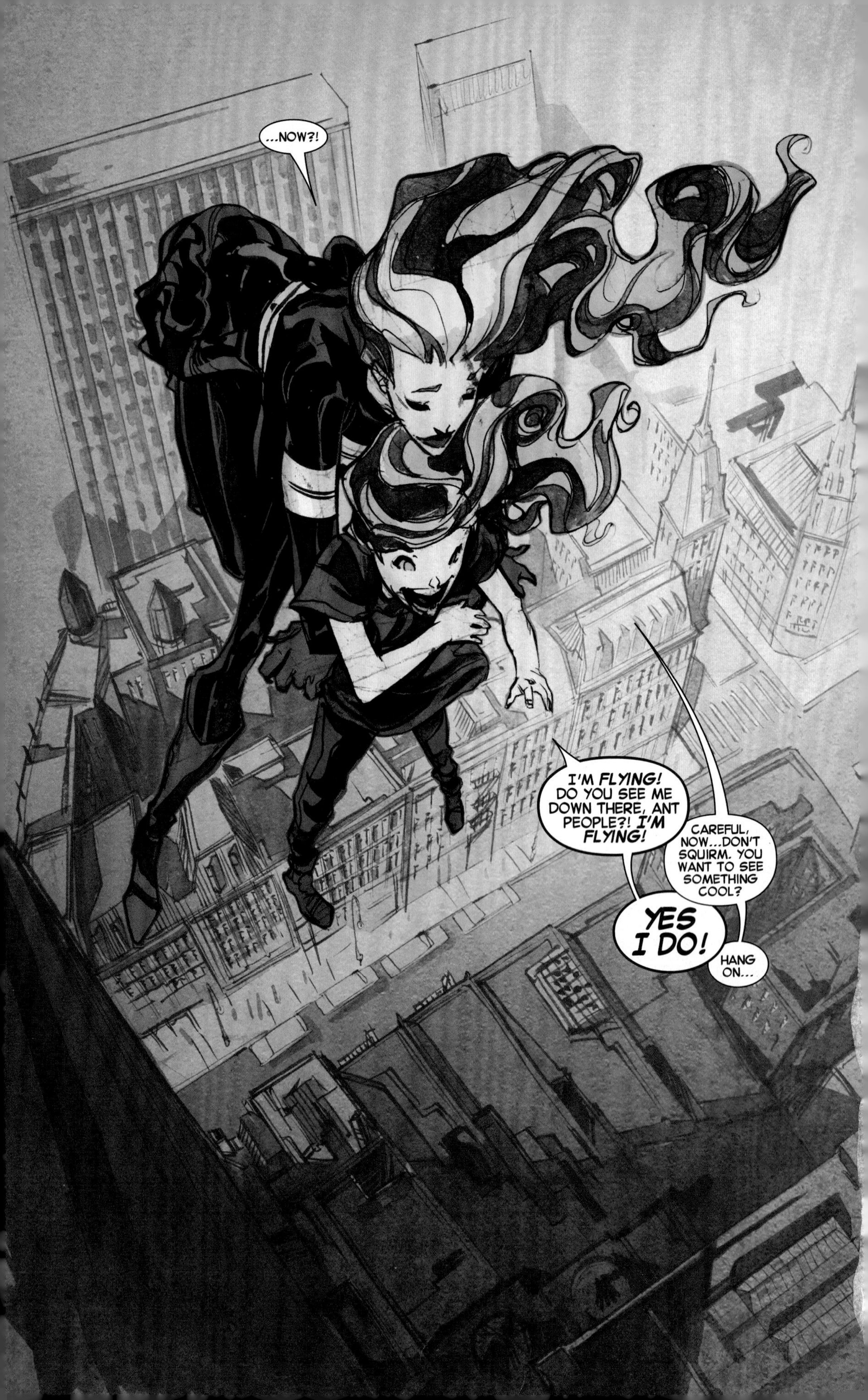
...NOW?!
I'M *FLYING!* DO YOU SEE ME DOWN THERE, ANT PEOPLE?! *I'M FLYING!*
CAREFUL, NOW...DON'T SQUIRM. YOU WANT TO SEE SOMETHING COOL?
YES I DO!
HANG ON...

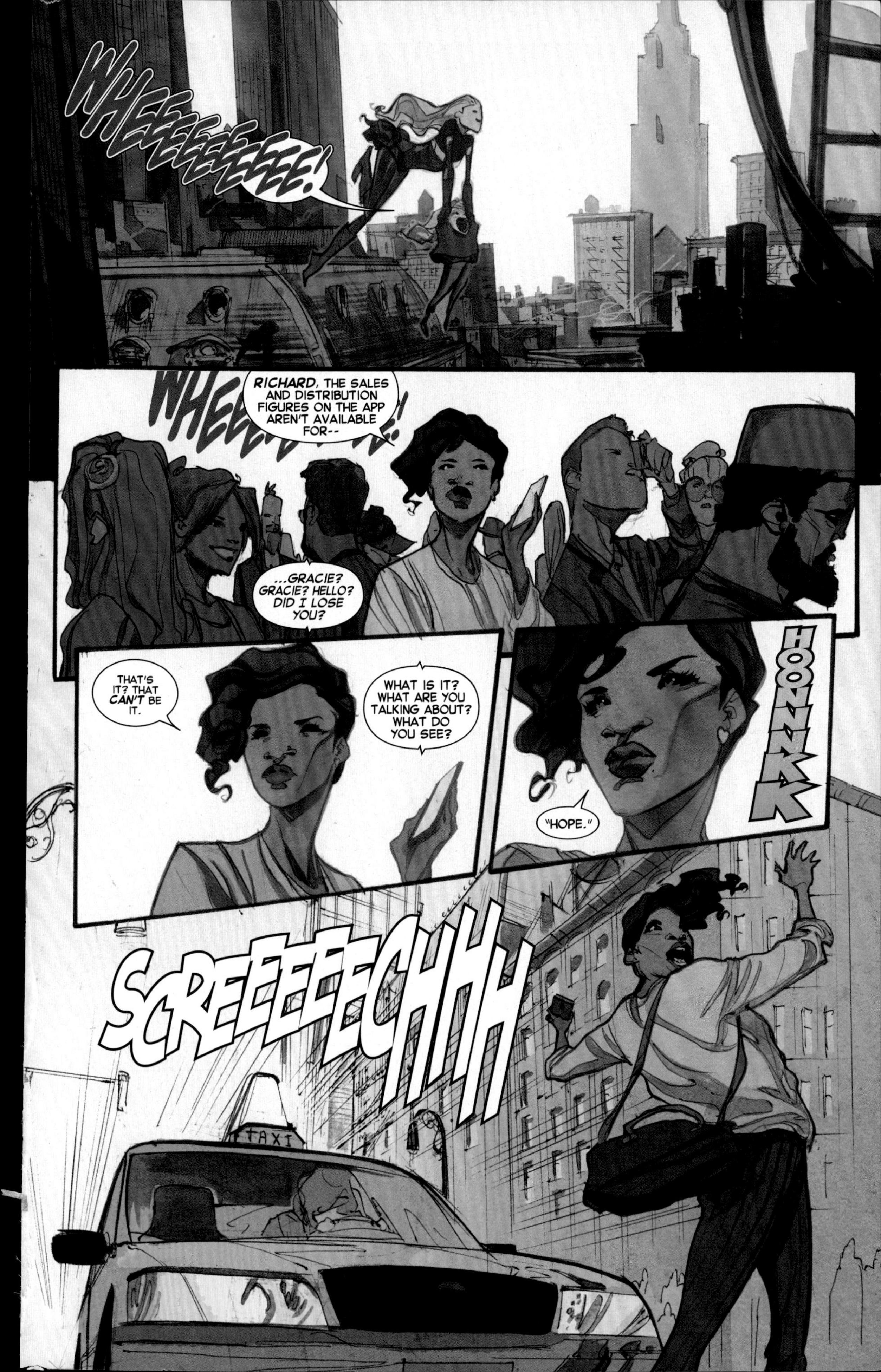
WHEEEEEEEEEEEEE!
WHEEEEEEEE!
RICHARD, THE SALES AND DISTRIBUTION FIGURES ON THE APP AREN'T AVAILABLE FOR--
...GRACIE? GRACIE? HELLO? DID I LOSE YOU?
THAT'S IT? THAT CAN'T BE IT.
WHAT IS IT? WHAT ARE YOU TALKING ABOUT? WHAT DO YOU SEE?
HOONNKK
"HOPE."
SCREEEEEECHHH
TAXI

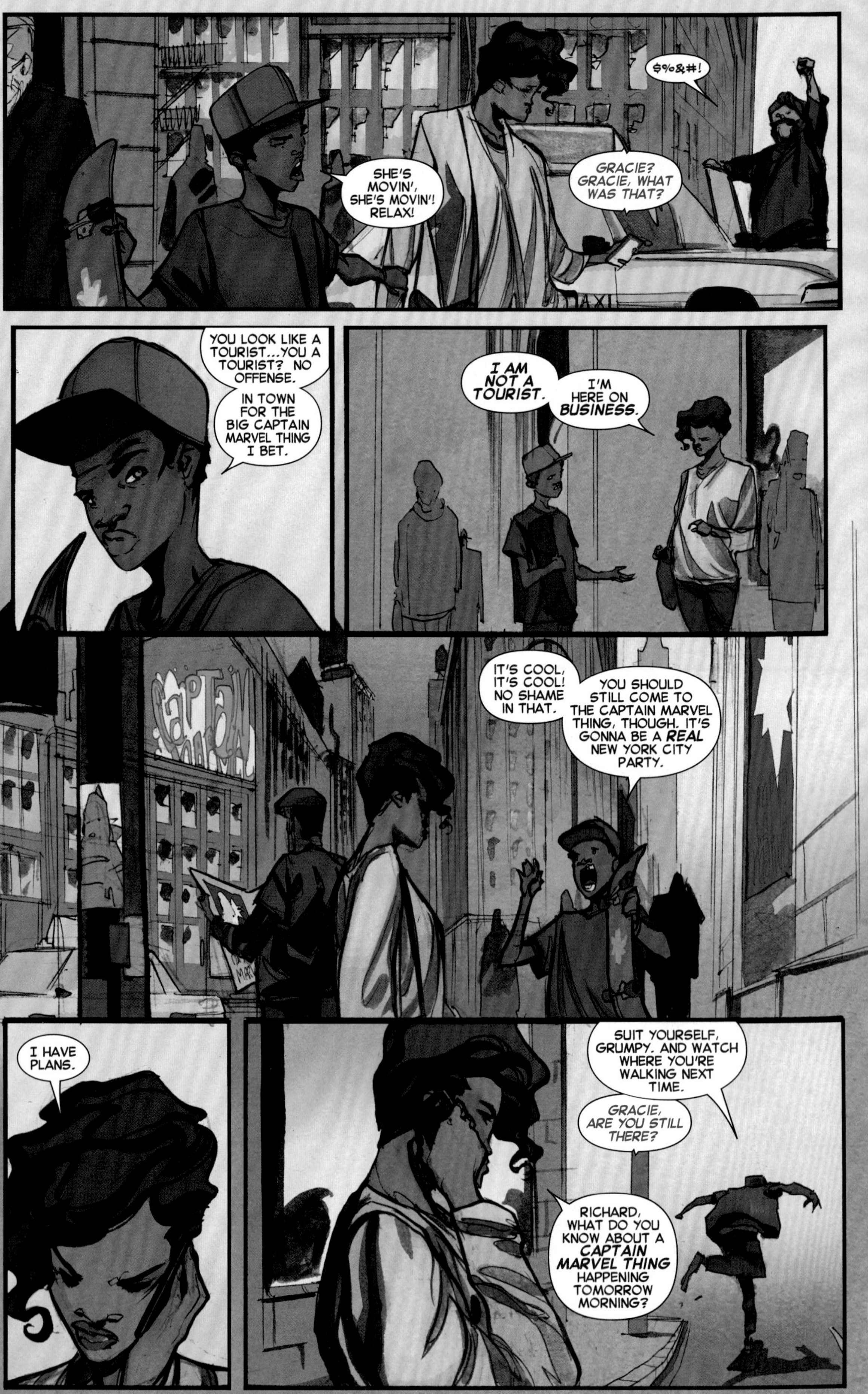
$%&#!
SHE'S MOVIN', SHE'S MOVIN'! RELAX!
GRACIE? GRACIE, WHAT WAS THAT?
TAXI
YOU LOOK LIKE A TOURIST...YOU A TOURIST? NO OFFENSE.
IN TOWN FOR THE BIG CAPTAIN MARVEL THING I BET.
I AM NOT A TOURIST.
I'M HERE ON BUSINESS.
IT'S COOL, IT'S COOL! NO SHAME IN THAT.
YOU SHOULD STILL COME TO THE CAPTAIN MARVEL THING, THOUGH. IT'S GONNA BE A REAL NEW YORK CITY PARTY.
I HAVE PLANS.
SUIT YOURSELF, GRUMPY. AND WATCH WHERE YOU'RE WALKING NEXT TIME.
GRACIE, ARE YOU STILL THERE?
RICHARD, WHAT DO YOU KNOW ABOUT A CAPTAIN MARVEL THING HAPPENING TOMORROW MORNING?

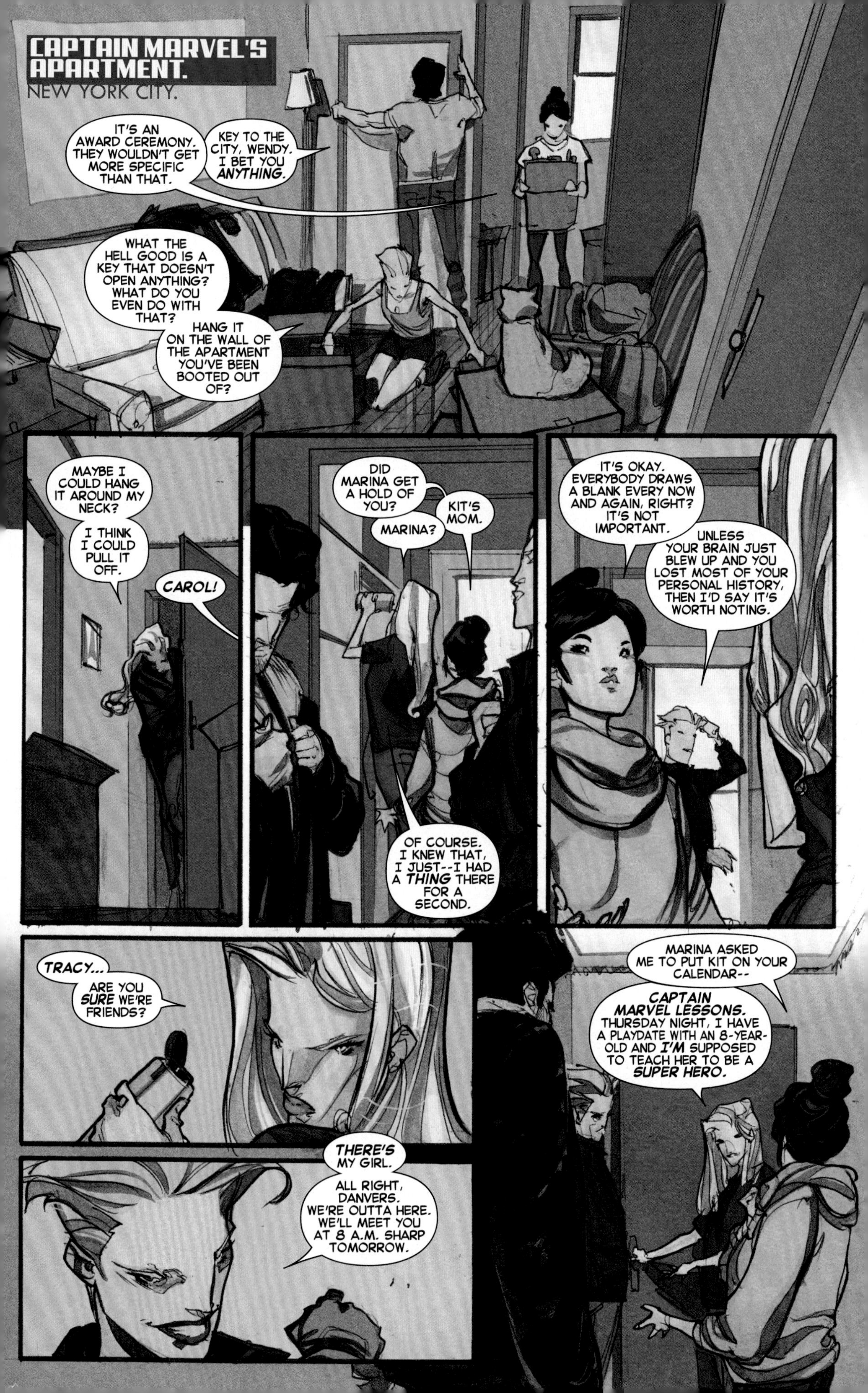

CAPTAIN MARVEL'S APARTMENT.
NEW YORK CITY.
KEY TO THE CITY, WENDY. I BET YOU ANYTHING.
IT'S AN AWARD CEREMONY. THEY WOULDN'T GET MORE SPECIFIC THAN THAT.
WHAT THE HELL GOOD IS A KEY THAT DOESN'T OPEN ANYTHING? WHAT DO YOU EVEN DO WITH THAT?
HANG IT ON THE WALL OF THE APARTMENT YOU'VE BEEN BOOTED OUT OF?
MAYBE I COULD HANG IT AROUND MY NECK?
I THINK I COULD PULL IT OFF.
CAROL!
DID MARINA GET A HOLD OF YOU?
MARINA?
KIT'S MOM.
OF COURSE. I KNEW THAT, I JUST--I HAD A THING THERE FOR A SECOND.
IT'S OKAY. EVERYBODY DRAWS A BLANK EVERY NOW AND AGAIN, RIGHT? IT'S NOT IMPORTANT.
UNLESS YOUR BRAIN JUST BLEW UP AND YOU LOST MOST OF YOUR PERSONAL HISTORY, THEN I'D SAY IT'S WORTH NOTING.
TRACY...
ARE YOU SURE WE'RE FRIENDS?
MARINA ASKED ME TO PUT KIT ON YOUR CALENDAR--
CAPTAIN MARVEL LESSONS. THURSDAY NIGHT, I HAVE A PLAYDATE WITH AN 8-YEAR-OLD AND I'M SUPPOSED TO TEACH HER TO BE A SUPER HERO.
THERE'S MY GIRL.
ALL RIGHT, DANVERS. WE'RE OUTTA HERE. WE'LL MEET YOU AT 8 A.M. SHARP TOMORROW.

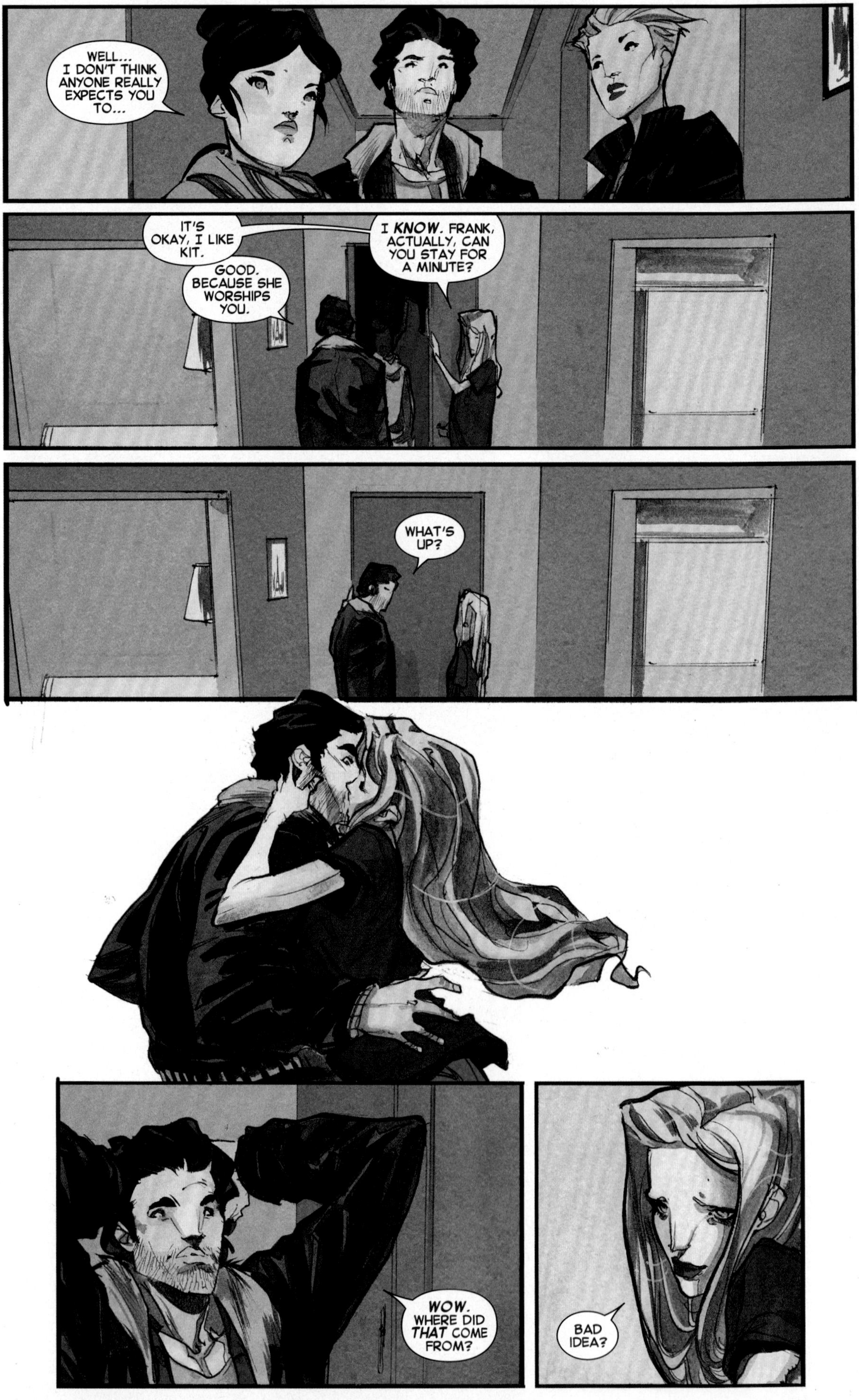
WELL... I DON'T THINK ANYONE REALLY EXPECTS YOU TO...
IT'S OKAY, I LIKE KIT.
GOOD. BECAUSE SHE WORSHIPS YOU.
I KNOW. FRANK, ACTUALLY, CAN YOU STAY FOR A MINUTE?
WHAT'S UP?
WOW. WHERE DID THAT COME FROM?
BAD IDEA?

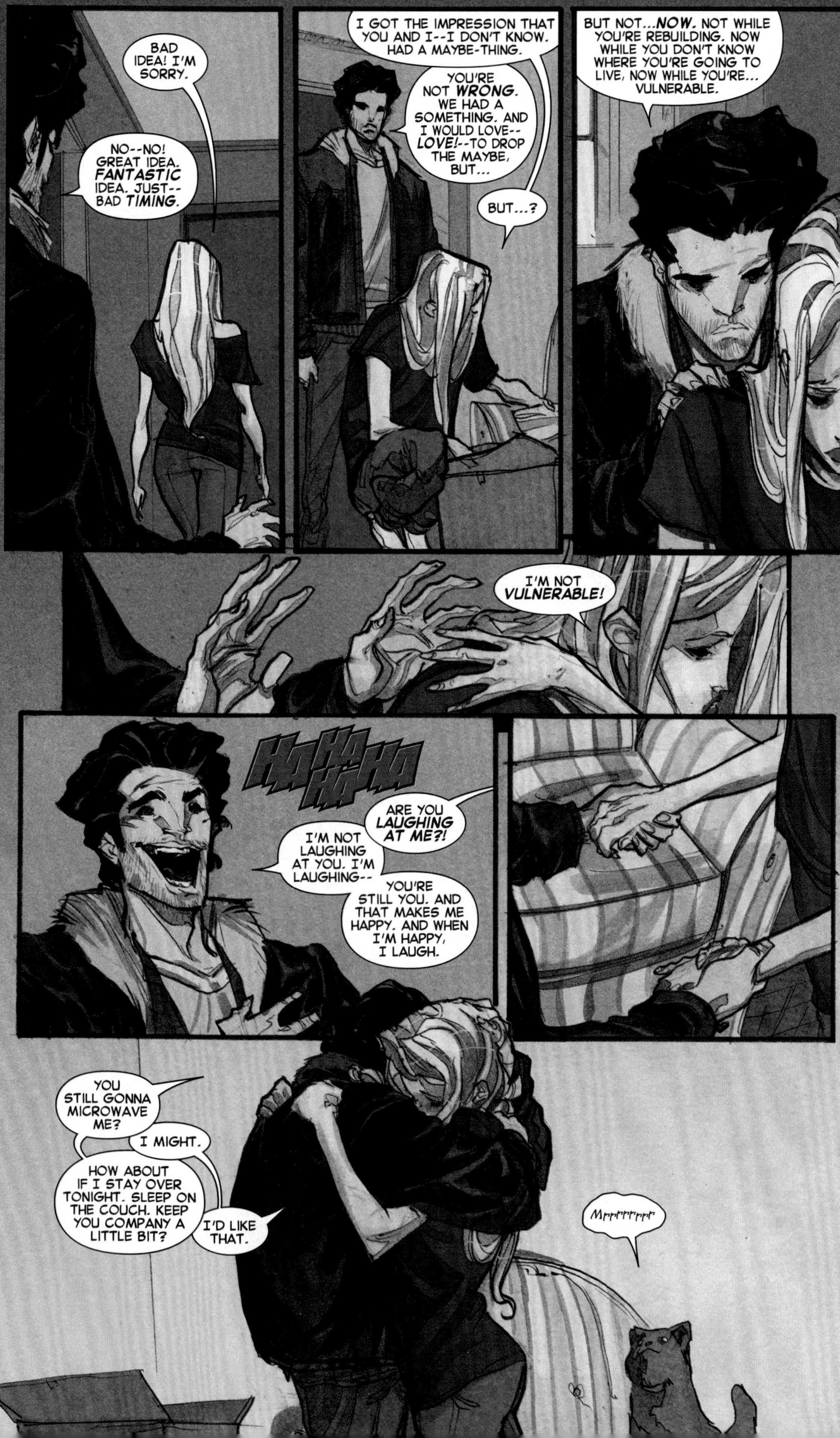
BAD IDEA! I'M SORRY.
NO--NO! GREAT IDEA. FANTASTIC IDEA. JUST--BAD TIMING.
I GOT THE IMPRESSION THAT YOU AND I--I DON'T KNOW. HAD A MAYBE-THING.
YOU'RE NOT WRONG. WE HAD A SOMETHING. AND I WOULD LOVE--LOVE!--TO DROP THE MAYBE, BUT...
BUT...?
BUT NOT...NOW. NOT WHILE YOU'RE REBUILDING. NOW WHILE YOU DON'T KNOW WHERE YOU'RE GOING TO LIVE, NOW WHILE YOU'RE... VULNERABLE.
I'M NOT VULNERABLE!
HA HA HA HA
ARE YOU LAUGHING AT ME?!
I'M NOT LAUGHING AT YOU. I'M LAUGHING--
YOU'RE STILL YOU. AND THAT MAKES ME HAPPY. AND WHEN I'M HAPPY, I LAUGH.
YOU STILL GONNA MICROWAVE ME?
I MIGHT.
HOW ABOUT IF I STAY OVER TONIGHT. SLEEP ON THE COUCH. KEEP YOU COMPANY A LITTLE BIT?
I'D LIKE THAT.
Mrrrrrrrr

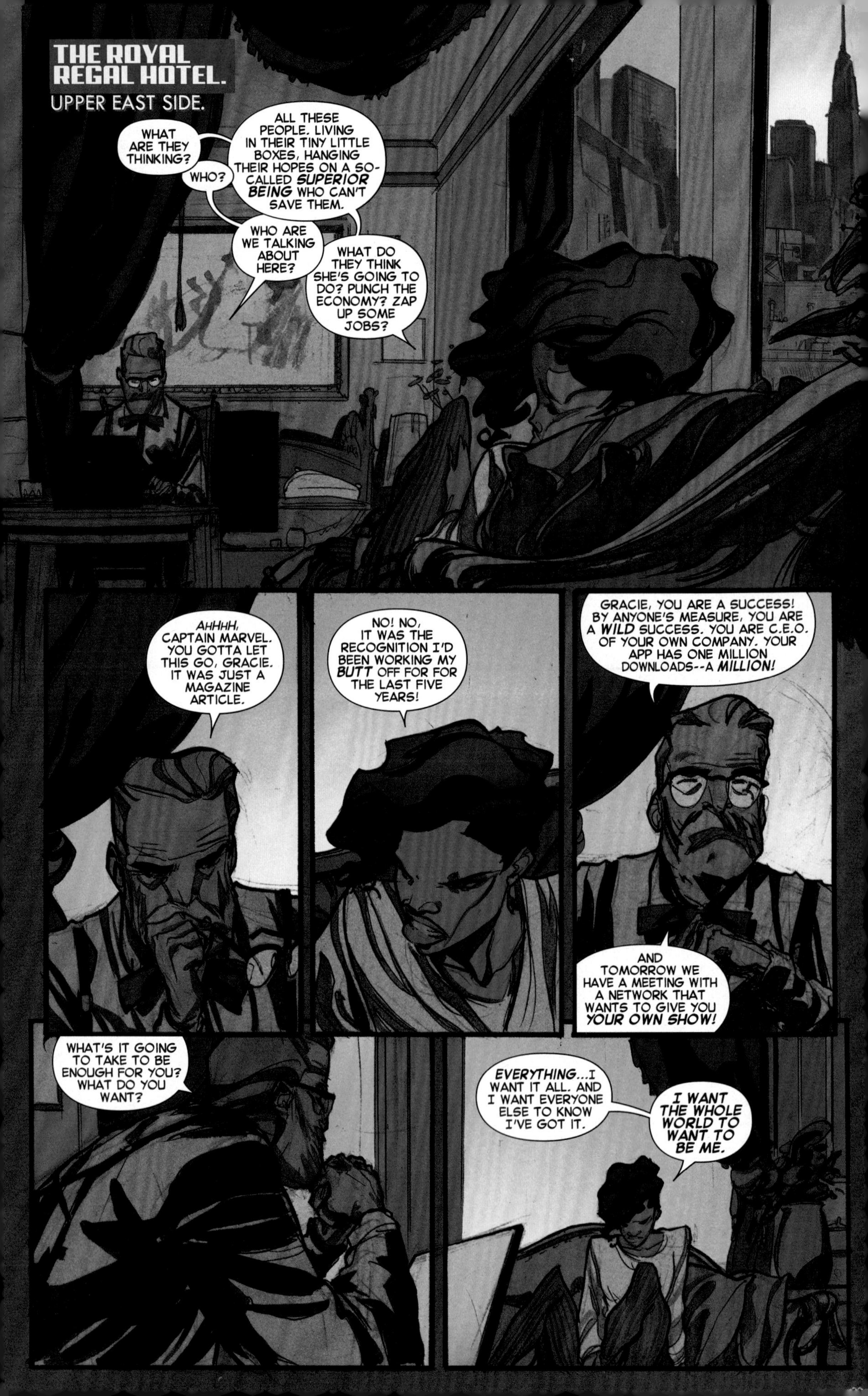
THE ROYAL REGAL HOTEL.
UPPER EAST SIDE.
WHAT ARE THEY THINKING?
ALL THESE PEOPLE. LIVING IN THEIR TINY LITTLE BOXES, HANGING THEIR HOPES ON A SO-CALLED SUPERIOR BEING WHO CAN'T SAVE THEM.
WHO?
WHO ARE WE TALKING ABOUT HERE?
WHAT DO THEY THINK SHE'S GOING TO DO? PUNCH THE ECONOMY? ZAP UP SOME JOBS?
AHHHH, CAPTAIN MARVEL. YOU GOTTA LET THIS GO, GRACIE. IT WAS JUST A MAGAZINE ARTICLE.
NO! NO, IT WAS THE RECOGNITION I'D BEEN WORKING MY BUTT OFF FOR FOR THE LAST FIVE YEARS!
GRACIE, YOU ARE A SUCCESS! BY ANYONE'S MEASURE, YOU ARE A WILD SUCCESS. YOU ARE C.E.O. OF YOUR OWN COMPANY. YOUR APP HAS ONE MILLION DOWNLOADS--A MILLION!
AND TOMORROW WE HAVE A MEETING WITH A NETWORK THAT WANTS TO GIVE YOU YOUR OWN SHOW!
WHAT'S IT GOING TO TAKE TO BE ENOUGH FOR YOU? WHAT DO YOU WANT?
EVERYTHING...I WANT IT ALL. AND I WANT EVERYONE ELSE TO KNOW I'VE GOT IT.
I WANT THE WHOLE WORLD TO WANT TO BE ME.

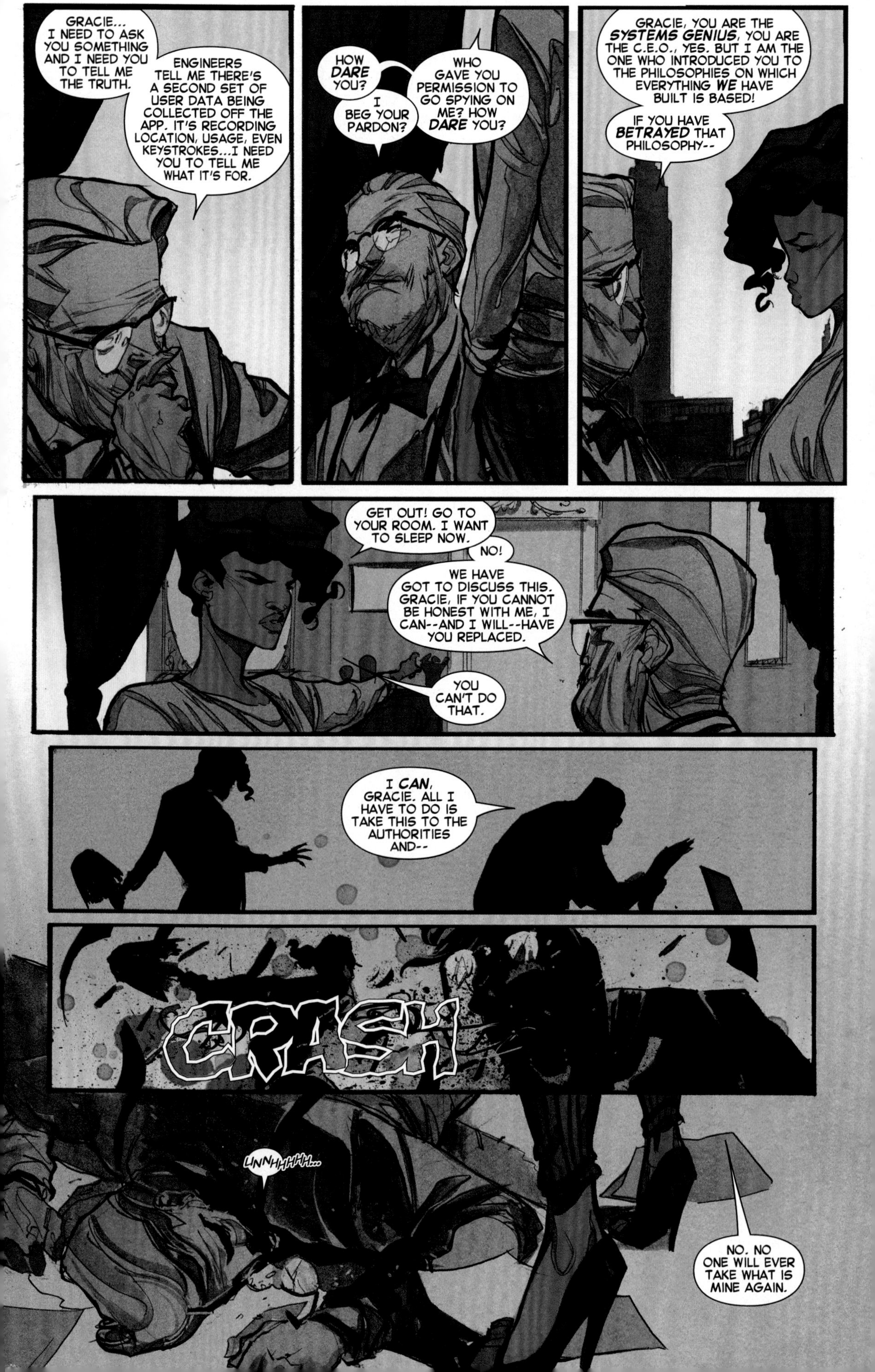
GRACIE... I NEED TO ASK YOU SOMETHING AND I NEED YOU TO TELL ME THE TRUTH.
ENGINEERS TELL ME THERE'S A SECOND SET OF USER DATA BEING COLLECTED OFF THE APP. IT'S RECORDING LOCATION, USAGE, EVEN KEYSTROKES...I NEED YOU TO TELL ME WHAT IT'S FOR.
HOW DARE YOU?
I BEG YOUR PARDON?
WHO GAVE YOU PERMISSION TO GO SPYING ON ME? HOW DARE YOU?
GRACIE, YOU ARE THE SYSTEMS GENIUS, YOU ARE THE C.E.O., YES. BUT I AM THE ONE WHO INTRODUCED YOU TO THE PHILOSOPHIES ON WHICH EVERYTHING WE HAVE BUILT IS BASED!
IF YOU HAVE BETRAYED THAT PHILOSOPHY--
GET OUT! GO TO YOUR ROOM. I WANT TO SLEEP NOW.
NO!
WE HAVE GOT TO DISCUSS THIS. GRACIE, IF YOU CANNOT BE HONEST WITH ME, I CAN--AND I WILL--HAVE YOU REPLACED.
YOU CAN'T DO THAT.
I CAN, GRACIE. ALL I HAVE TO DO IS TAKE THIS TO THE AUTHORITIES AND--
CRASH
UNNHHHHH...
NO. NO ONE WILL EVER TAKE WHAT IS MINE AGAIN.

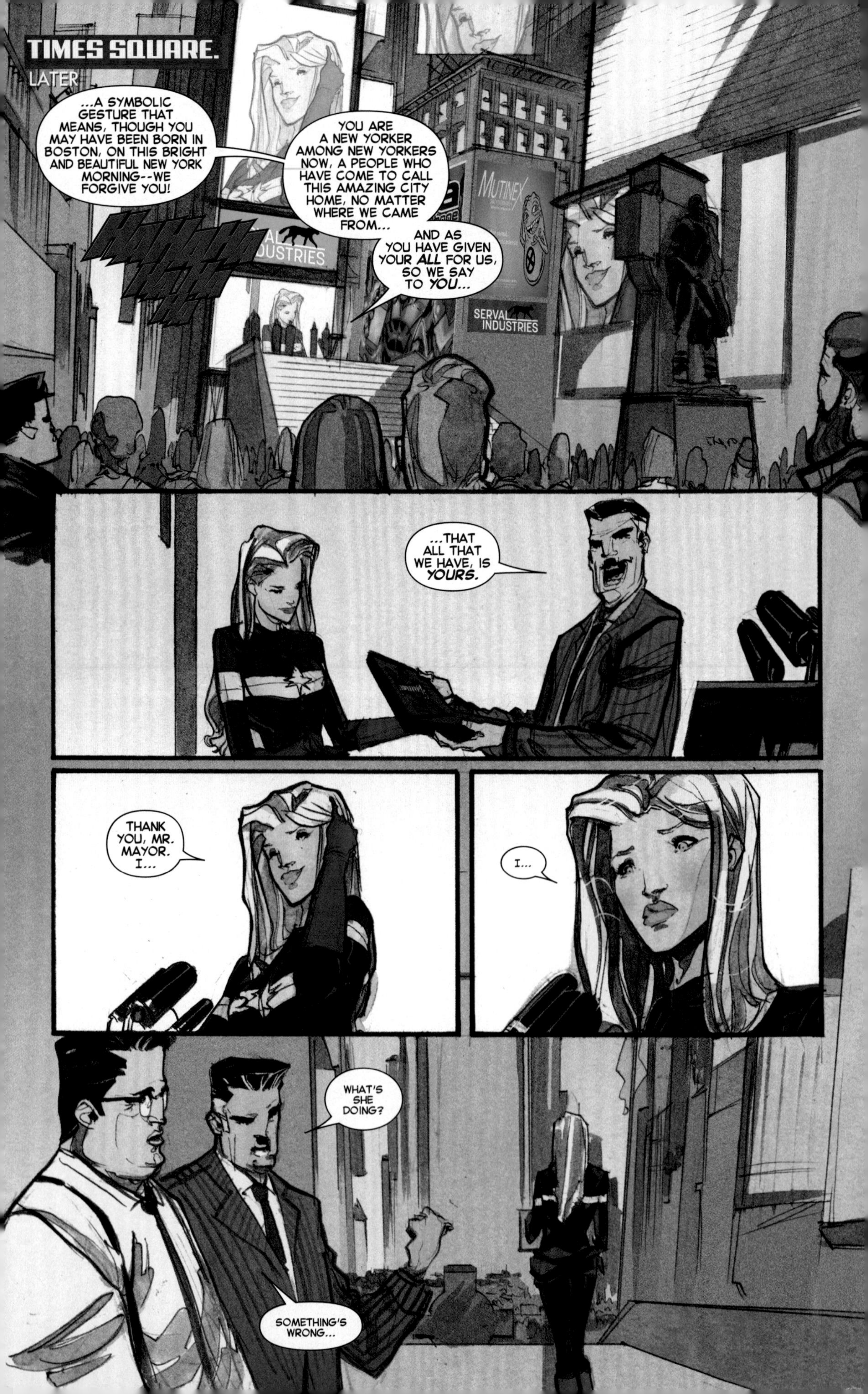
TIMES SQUARE.
LATER
...A SYMBOLIC GESTURE THAT MEANS, THOUGH YOU MAY HAVE BEEN BORN IN BOSTON, ON THIS BRIGHT AND BEAUTIFUL NEW YORK MORNING--WE FORGIVE YOU!
YOU ARE A NEW YORKER AMONG NEW YORKERS NOW, A PEOPLE WHO HAVE COME TO CALL THIS AMAZING CITY HOME, NO MATTER WHERE WE CAME FROM...
AND AS YOU HAVE GIVEN YOUR ALL FOR US, SO WE SAY TO YOU...
MUTINEX
SERVAL INDUSTRIES
...THAT ALL THAT WE HAVE, IS YOURS.
THANK YOU, MR. MAYOR. I...
I...
WHAT'S SHE DOING?
SOMETHING'S WRONG...

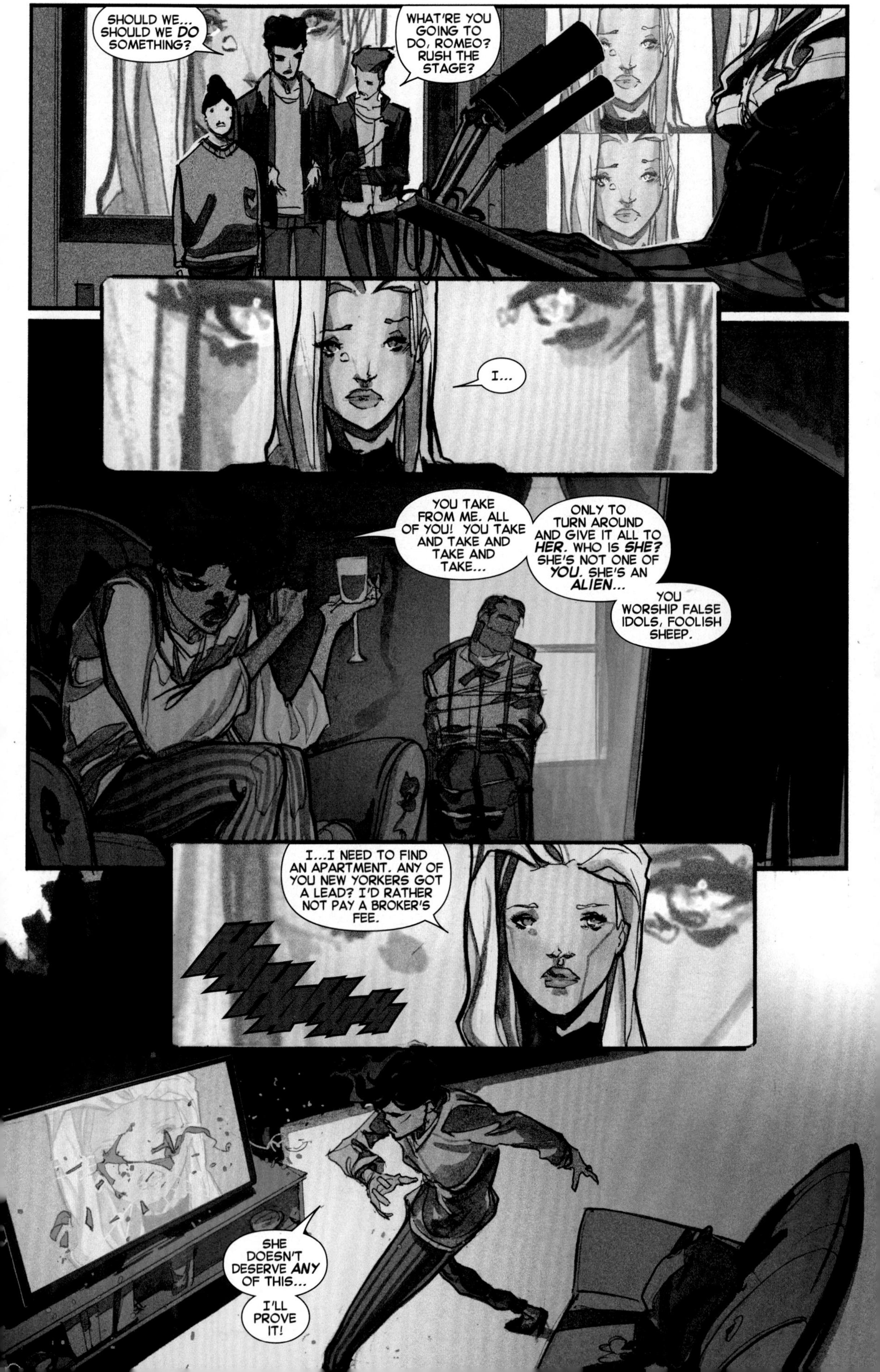
SHOULD WE... SHOULD WE DO SOMETHING?
WHAT'RE YOU GOING TO DO, ROMEO? RUSH THE STAGE?
I...
YOU TAKE FROM ME. ALL OF YOU! YOU TAKE AND TAKE AND TAKE AND TAKE...
ONLY TO TURN AROUND AND GIVE IT ALL TO HER. WHO IS SHE? SHE'S NOT ONE OF YOU. SHE'S AN ALIEN...
YOU WORSHIP FALSE IDOLS, FOOLISH SHEEP.
I...I NEED TO FIND AN APARTMENT. ANY OF YOU NEW YORKERS GOT A LEAD? I'D RATHER NOT PAY A BROKER'S FEE.
SHE DOESN'T DESERVE ANY OF THIS...
I'LL PROVE IT!

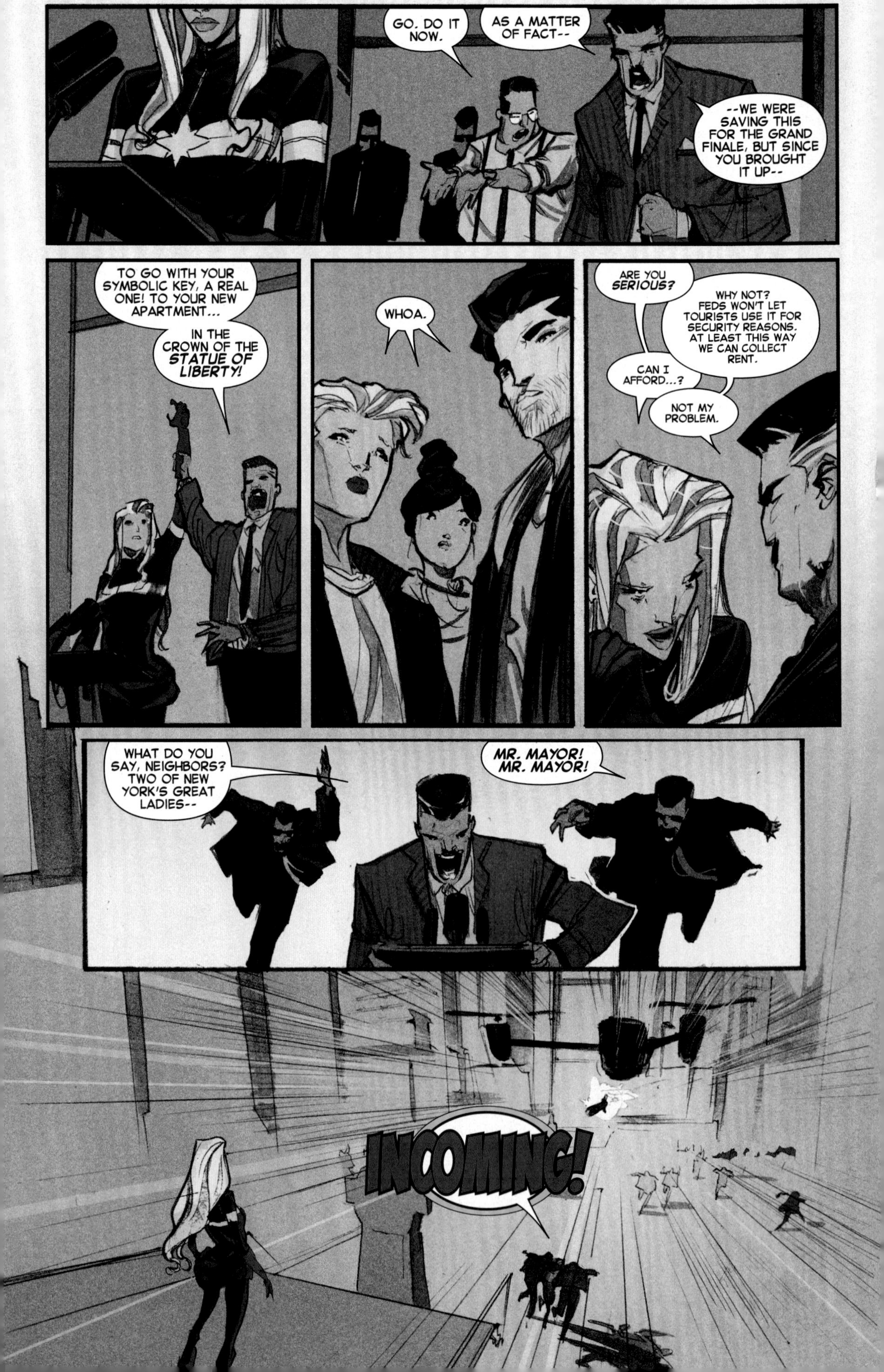
GO. DO IT NOW.
AS A MATTER OF FACT--
--WE WERE SAVING THIS FOR THE GRAND FINALE, BUT SINCE YOU BROUGHT IT UP--
TO GO WITH YOUR SYMBOLIC KEY, A REAL ONE! TO YOUR NEW APARTMENT...
IN THE CROWN OF THE STATUE OF LIBERTY!
WHOA.
ARE YOU SERIOUS?
WHY NOT? FEDS WON'T LET TOURISTS USE IT FOR SECURITY REASONS. AT LEAST THIS WAY WE CAN COLLECT RENT.
CAN I AFFORD...?
NOT MY PROBLEM.
WHAT DO YOU SAY, NEIGHBORS? TWO OF NEW YORK'S GREAT LADIES--
MR. MAYOR! MR. MAYOR!
INCOMING!

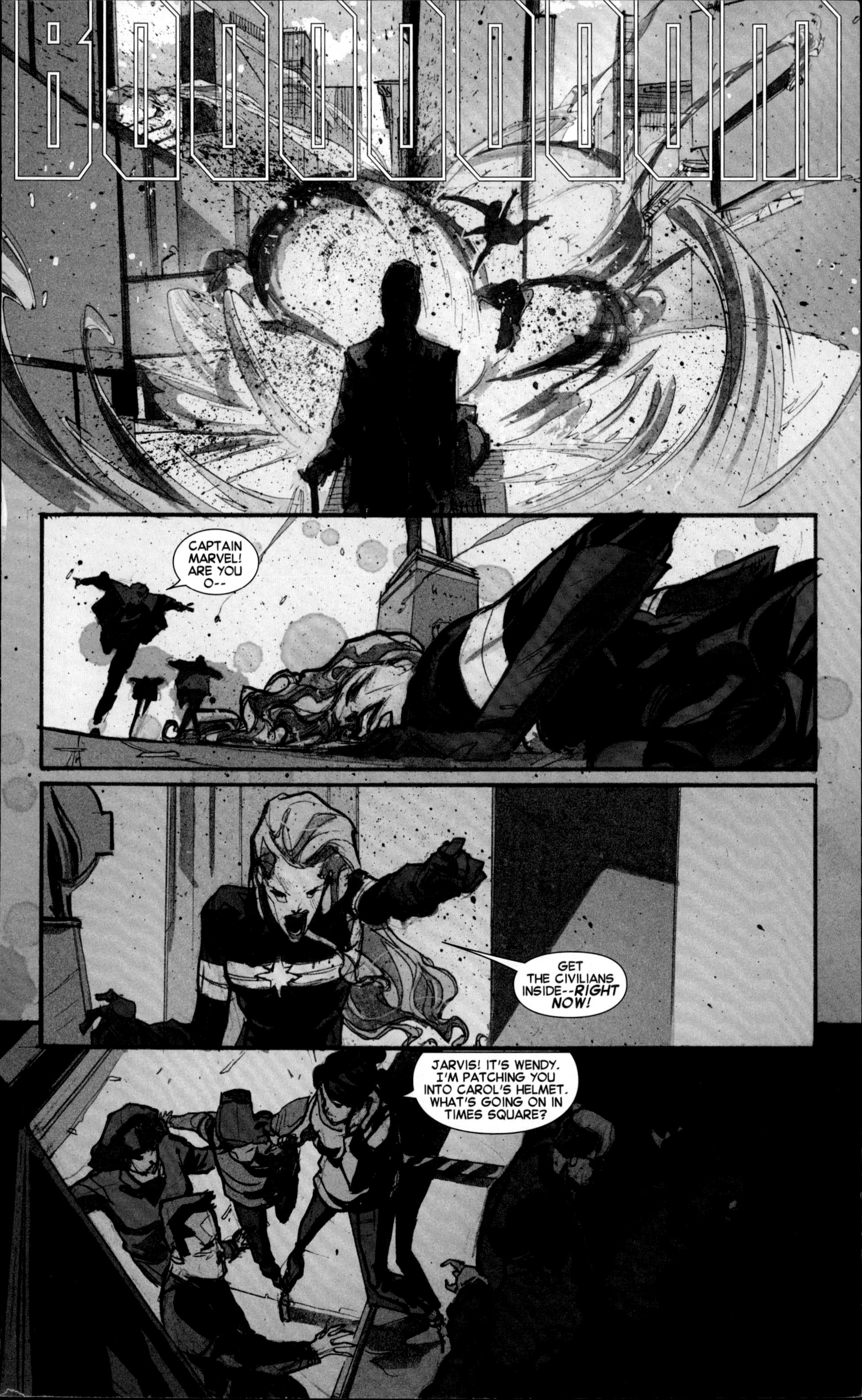
CAPTAIN MARVEL! ARE YOU O--
GET THE CIVILIANS INSIDE--RIGHT NOW!
JARVIS! IT'S WENDY. I'M PATCHING YOU INTO CAROL'S HELMET. WHAT'S GOING ON IN TIMES SQUARE?

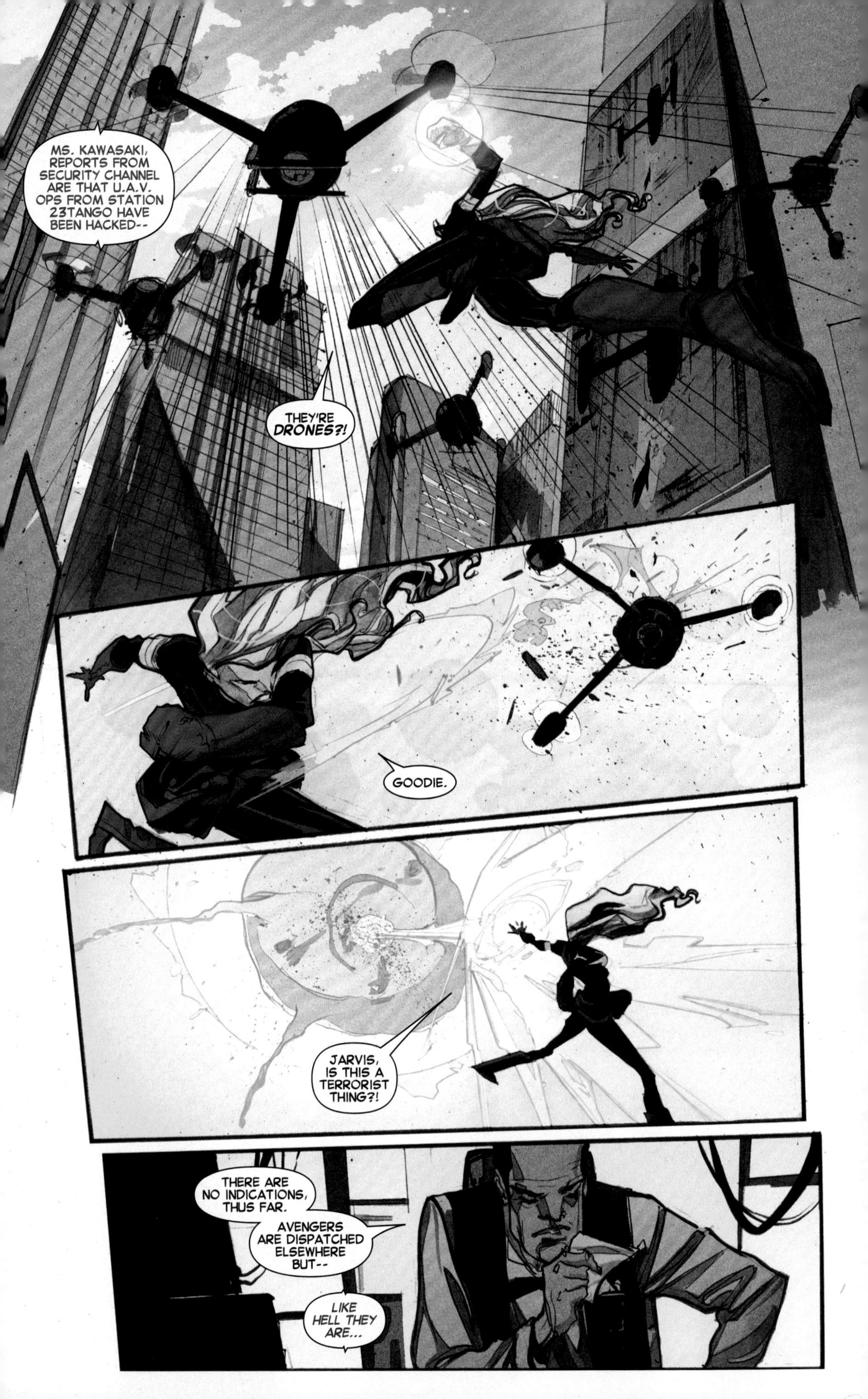
MS. KAWASAKI, REPORTS FROM SECURITY CHANNEL ARE THAT U.A.V. OPS FROM STATION 23TANGO HAVE BEEN HACKED--
THEY'RE *DRONES?!*
GOODIE.
JARVIS, IS THIS A TERRORIST THING?!
THERE ARE NO INDICATIONS, THUS FAR.
AVENGERS ARE DISPATCHED ELSEWHERE BUT--
LIKE HELL THEY ARE...

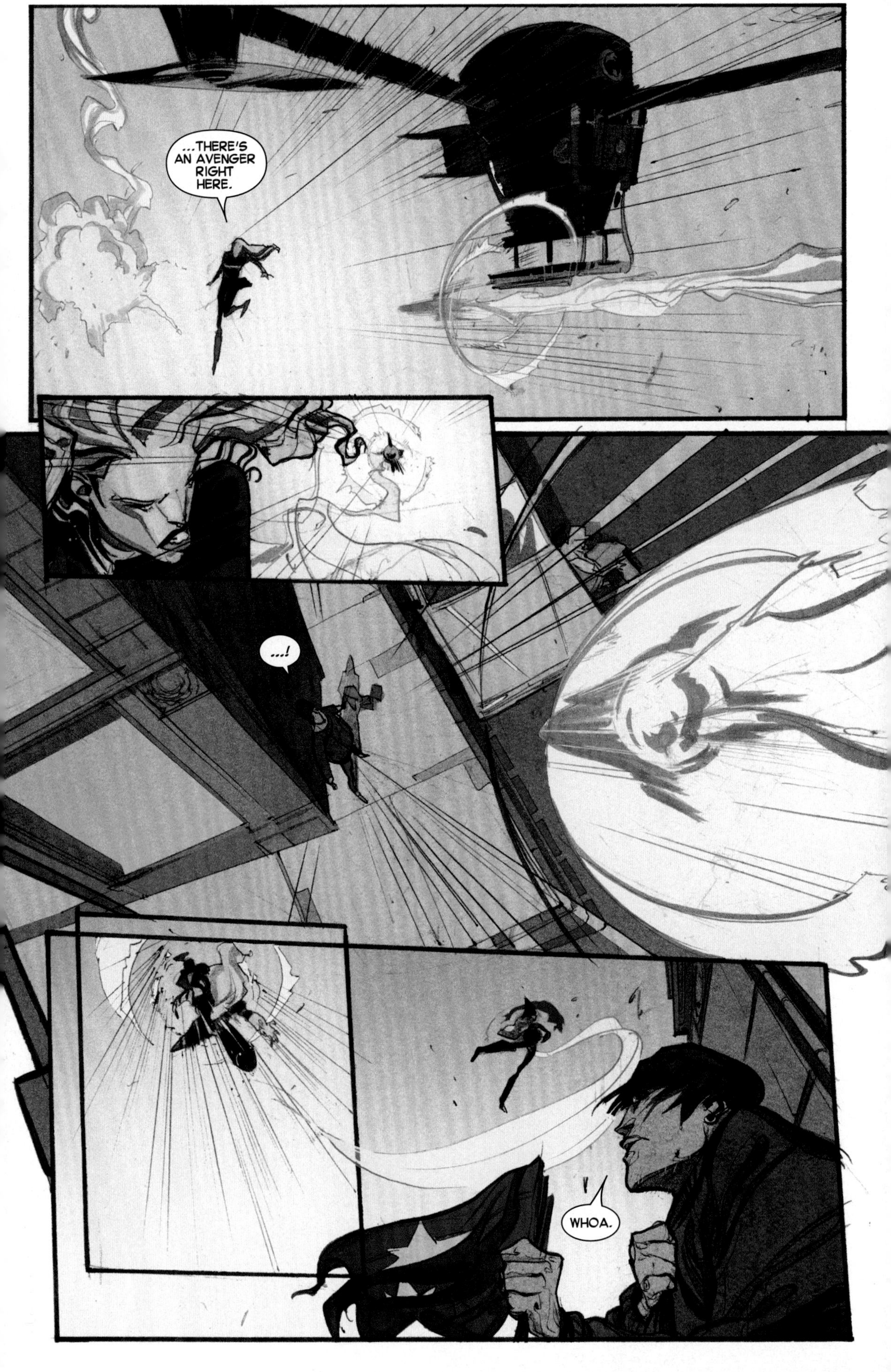
...THERE'S AN AVENGER RIGHT HERE.
...!
WHOA.

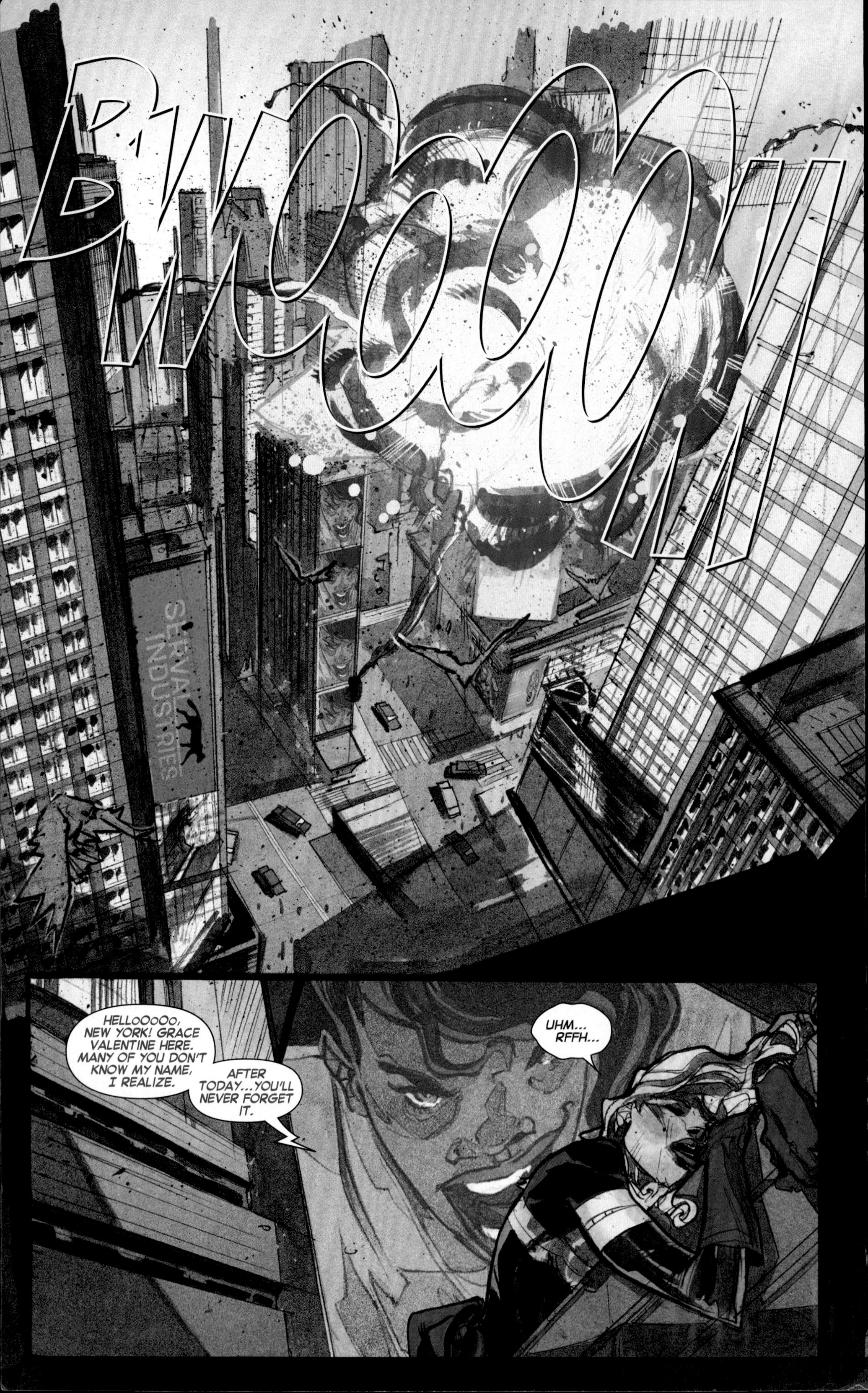

BWOOOOM!!
SERVAL INDUSTRIES
HELLOOOOO, NEW YORK! GRACE VALENTINE HERE. MANY OF YOU DON'T KNOW MY NAME, I REALIZE.
AFTER TODAY...YOU'LL NEVER FORGET IT.
UHM... RFFH...

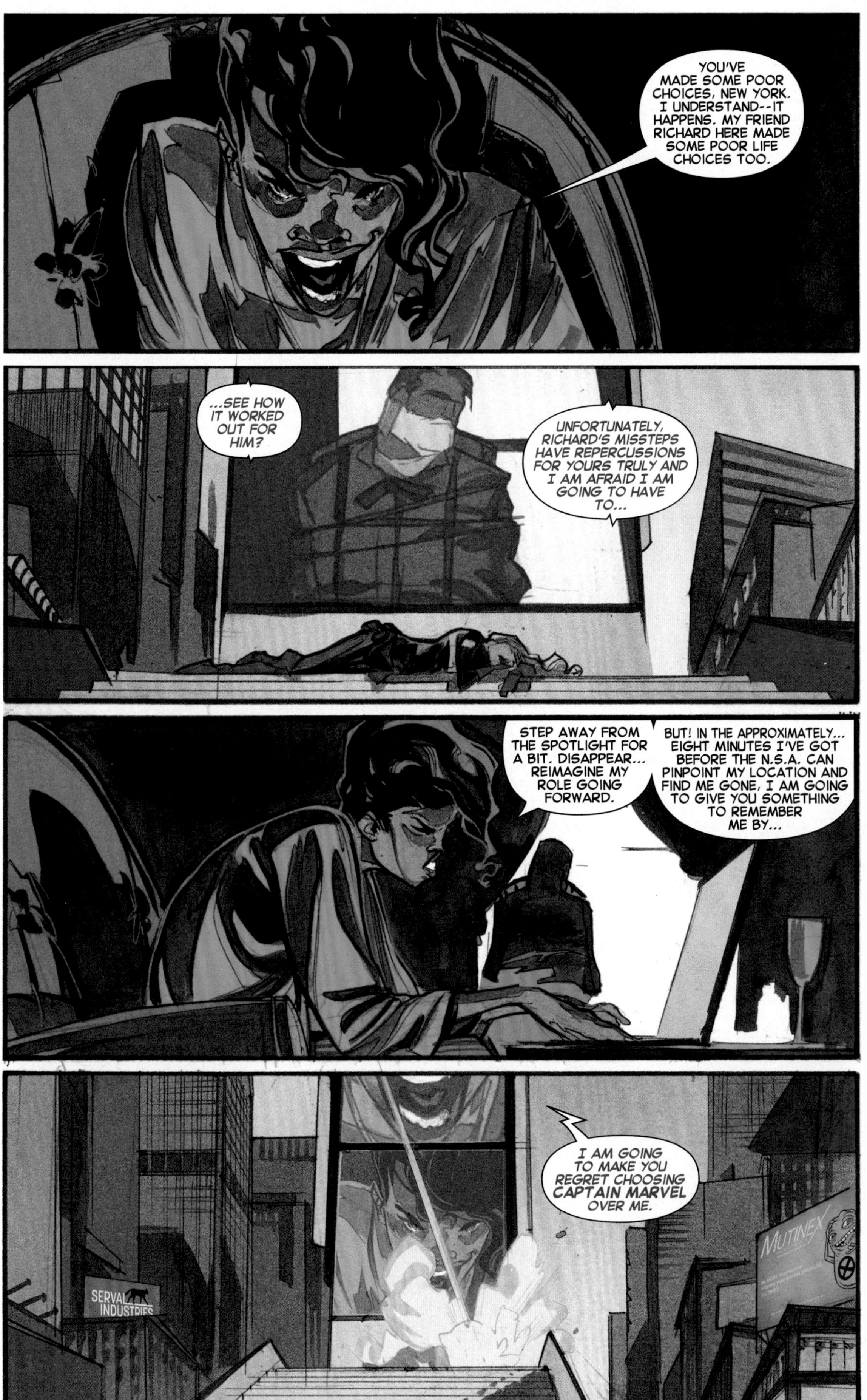
YOU'VE MADE SOME POOR CHOICES, NEW YORK. I UNDERSTAND--IT HAPPENS. MY FRIEND RICHARD HERE MADE SOME POOR LIFE CHOICES TOO.
...SEE HOW IT WORKED OUT FOR HIM?
UNFORTUNATELY, RICHARD'S MISSTEPS HAVE REPERCUSSIONS FOR YOURS TRULY AND I AM AFRAID I AM GOING TO HAVE TO...
STEP AWAY FROM THE SPOTLIGHT FOR A BIT. DISAPPEAR... REIMAGINE MY ROLE GOING FORWARD.
BUT! IN THE APPROXIMATELY... EIGHT MINUTES I'VE GOT BEFORE THE N.S.A. CAN PINPOINT MY LOCATION AND FIND ME GONE, I AM GOING TO GIVE YOU SOMETHING TO REMEMBER ME BY...
I AM GOING TO MAKE YOU REGRET CHOOSING CAPTAIN MARVEL OVER ME.
SERVAL INDUSTRIES
MUTINEX

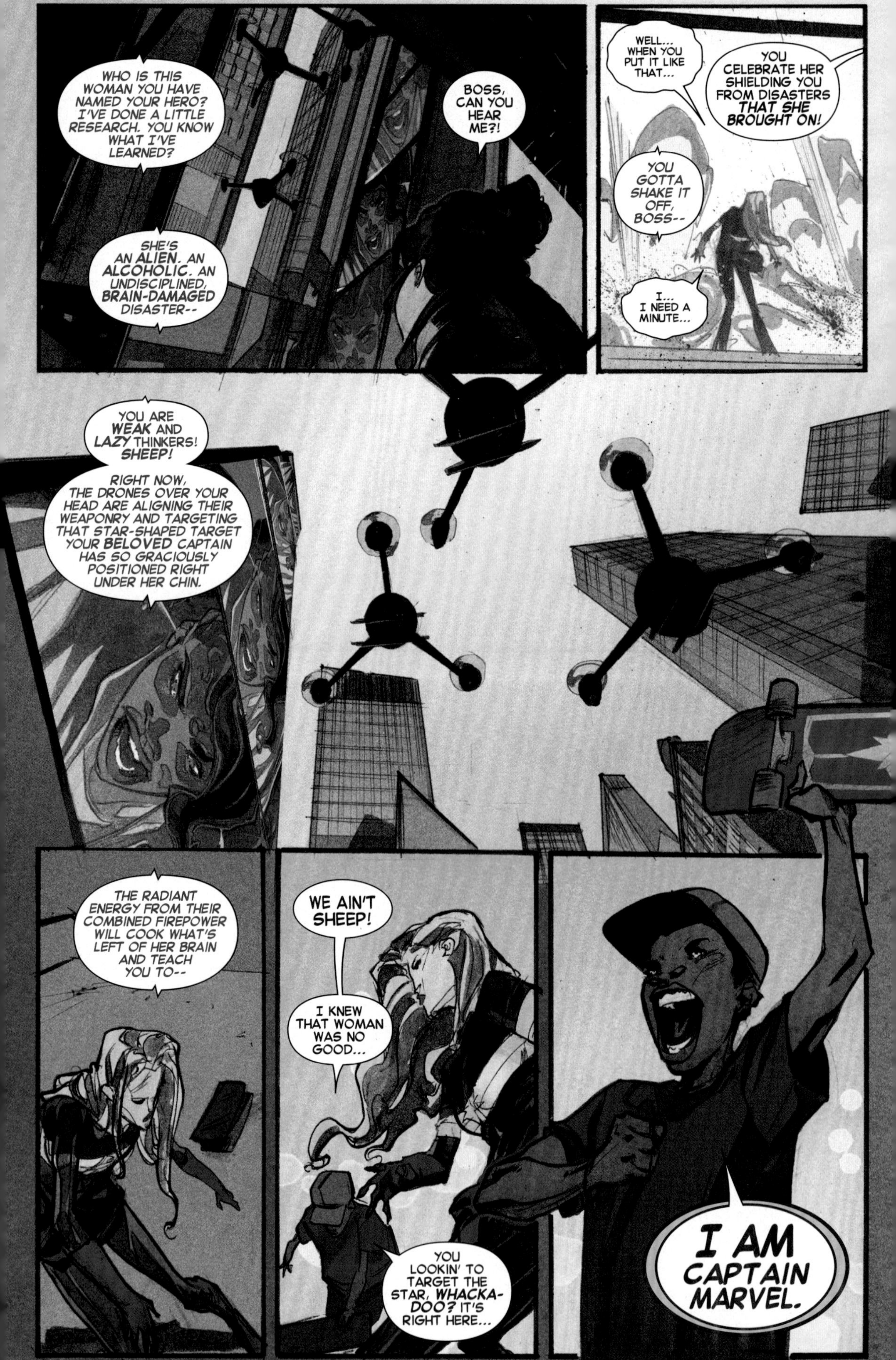
WHO IS THIS WOMAN YOU HAVE NAMED YOUR HERO? I'VE DONE A LITTLE RESEARCH. YOU KNOW WHAT I'VE LEARNED?
SHE'S AN ALIEN. AN ALCOHOLIC. AN UNDISCIPLINED, BRAIN-DAMAGED DISASTER--
BOSS, CAN YOU HEAR ME?!
WELL... WHEN YOU PUT IT LIKE THAT...
YOU CELEBRATE HER SHIELDING YOU FROM DISASTERS THAT SHE BROUGHT ON!
YOU GOTTA SHAKE IT OFF, BOSS--
I... I NEED A MINUTE...
YOU ARE WEAK AND LAZY THINKERS! SHEEP!
RIGHT NOW, THE DRONES OVER YOUR HEAD ARE ALIGNING THEIR WEAPONRY AND TARGETING THAT STAR-SHAPED TARGET YOUR BELOVED CAPTAIN HAS SO GRACIOUSLY POSITIONED RIGHT UNDER HER CHIN.
THE RADIANT ENERGY FROM THEIR COMBINED FIREPOWER WILL COOK WHAT'S LEFT OF HER BRAIN AND TEACH YOU TO--
WE AIN'T SHEEP!
I KNEW THAT WOMAN WAS NO GOOD...
YOU LOOKIN' TO TARGET THE STAR, WHACKA-DOO? IT'S RIGHT HERE...
I AM CAPTAIN MARVEL.

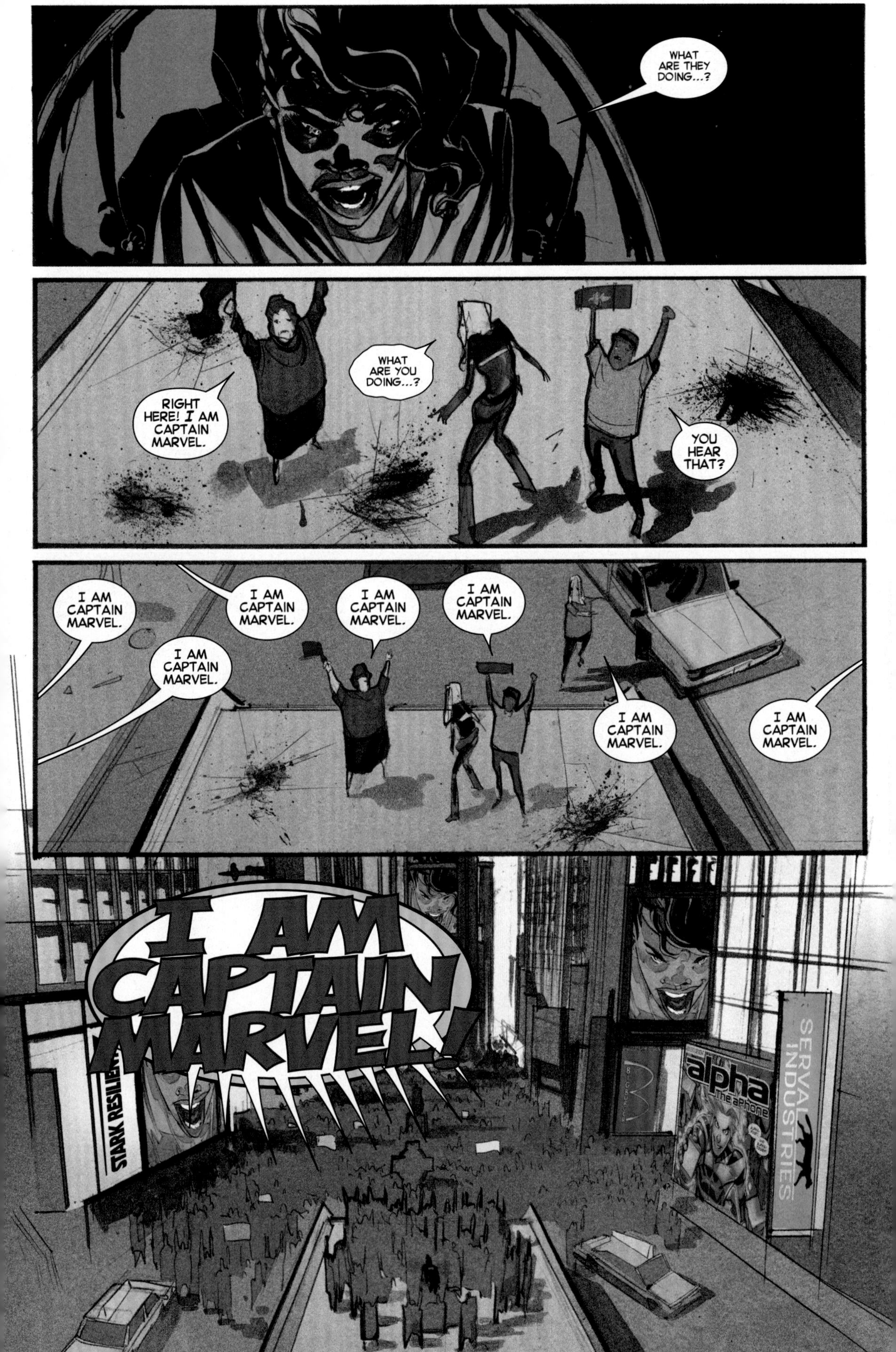
WHAT ARE THEY DOING...?
RIGHT HERE! *I* AM CAPTAIN MARVEL.
WHAT ARE YOU DOING...?
YOU HEAR THAT?
I AM CAPTAIN MARVEL.
I AM CAPTAIN MARVEL.
I AM CAPTAIN MARVEL.
I AM CAPTAIN MARVEL.
I AM CAPTAIN MARVEL.
I AM CAPTAIN MARVEL.
I AM CAPTAIN MARVEL.
I AM CAPTAIN MARVEL!
STARK RESILIEN
alpha
The aPhone
SERVAL INDUSTRIES

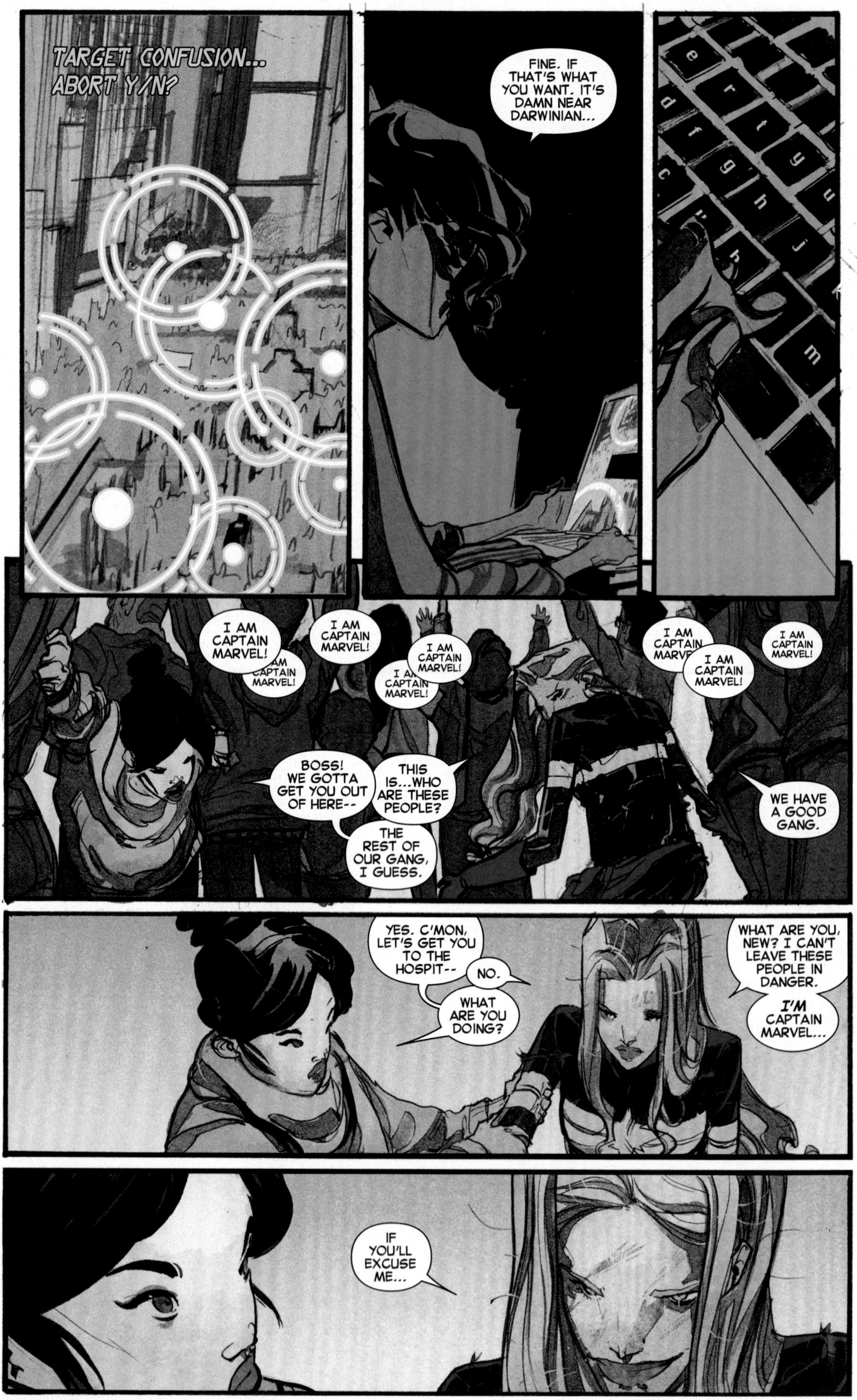
TARGET CONFUSION... ABORT Y/N?
FINE. IF THAT'S WHAT YOU WANT. IT'S DAMN NEAR DARWINIAN...
I AM CAPTAIN MARVEL!
AM CAPTAIN MARVEL!
I AM CAPTAIN MARVEL!
I AM CAPTAIN MARVEL!
I A CAPTAIN MARVEL!
I AM CAPTAIN MARVE
I AM CAPTAIN MARVEL!
I AM CAPTAIN MARVEL!
BOSS! WE GOTTA GET YOU OUT OF HERE--
THIS IS...WHO ARE THESE PEOPLE?
THE REST OF OUR GANG, I GUESS.
WE HAVE A GOOD GANG.
YES. C'MON, LET'S GET YOU TO THE HOSPIT--
NO.
WHAT ARE YOU DOING?
WHAT ARE YOU, NEW? I CAN'T LEAVE THESE PEOPLE IN DANGER.
I'M CAPTAIN MARVEL...
IF YOU'LL EXCUSE ME...

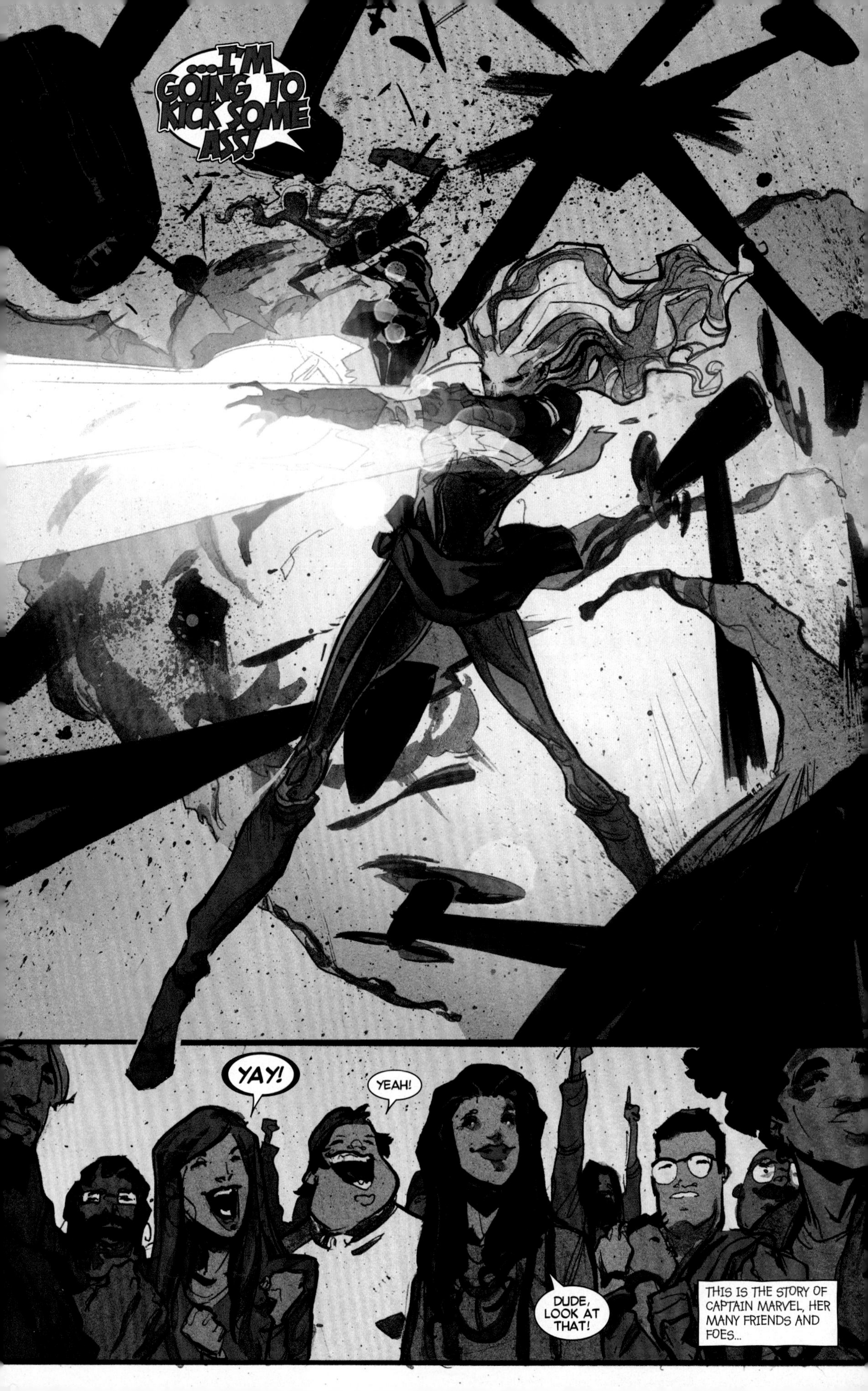
...I'M GOING TO KICK SOME ASS!
YAY!
YEAH!
DUDE, LOOK AT THAT!
THIS IS THE STORY OF CAPTAIN MARVEL, HER MANY FRIENDS AND FOES...

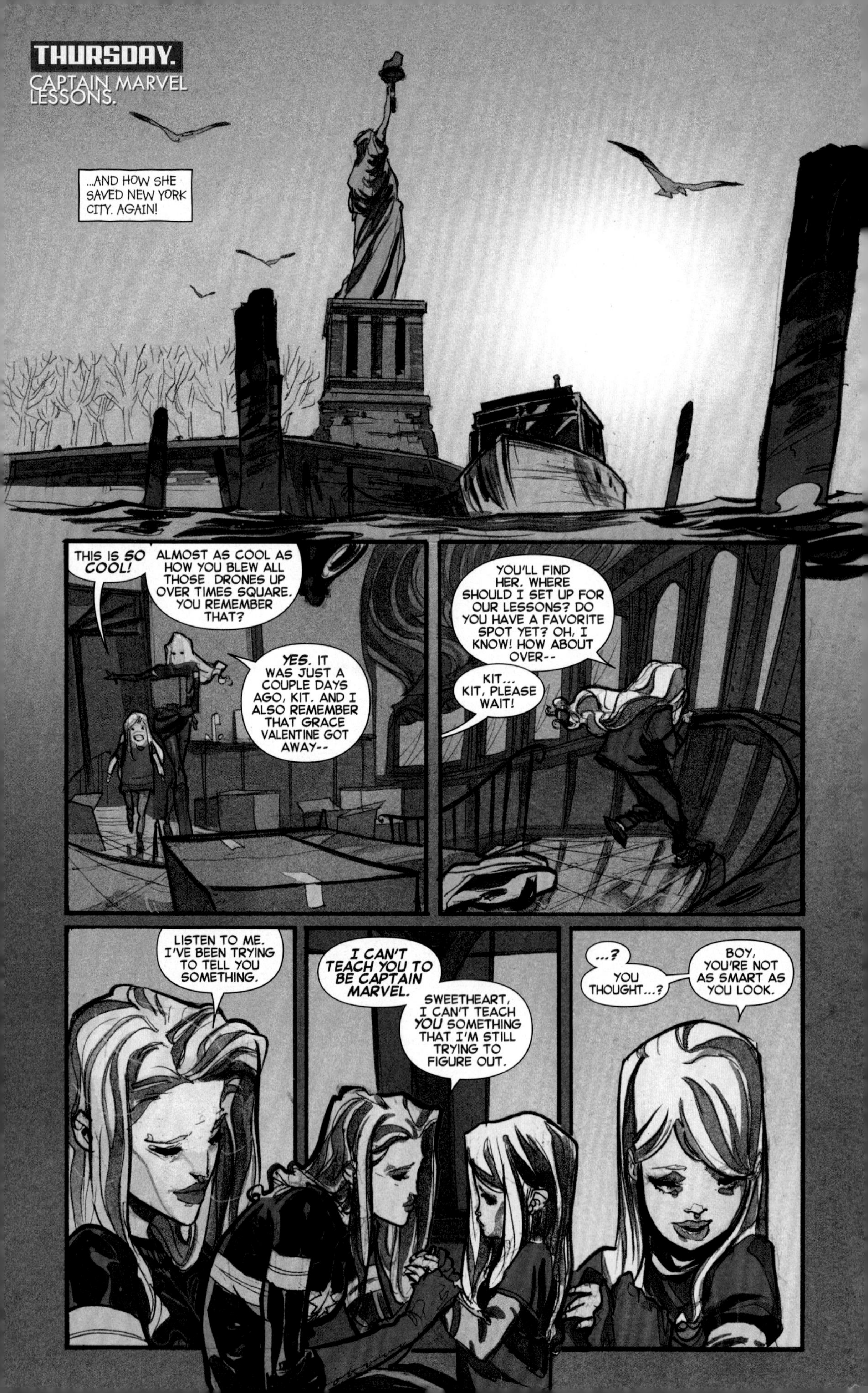

THURSDAY.
CAPTAIN MARVEL LESSONS.
...AND HOW SHE SAVED NEW YORK CITY. AGAIN!
THIS IS SO COOL!
ALMOST AS COOL AS HOW YOU BLEW ALL THOSE DRONES UP OVER TIMES SQUARE. YOU REMEMBER THAT?
YES. IT WAS JUST A COUPLE DAYS AGO, KIT. AND I ALSO REMEMBER THAT GRACE VALENTINE GOT AWAY--
YOU'LL FIND HER. WHERE SHOULD I SET UP FOR OUR LESSONS? DO YOU HAVE A FAVORITE SPOT YET? OH, I KNOW! HOW ABOUT OVER--
KIT... KIT, PLEASE WAIT!
LISTEN TO ME. I'VE BEEN TRYING TO TELL YOU SOMETHING.
I CAN'T TEACH YOU TO BE CAPTAIN MARVEL.
SWEETHEART, I CAN'T TEACH YOU SOMETHING THAT I'M STILL TRYING TO FIGURE OUT.
...?
YOU THOUGHT...?
BOY, YOU'RE NOT AS SMART AS YOU LOOK.

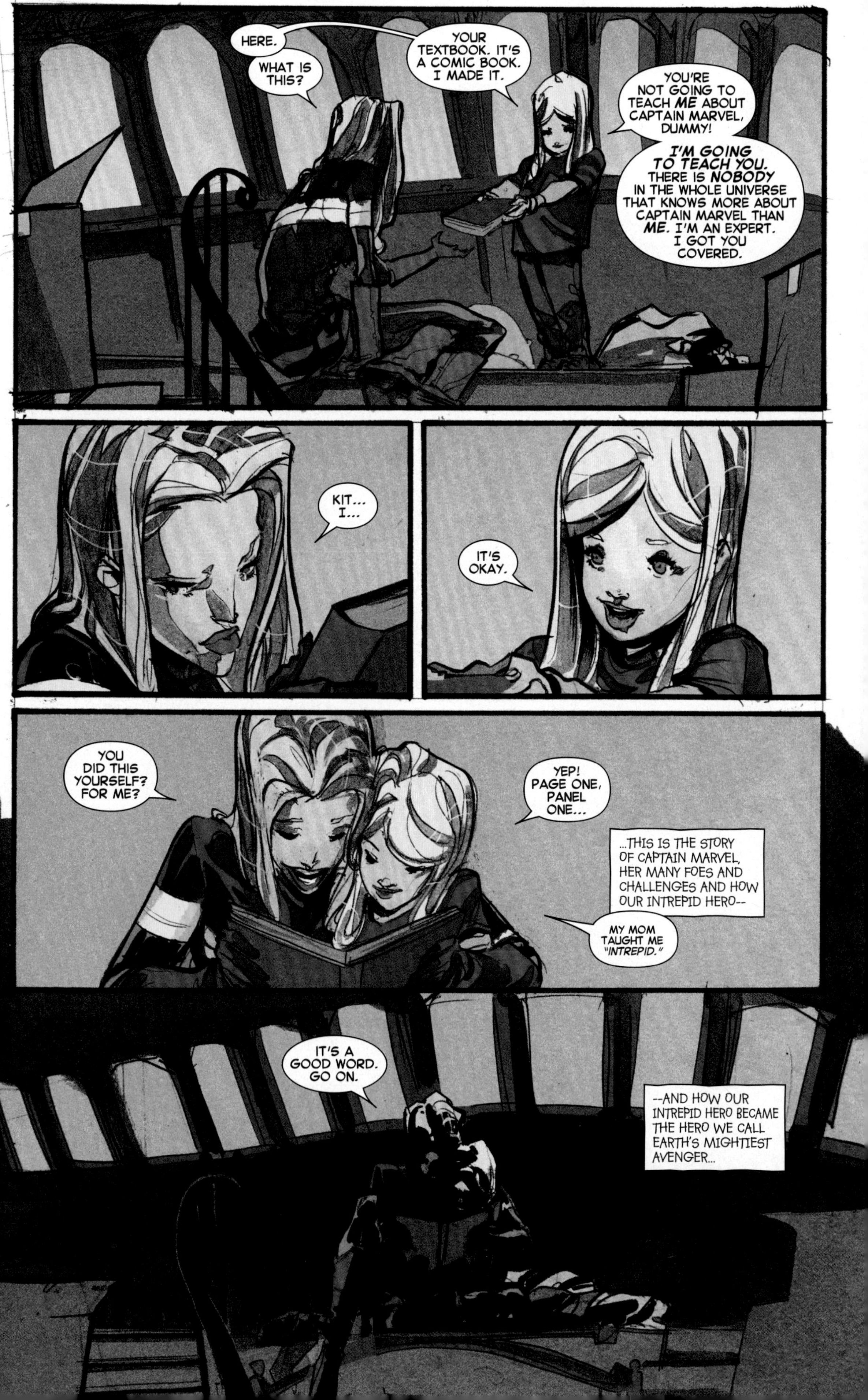
HERE.
WHAT IS THIS?
YOUR TEXTBOOK. IT'S A COMIC BOOK. I MADE IT.
YOU'RE NOT GOING TO TEACH ME ABOUT CAPTAIN MARVEL, DUMMY!
I'M GOING TO TEACH YOU. THERE IS NOBODY IN THE WHOLE UNIVERSE THAT KNOWS MORE ABOUT CAPTAIN MARVEL THAN ME. I'M AN EXPERT. I GOT YOU COVERED.
KIT... I...
IT'S OKAY.
YOU DID THIS YOURSELF? FOR ME?
YEP! PAGE ONE, PANEL ONE...
...THIS IS THE STORY OF CAPTAIN MARVEL, HER MANY FOES AND CHALLENGES AND HOW OUR INTREPID HERO--
MY MOM TAUGHT ME "INTREPID."
IT'S A GOOD WORD. GO ON.
--AND HOW OUR INTREPID HERO BECAME THE HERO WE CALL EARTH'S MIGHTIEST AVENGER...

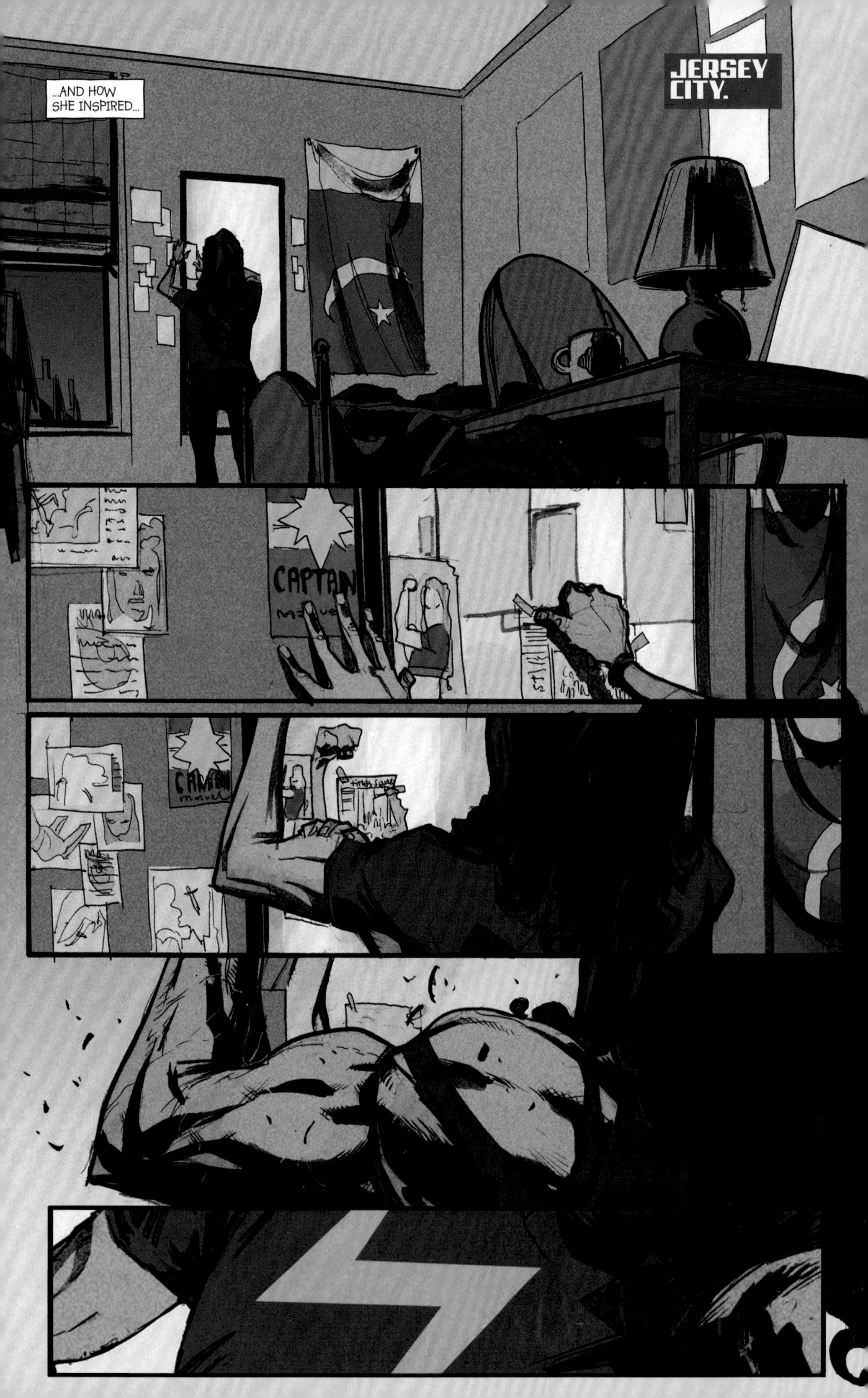
...AND HOW
SHE INSPIRED...
JERSEY
CITY.
CAPTAIN
marvel

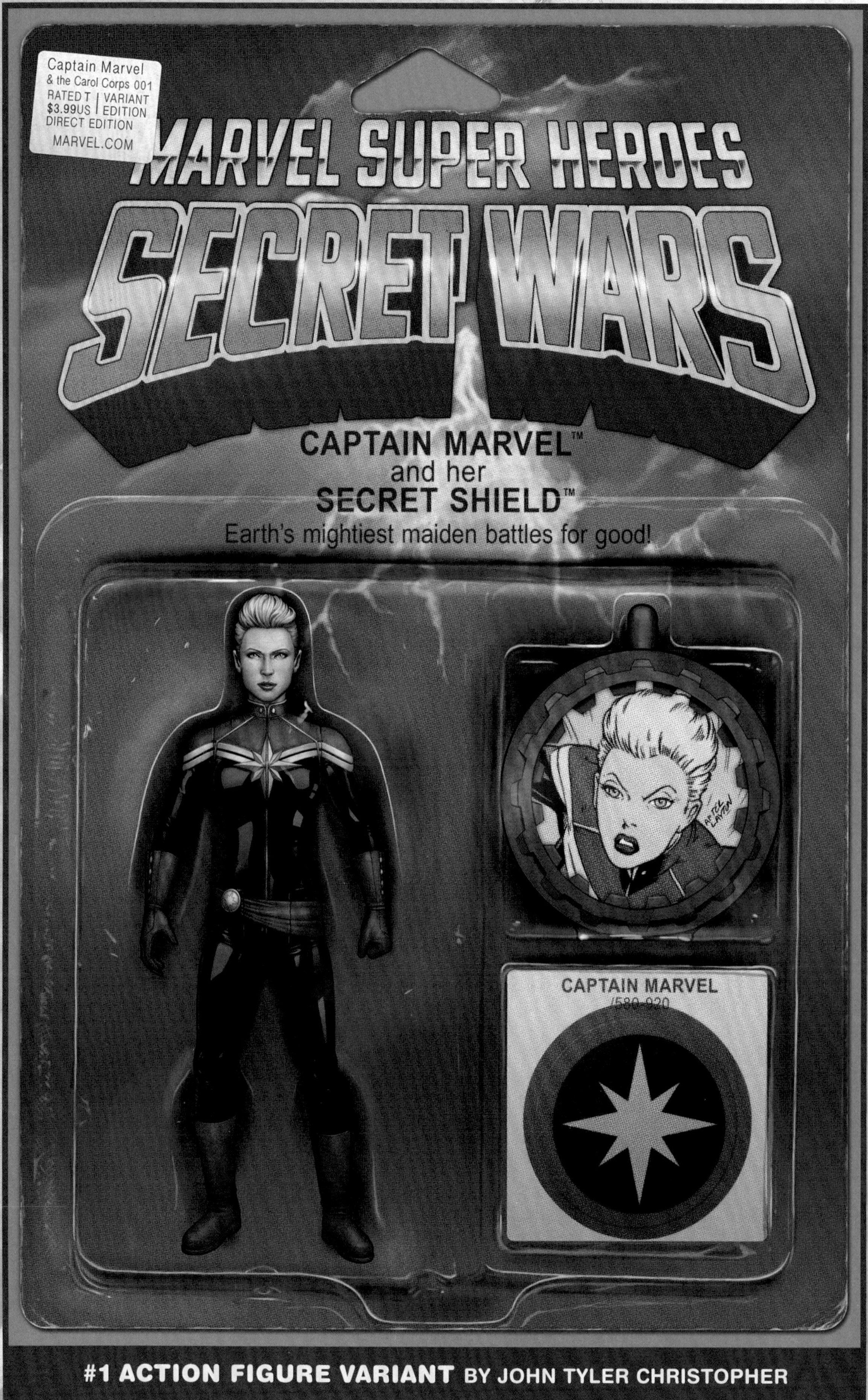
Captain Marvel
& the Carol Corps 001
RATED T | VARIANT
$3.99US | EDITION
DIRECT EDITION
MARVEL.COM
MARVEL SUPER HEROES
SECRET WARS
CAPTAIN MARVEL™
and her
SECRET SHIELD™
Earth's mightiest maiden battles for good!
CAPTAIN MARVEL

#1 ACTION FIGURE VARIANT BY JOHN TYLER CHRISTOPHER

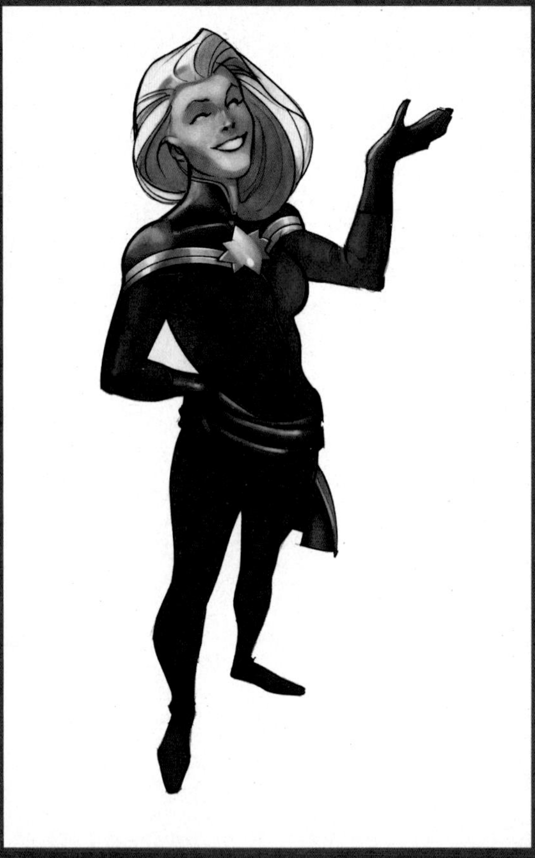

#1 ANT-SIZED VARIANT
BY PASQUAL FERRY

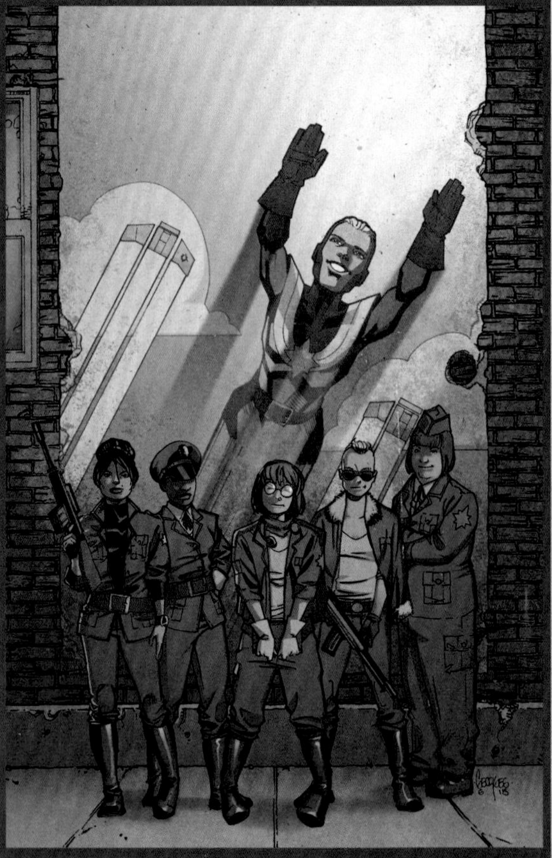

#2 VARIANT BY GEORGES JEANTY
& WIL QUINTANA

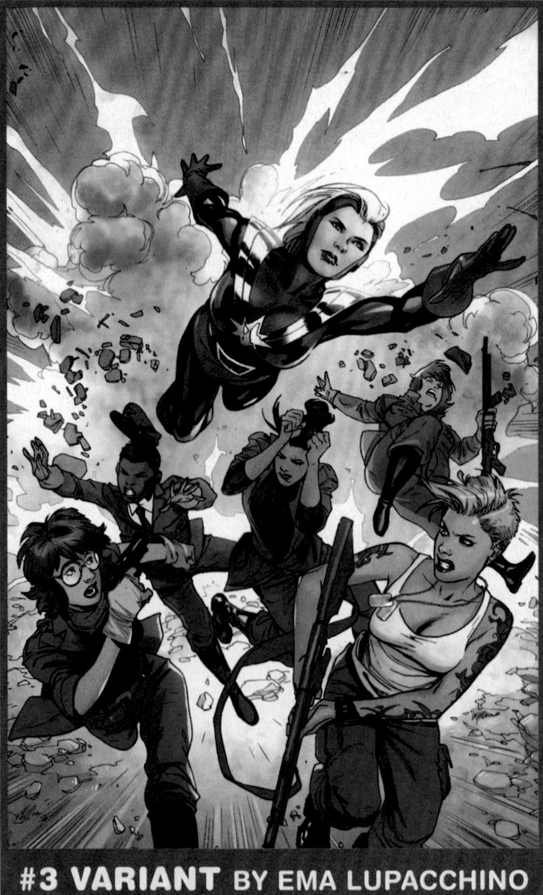

#3 VARIANT BY EMA LUPACCHINO
& JASON KEITH